Spotlight on Security for Real Estate Managers

Spotlight on Security for Real Estate Managers

Lawrence J. Fennelly, CPO
John H. Lombardi, Ph.D.

IREM Institute of Real Estate Management

CHICAGO

Library of Congress Cataloging-in-Publication Data

Fennelly, Lawrence J., 1940-
    Spotlight on security for real estate managers / Lawrence J.
Fennelly, John H. Lombardi.
      p. cm.
    Includes bibliographical references and index.
    ISBN 1-57203-052-6
    1. Real estate management--United States.   2. Residential real
estate--Security measures--United States.   3. Commercial real
estate--Security measures--United States.   4. Security systems-
-United States.   5. Crime prevention--United States.   6. Liability
for building accidents--United States.   I. Lombardi, John H., 1944-
. II. Title.
HD1394.5.U6F46   1996   96-38549
333.33'068'4--dc20   CIP

Printed in the United States of America

1 2 3 4 5 6 7 8 9 10 Printing / Year 06 05 04 03 02 01 00 99 98 97

To Annmarie, Alison, Charlie, Larry, Jr.,
Bill, Stephen, and especially Billy Boyce for their
patience and understanding of time spent apart from them.

L.J.F.

To my lovely wife, Rosemary, whose nurturing is a constant motivation;
my most wonderful mother, Lorraine, who gave me the love of ethical
inquiry and honest openness and has always been my biggest fan;
my father, John, who was a role model of reliable, aggressive persistence
that only a truck driver's son can understand and whom I greatly miss;
and Mr. Chester Pucci, Dr. Bryant Feather, Dr. Marc Gertz,
Dr. Gene Czajkoski, Dr. Vernon Fox, and Ms. Gwendolyn Brooks, mentors all,
who taught me the difference between practice and theory
and the necessity for accuracy and inclusion of both in the real world.

J.H.L.

To our consultant and technical assistant, Jan Rossi.
We would not have done this without you.

Preface

The most recent statistics published by the U.S. Department of Justice in its annual Uniform Crime Reports, *Crime in the United States 1994,* show the following:

One crime index offense every 2 seconds
One violent crime every 17 seconds
One property crime every 3 seconds
One murder every 23 minutes
One forcible rape every 5 minutes
One robbery every 51 seconds
One aggravated assault every 28 seconds
One burglary every 12 seconds
One larceny-theft every 4 seconds
One motor vehicle theft every 20 seconds

Crimes do not just occur. They involve people (the perpetrator of the crime as well as the victim) and property (the site of the crime). More often than not, the location is a managed property and the victims are residents or tenants or employees at the property. Worst of all, the property owner or the real estate manager, or both, may be held liable for personal injuries and/or property damage that results from crime committed on the property. The liability arises out of claims of ownership and management's negligence in providing security.

Our goal in writing this book was to help real estate managers understand the issues that form the basis for such liability claims. We also wanted to provide some tools they can use to minimize the likelihood of the properties they manage becoming crime sites and to be prepared to deal with the consequences in the event a crime occurs at or near their property. Things you, as real estate managers, need to understand about crime and its impact on your business and personal interests include the following:

- You may be held liable if your employees, your residents or tenants, or guests at the property you manage are attacked or otherwise criminally assaulted—or if their personal property is damaged or destroyed.
- You are *not* expected to *predict* crimes against people or against property at your managed premises; however,
- You are expected to be able to anticipate such crimes.

The same management skills and tools that you use to generate profits from the property's operations provide the means for defending against crime and liability—i.e., security and crime prevention are good business. This is true because:

Even though your property may not have been the site of a violent crime, violent crimes are still *foreseeable.*

Even though you may not have had certain knowledge about a criminal incident, you could still be engaged in civil litigation and held liable for crimes committed against the people who are on your premises.

Consequently, you need to know what to expect *before*—and *after*—any possible litigation. To be able to reasonably protect your managed premises from crime, you need not be an attorney or criminologist or security expert—you only need to be a good businessperson.

The concept of "broken windows" provides an important insight: Crime prevention at managed properties is similar to preventive maintenance. When a property is unoccupied, broken windows are the most obvious indication of a lack of guardianship. A vacant property becomes a magnet for all types of problems, including and especially crime; and if it is next door or around the corner, those problems can easily migrate to your managed property if you are not ceaselessly vigilant. Professional real estate managers usually fight deferred maintenance because it diminishes the market value of the managed property. As crime continues to increase, in general, maintenance must become an integral part of security, not only to protect the value of the property, but to protect the lives of the people on it.

Failure to anticipate the need for either crime prevention or preventive maintenance can result in people being hurt and ownership and management of the property losing profits. While real estate owners and managers may often consider security a *cost center* (i.e., a loss), this book spells out the role of security in maintaining the viability and value of an investment property, which is why security should be considered a *profit center.*

An Array of Topics and Tools

In writing this book, we have tried to provide information that will assist the real estate manager in evaluating the security needs of a property and identifying security measures that will meet those needs within the available budget. While some chapters focus on a single property type, most of the strategies presented in the text can be adapted or considered for all types of properties. The nature of a work that addresses property types separately and looks at different approaches to accomplish the same goal cannot selectively exclude from one chapter strategies or devices that are mentioned elsewhere. In general, each separate treatment of a topic adds a unique perspective because of the context in which it is presented.

As the book was being developed, it became clear that we were dealing with many different kinds of things—i.e., with properties and their occupants as well as specific security measures. In the meantime, friends and professional colleagues who became aware of our project offered to write about some of the highly specialized topics, and we welcomed their contributions and their expertise. Working with these experts created an additional challenge in that it meant a contributor's unique chapter was likely to mention some point that would be made differently by another writer. However, such repetition has generally occurred within completely different contexts, and the details tend to be cumulative as each writer brought a particular perspective to his or her contribution. We think this repetition adds to the value of our book because it has allowed us to focus on larger issues and specific strategies, on unique aspects of different types of managed properties rather than emphasize the devices and technologies. (The latter have been covered in great depth in topic-specific books. We have included a selection of recommended reading so that those who need or want specific details and technical comparisons can pursue their information needs independently.)

To organize the variety of topics and guide the reader, we chose to arrange the contents of the book in five sections. Each section includes an introduction that identifies the component chapters and contributing authors. It also provides an overview and includes adjunct information related to the unifying theme of the section.

First and foremost are the issues of negligence and liability. The section on legal issues describes the challenge to the real estate manager and provides information about civil and criminal law, giving a deposition, and being proactive in preventing crime and minimizing liability. These chapters focus on why security is an issue.

The second section addresses security needs. Chapters describe the security survey and provide sample checklists for evaluating different types of properties. One type of survey is specific to offices; another offers a more general perspective and includes items that can apply to both residential and commercial properties. The focus here is on identifying what security measures are or should be in place and their effectiveness now and for the future.

Crime and the prevention of crime are major concerns of all citizens. Chapters in this third section explore various proactive approaches to crime prevention. One discusses design issues in shopping centers and malls. Another addresses watch programs in a mostly residential context. The overall emphasis in this section is on planning.

The fourth section addresses protection of assets—people and property—with an emphasis on operational strategies. Individual chapters focus on strategies for providing security for different types of properties and their occupants or users.

In discussing crime prevention and protection of assets, a variety of strategies and devices are identified. In particular, the roles of such security measures as access control, alarm systems, closed-circuit television, and security guards are mentioned repeatedly. The fifth and last section provides background information on these security measures, including some basic data on different types of devices and how they work. The focus here is on effective measures to accomplish the goal of providing reasonable security in a cost-effective manner.

ACKNOWLEDGMENTS

This book would have been less comprehensive without the specific contributions of our friends and colleagues named below (see also the section titled Contributors). These chapters are published here by permission of the respective authors.

"The Property Manager as Juggler" by J. Scott Harr

"The Security Audit and Premises Liability" by Randall I. Atlas

"A General Security Checklist" by Dana Perrin

"Crime Prevention Concepts" by Patrick J. Lenaghan

"Crime Prevention Through Environmental Design" by Timothy D. Crowe

"Community-Oriented Policing" by David Struckhoff

"Recognizing Potential Problems: A Police Officer's Perspective" by Michelle Richter

"Security Issues in 'The Residents' Guidebook'" by Steven J. Rizzuto

"Fire Alarms" by James H. Cullity

"Visual Monitoring via CCTV" by John I. Kostanoski

"Security Training" by Christopher A. Hertig

In addition, the chapter titled "Security Guards" includes two adjunct lists ("Qualifying a Security Guard Company" and "Characteristics of Different Levels or Qualities of Security Guard Service"), which are from "Legal Aspects of Real Property Crime," copyright 1994 by Jeffrey R. Mazor and reprinted by permission of the author.

Our deepest gratitude to all of these individuals for their continued interest in and support of this project, and special thanks to Jim Cullity for his invaluable assistance in developing the chapter titled "Intrusion Alarms."

We also wish to acknowledge the additional insights and encouragement shared with us by other professionals—colleagues and friends—including Carl Bennett, John Borman, Corey Gordon, Celeste Grant, Rosemary Jenkins, Richard Kobetz, and Randy Robertson.

The entire manuscript was reviewed by the following editorial consultants whose questions and feedback were invaluable: Laurence C. Harmon, CPM®, Attorney at Law, The Griffin Companies in Minneapolis, Minnesota; W. Alan Huffman, CPM®, President of Key Management in Wichita, Kansas; Joseph W. Karp, CPM®, SCSM, President of Realty/REIT Advisors, Inc., in Kerrville, Texas; and Henry M. Schaffer, Attorney at Law, Howe & Hutton, Ltd., in Chicago, Illinois.

We wish to thank Caroline Scoulas and other IREM staff members for all their assistance. We also thank Charles A. Goding, Jr., of Goding Design in Evanston, Illinois, for his work in preparing the book cover.

Finally a special thank you to our own special consultant, Jan Rossi, who was with us every step of the way.

Lawrence J. Fennelly, CPO
John H. Lombardi, PH.D., CST, CPO, NAPS, IAPSC

About the Authors

Lawrence J. Fennelly is a Certified Protection Officer (CPO) affiliated with the International Foundation for Protection Officers. He has a bachelor's degree in law enforcement and extensive training and experience in different aspects of security.

Mr. Fennelly is recently retired after more than 30 years with the Harvard University Police Department where he served as a crime prevention specialist and training officer. As the principal of Assets Protection Training Institute, Inc., in Milton, Massachusetts, he also serves as a professional consultant specializing in crime prevention, security planning and analysis, and litigation (expert witness testimony).

Mr. Fennelly is an active member of the American Society for Industrial Security and a charter member of the International Crime Prevention Practitioners Association. He is also a member of the International Association of Professional Security Consultants, Inc., a member of the Advisory Board of the International Security Management and Crime Prevention Institute based in Australia, and a Senior Consultant for Loyal Security, Inc, based in Fayetteville, North Carolina.

His prior experience includes service as a consultant for a year-long Priority One Program on Crime Prevention for WNEV-TV and appointment to President Reagan's Task Force on Crime Prevention and Violent Crime. He has written numerous articles and is the author or editor of several books, including *Handbook of Loss Prevention and Crime Prevention,* third edition, and *Office and Office Building Security,* second edition.

John H. Lombardi is a professional criminologist with a doctorate from The Florida State University School of Criminology and a master's degree in criminal psychology. He is professionally board certified by the National Academy of Police Specialists, Academy of Security Educators and Trainers, International Foundation of Protection Officers, and the International Association of Private Security Consultants.

Dr. Lombardi has been a professor of criminology at several universities over the past 15 years and is currently chairman of the criminal justice department for Troy State University – King's Bay Naval Submarine Base in St. Mary's, Georgia, a suburb of Jacksonville, Florida. He was also training director of the police academy in north Florida's Panhandle in Panama City, Florida, and chief investigator for the State of Illinois Violent Crimes Parole Unit in Chicago.

He is an active member and participating board member in several national and international professional associations, including the American Society for Industrial Security, the Justice Research Institute of Chicago, the Academy of Security Educators and Trainers, and the International Security Management and Crime Prevention Institute based in Australia. He is a senior consultant for Loyal Security, Inc., based in Fayetteville, North Carolina.

A frequent speaker on security issues, including civil litigation resulting from acts of violence and security and police operations, Dr. Lombardi has authored numerous articles and contributed chapters to several prominent books on security. As a principal of Lombardi and Associates, Inc., in Tallahassee and Jacksonville, Florida, he also serves as a security consultant and expert witness in litigation on premises security liability and as a consultant to governmental agencies and private companies.

Contributors

Randall I. Atlas, Ph.D., AIA, CPP, an architect with a doctorate in criminology, is Vice President of Atlas Safety & Security Design Inc., in Miami, Florida.

Timothy D. Crowe, M.S., author of numerous publications on criminal justice and loss prevention subjects, is a professional consultant on Crime Prevention Through Environmental Design (CPTED) working out of Louisville, Kentucky.

James H. Cullity, Manager, Engineered Systems Division of American Alarm and Communications in Arlington, Massachusetts, is a specialist in alarm systems and technologies.

J. Scott Harr, J.D., Public Safety Director for the City of Chanhassen, Minnesota, is responsible for law enforcement, fire and rescue services, building and fire inspections, crime prevention, and code enforcement in this suburb of Minneapolis.

Christopher A. Hertig, M.S., CPP, CPO, has written several books on security subjects, including training, and is on the faculty of York College of Pennsylvania where he teaches security management and criminal justice courses.

John I. Kostanoski, M.A., C.S.T., is Professor and Chair of the Department of Criminal Justice and Director of the Security-Imaging Systems Laboratory at the State University of New York at Farmingdale.

Patrick J. Lenaghan, Lt. Col. (Ret.), U.S. Army Special Forces, has an M.A. degree in Security Management and is President of Loyal Security, Inc., in Fayetteville, North Carolina.

Jeffrey R. Mazor, J.D., Senior Partner, Jeffrey R. Mazor and Associates P.A., Attorneys at Law, in North Miami Beach, Florida, frequently writes about legal aspects of crime on managed properties for publication in real estate journals.

Dana Perrin is an Administrator for the University of Rochester (N.Y.) Security Services Division assigned to the Crime Prevention Program. He has extensive background and training in criminal justice and CPTED.

Michelle Richter is a police officer with the Metropolitan Nashville (Tennessee) Police Department with several years experience patrolling in high-crime low-income housing areas. She has a B.S. degree in criminal justice.

Steven J. Rizzuto, CPM®, RPA, a senior property manager with 15 years experience in all aspects of property management, is also a licensed real estate broker.

David R. Struckhoff, Ph.D., Director, Justice Research Institute in Joliet, Illinois, is also Associate Professor, Loyola University, Chicago, where he teaches theoretical criminology, and has written extensively on crime and criminals.

Contents

Strategy in a Society of "Broken Windows"

The concept of "broken windows" described by Wilson and Kelling back in 1982[1] indicates that anonymity, the frequency of "no one caring," disorder, and crime are linked in a developmental sequence: If a single window is broken and left unrepaired, "all of the rest of the windows will soon be broken." Untended or unguarded property becomes "fair game" for criminal activity. Lack of guardianship results in the breakdown of community controls, as well as the individual controls at individual properties. It is possible to have a low-crime property in a high-crime area and vice versa. Deferred maintenance can lower the value of a property, as well as people's perceptions of it, and lessen one's pride of ownership. When the property tax rate is coupled with market value, it most often directly impacts the crime rate: Public service (number of police), school systems (quality of education), and zoning effects (market values) are linked together through real estate taxation.

It is most important that property owners and managers understand the difference between "order maintenance" and "crime control." *Order maintenance* existed prior to the 1950s when police functioned more informally to support community controls. These informal resources and reinforcements have been superseded by stricter police procedures for dealing with suspected criminals—the replacement police strategy of "crime control" focuses on due process and fair treatment. (Law enforcement organizational research indicates that police departments have a stronger vested interest in "crime control" strategies for general deterrence in a city than in "order maintenance" for situational crime prevention on individual properties.)

Current police strategy focuses on the Uniform Crime Reports, which lists seven felonies that comprise the Crime Index. These data are collected

1

from police departments by the Federal Bureau of Investigation (FBI). Because lesser crimes are not counted in the Crime Index, police man-hours are more closely accounted in relation to the Crime Index and more serious crimes. This means it is up to individuals to anticipate when serious crime will actually be the outcome from less-serious infractions or disorder.

The climate of real estate management is continually changing. Violence has continued to increase each year, and there is a high probability that it will continue to increase. Civil litigation pertaining to premises security also has drastically increased. In addition, the growth of security forces (private police) has exceeded that of law enforcement personnel (public police) by more than 350 percent.[2]

Adequate security and security awareness have a foundation in supportive management, and together they anticipate potential risk exposures of residents and/or tenants and property. This is proactive management, not reactive policing. The longer your properties are unprotected against predatory crime, the higher the probability that crime will be displaced to your property from other properties that are better secured. This is so because (a) violent crimes are foreseeable, and (b) "crime prevention" tends to work better where it is needed least. In locales where virtually all categories of crime continue to be on the increase, it would seem that one consequence of proactive strategies (e.g., security surveys, police liaison, neighborhood watch programs) is a displacement of crime to less secure areas.[3,4]

Efforts to increase security measures on managed properties are less expensive and easier to implement than trying to change social conditions generally. The guardianship over your premises determines whether criminal opportunity will be displaced to other properties that are not as secure as yours—or vice versa—or if a criminal will be discouraged because the effort to commit a crime outweighs the reward. The probability is that criminals will avoid increased risks at protected properties and seek opportunities at less-protected targets. Because security is good management and good management is good business, security is good business. Just as selling more product generates more profit, reducing loss also generates more profit.

Throughout this book, many topics will be discussed that have an impact on the incidence of crime or the potential for crime occurring at your managed property. By shining a spotlight on legal issues, identification of security needs, crime prevention strategies, asset protection strategies, and specific security measures, the book provides a big picture view of the guardianship of managed property.

Notes

1. Wilson, James Q., and Kelling, George L.: Broken Windows, *Atlantic Monthly* 249(3):29, March 1982.

2. Cunningham, W. C.; Strauchs, J. G., and Van Meter, C. W.: *Private Security Trends 1970– 2000: Hallcrest Report II* (Boston: Butterworth-Heinemann, 1990).

3. Bennett, J.: Factors Related to Participation in Neighborhood Watch, *British Journal of Criminology* 29(3):207, 1989.

4. Rosenbaum, D.: Community Crime Prevention: A Review and Synthesis of the Literature, *Justice Quarterly* 5(3):323, 1988.

Spotlight
on
Legal Issues

Negligence, Liability, and the Law

Negligence and liability are defined in the law. Real estate managers need to know what constitutes negligence and how their actions and the property owner's actions—or their respective failures to take action—can make them liable for injuries to people and damage to others' property. Liability is assigned under civil law, which differentiates between intentional and negligent torts, weighs the evidence of injury, and exacts monetary damages to compensate the injured party. This is the realm of lawsuits.

Liability under civil law may also accrue from criminal acts, which are defined as to differing degrees of severity based on the evidence. The perpetrator of a criminal act is punished (e.g., imprisoned) or required to make restitution. The punishment for a crime is completely separate from any liability for injuries caused by the criminal while committing the crime (e.g., a robber shoots a store employee during a holdup) or as a consequence of the criminal incident (e.g., fleeing from the crime scene, the robber knocks down a pedestrian on the sidewalk outside the store, and in the fall, the pedestrian's arm is broken, and a piece of broken glass cuts the person's face leaving a gash that requires stitches). Strange as it may seem, the robbery victim—the store employee—could sue the storekeeper and the owner of the building for negligence in providing security, and both the storekeeper and the building owner could be held liable for the employee's and the pedestrian's injuries while the robber, if caught, might only be subject to prosecution for the criminal act. In fact, if the perpetrator of the crime were injured on the premises during the commission of the crime (e.g., in a fall), the storekeeper and the building owner could be held liable for the robber's injuries as well.

Although the real estate manager's concern is for his or her own liability,

The Language of Negligence and Liability

Following are definitions of some of the legal terms that are used in this book, which are not always explained in context. These are general descriptions in common language to facilitate reader understanding and not precise legal definitions; *Black's Law Dictionary* is a definitive resource for specific definitions. Most other relevant terms are defined in place.

Damages Money to be paid to the injured party as compensation. Often specified as *compensatory damages* to pay the victim for the actual loss (value of the property damaged/cost of replacement) or injury (cost of medical treatment/wages lost) or *punitive damages* to be paid over and above the amount of actual loss. The first, also called *actual damages,* is intended to compensate the injured party for loss or damage; the second, also called *exemplary damages,* is intended to punish the person at fault. (Insurance can only pay compensatory or actual damages, not punitive damages.)

Defendant The party who is sued; the wrongdoer or person alleged to be at fault.

Deposition Testimony required for a lawsuit but not taken in open court. A deposition is taken during "discovery" before a court reporter who records and transcribes the testimony.

Foreseeability The reasonable anticipation that a certain act or failure to act is likely to have certain results, including possible injury or property damage.

Invitee Any person who has been invited onto a property or has a business reason to be there. Examples include vendors' representatives (sales or delivery personnel), clients or customers of commercial tenants, residents' guests or other visitors.

both personally and as the agent of the property owner, it is important to understand some of the rudiments of criminal law because managed properties can be and often are the sites of criminal acts. Moreover, the perpetrators of criminal acts on managed properties are not exclusively unrelated third parties. A resident, a site employee, or the manager, or a visitor to any of these people, might have a criminal history (possibly including time served in jail) and prey upon others at the property, residents or staff members alike. A crime against people or property, if committed on or near a property you manage, can involve you in the prosecution of the criminal. (You may have to give testimony in a deposition or at trial.) You may also be sued by the victim—or the perpetrator—of the crime, by the heirs of either party, or by a bystander. The following chapters address these concerns in detail.

First, "The Property Manager as Juggler" by J. Scott Harr provides a brief overview of some of the specific issues and preventive measures (CPTED and watch programs) that will be discussed in detail in later chapters. In ad-

---

The Language of Negligence and Liability *(concluded)*

Liability A finding that someone is responsible for something and therefore obligated to take action or pay damages.

Negligence In general, the failure to use *reasonable care*. As a *tort* (legal wrong), however, negligence comprises a duty owed, a breach of that duty, an injury or property damage directly resulting from the breach of duty, and financial compensation to the injured party (damages).

Perpetrator A person who commits a crime or tort. (Sometimes shortened to "perp.")

Plaintiff The party who complains or files a lawsuit.

Prior Similar Acts Previous occurrences of the same or a comparable crime in or near a particular location. This may be interpreted broadly to encompass any previous occurrences of criminal acts: A particular crime having occurred at a managed property or within its neighborhood could be considered a prior similar act in the event of any specific crime occurring in the same general area some time later.

Reasonable Care The ordinary precautions expected or required because of the nature of an action or the circumstances surrounding it.

Totality of the Circumstances A "big picture" look at all the circumstances of an incident, rather than a focus on any one factor.

NOTE: The implications of a particular incident in which a real estate manager may become involved will require understanding of specifics that should be explained by his or her legal counsel.

---

dition to a perspective on foreseeability, he defines and provides examples of negligent hiring, supervision, and retention. These employment considerations can lead to all sorts of problems, including workplace violence.

Next, "Civil Law: A Foundation in Torts" provides some examples of negligent acts and explains how damages are determined. Then, "Giving a Deposition" describes the deposition process and what is expected of the person being deposed. It also provides some cautions and gives some tips on how to prepare for a deposition.

"Crime and Criminal Law" identifies and characterizes some of the more frequently occurring crimes against people and against property. It also discusses the crime scene and provides tips on target hardening.

"The Issue of Foreseeability" takes a more detailed look at foreseeability and identifies some of the ways real estate managers can minimize liability through appropriate documentation of security efforts. In particular, foreseeability is discussed in terms of "prior similar acts" and the "totality of the circumstances" rules that are applied in a court of law. Also included are factors utilized in establishing general and specific foreseeability and a listing of items that comprise documentation of security.

Finally, "Strategizing Proactivity: The Predatory Prevention Matrix" introduces a new concept that is being utilized as a working tool in developing

---

Crime and Liability

Crime, the prevention of crime, and the handling of the perpetrators of crimes are issues that have perplexed society since Biblical times. Not surprisingly, the legal system has had a major impact, if not in proposing solutions to the problem of crime, at least in allocating responsibility for its consequences.

Historically, owners and managers of commercial and residential premises enjoyed some insulation from liability for criminal acts committed on their sites. Courts were reluctant to impose responsibility, most often for the reason that criminal behavior is inherently random and unpredictable. Landlords, the courts reasoned, could not be expected to anticipate that crimes would occur on their premises and therefore should not be held liable when they did.

Increasingly, however, there has been a trend to find owners and their agents responsible for criminal activity that occurs at their sites. In an increasingly litigious society, and one that is increasingly plagued by criminal behavior, it is hardly surprising that the courts are willing to hold owners and their surrogates responsible despite the fact that they were not involved in the act itself and arguably could have done little to prevent the crime or to minimize its consequences.

---

and evaluating evidence for both plaintiff and defense cases in lawsuits. It also provides a starting point for avoiding liability—and losses—at managed properties.

For individuals, real safety and security are as much a result of personal awareness and an attitude of caution as of devices and protocols. The latter, without the former, will not deter criminals. That said, the importance of preparedness cannot be overstated. Emergencies and criminal incidents are not exclusively the province of other people and others' properties. They are probabilities for any property.

There is always a likelihood that a particular person or property will be a "victim" at some time, and the likelihood increases as incidents escalate. Just as deferred maintenance increases the probability of roof leaks and potential structural damage to a building, perpetrators of criminal acts are emboldened when their acts are ignored or tolerated.

In addressing security issues, awareness of potential problems (possibilities) and the likelihood of their occurring (probabilities) is the first step. Examination of possibilities and probabilities provides a rationale for action or inaction—for prescribing or choosing to take specific actions. As pointed out in the discussion of the Predatory Prevention Matrix, *policy is static*. Proactive preparedness requires establishing procedures. Unless established procedures derived from the policy are spelled out clearly and implemented effectively—and communicated to all those who are affected by it—security policy remains an undeveloped idea.

Preparedness involves taking *reasonable* precautions. With regard to

---

Foreseeability

Foreseeability of risk requires the real estate manager to be able to recognize potential problems. A criminal act may injure one or more people or result in damage to property or both. Any crimes perpetrated on a property must be prosecuted under criminal law. A criminal incident is not likely to end with prosecution of the criminals. Apart from the individual who is the victim of a crime, others may claim some "injury" as a result, and any or all of these people could initiate a civil lawsuit against the property and its owner and manager, claiming negligence in the provision of security. In an increasingly litigious society, real estate managers must be continually on the alert for potential problems and ways to deal with them. This is not only being proactive but may prevent future crimes.

---

security policy, for example, one item to consider is a procedure for reporting incidents, which might read: "If you witness a crime being perpetrated on the property, notify the police *and* the management—in that order." Notice to the proper authority first speeds response—the reverse delays response; a less-knowledgeable "middle man" cannot communicate details about particulars of the incident as well as the eyewitness can.

This first section looks at some of the legal issues that can and do arise in the management of real estate. Many of the concepts and strategies that are briefly outlined here are revisited in later chapters in different contexts as they explore ways to identify security needs, outline various strategies for preventing crime and protecting people and property (assets), and describe different kinds of security measures that can be implemented at managed properties to reduce liability and minimize the attendant economic losses resulting from lawsuits.

The Property Manager as Juggler

J. Scott Harr

Anyone trying to operate a business these days has to be proficient at juggling. This is certainly the case for real estate managers. Not only do property managers want to create the safest environment for those they serve and with whom they do business, but it is a fact of life that, no matter how hard one tries, the odds of a lawsuit are increasing. What follows are some suggestions of ways to help minimize risk as you juggle the various concerns. They are based on my own experience and unique perspective as a licensed police officer, private investigator, and attorney. My goal is to provide you with a "nuts and bolts" approach to help you juggle the two goals ever in the real estate manager's mind:

1. To create a safe environment for those enjoying your property, and

2. To minimize your legal liability.

My first recommendation is simply to be observant and exercise good judgment. Everyone is busy, and everyone views the world around them from a very personal perspective. However, real estate managers must take the time to learn about pertinent safety and security issues that affect the properties they manage: They need to look at the big picture and view things practically.

The big picture revolves around two questions: "How could someone be injured on the premises?" and "What can I reasonably do to prevent it?" While these may seem easy questions to answer, especially to those who are trained in security, the problem is that for most people, being "safety and security conscious" means becoming more suspicious than most of them were brought up to be. You have to learn to change the way you look at things—and people—and you have to start asking yourself questions that you are not used to asking:

What is wrong with the way things are being done now?

Could someone get hurt because of something we are—or are not—doing?

How could a criminal take advantage of the property?

What is the worst thing that could happen?

and

What can be done to prevent it?

My second recommendation is a word of caution against going overboard. A little cynicism and suspicion is necessary in everyone's work. Not everyone is as careful as they should be, and not everyone is a law-abiding citizen. The reverse is also true: Not everyone is evil or waiting to take advantage of an opportunity to file a frivolous lawsuit. However, there are criminals, and there are people who sue over what others think is frivolous. It is part of your job to be prepared, as best you can, to deal with both groups.

Preventing Crime

A wonderful resource that is available to just about everyone is the crime prevention unit of the local law enforcement agency—i.e., the police. For years, crime prevention officers have been working hand-in-hand with property managers to help them learn more about the various factors that create a more-secure environment. Things like proper locks, security hardware, alarms, and lighting are critical, and police personnel trained in crime prevention will be more than happy to give you information about these measures. A particularly worthwhile service that police gladly provide is a premises survey, during which a crime prevention professional examines a property and makes recommendations that can help make it safer and more secure. Because crime prevention is their business, you can acquire a great deal of information by simply tagging along while your property is being surveyed or by taking the time to arrange a meeting with them.

Two relevant concepts come to mind regarding crime prevention as it applies to property managers. The first is Crime Prevention Through Environmental Design; the other is crime free multi-housing programs.

Crime Prevention Through Environmental Design (CPTED).
CPTED addresses exactly what I mentioned at the beginning of this discussion—thinking about what is going on around you. In designing a property, or when making changes to it, you should consider all of the "what if"

questions and plan accordingly. For example, you should avoid having bushes planted in front of windows because criminals can hide in them; nor do you want driveways to be totally hidden from view. On the safety side, it is not a good idea to have downspouts positioned so they drain melting snow onto a sidewalk where the water can freeze to a sheet of ice.

Crime Free Multi-Housing.   A very exciting idea that continues to gain momentum is that of programs developed through the mutual efforts and cooperation between local law enforcement personnel and property managers. This relationship offers tremendous benefits to tenants and property owners and managers, as well as the police. The result has been development of so-called *neighborhood watch* programs for multi-housing properties.

Crime free multi-housing, a concept that originated in Mesa, Arizona, offers strategies for keeping illegal activity out of rental properties. According to the Mesa Crime Free Multi-Housing Program, three key elements commonly used in traditional crime prevention have added to the success of the program:

1. Management training,
2. Security assessments, and
3. Resident training and involvement.

Developed with input from many perspectives, including property management associations, legal aid attorneys, resident advocates, police and public housing officials, the Crime Free Multi-Housing Program teaches property owners and managers how to deter illegal activity. The program delivers two important messages:

1. Effective property management can have a major impact on the health and welfare and/or safety of a community; and,
2. There are accessible, legitimate techniques that can be used to stop the spread of illegal activity on rental property.[1]

Negligence and Foreseeability.   The easiest way to learn about crime prevention is to pay attention to what is going on around you. Not only is this a precise way to know if there are things to take precautions against because they are indeed occurring around you, but the law expects and, in fact, demands it of you. *The essence of negligence is the failure to prevent harm from foreseeable risk.* For example, if a person is not paying attention while driving and does not stop for a stop sign, and someone is injured because the driver did not stop, that driver is *negligent.* (It is *foreseeable* that if one does not stop for a stop sign, someone may be hurt in an ensuing crash.) In real estate management, if you know (or should have known) that certain crime is occurring in or around your property, and you fail to respond by taking adequate safety measures—and someone is injured—you could be found liable.

The law expects anyone who has a legal responsibility to others to take *reasonable precautions* to prevent foreseeable harm. Property managers and owners clearly have a legal responsibility to those who work at, live on, and visit their properties. You have to provide adequate locks as well as keep ice off the sidewalk. You need to provide adequate lighting as well as keep the steps in repair. It is a truism that any competent defense attorney would argue why you may not be liable, but the operative word here is *may*. The goal of this book is to help you minimize your risk by learning how to prevent injury or damage before it occurs. You must also bear in mind that an injury which results from a crime committed on your property could be just as legally actionable as an injury from an accidental slip and fall under certain circumstances—*if it was reasonable that you could have prevented it.* The point is: You need to learn how to identify actual and potential risks, and there are people whom you can ask for help.

Avoiding Negligent Employment Practices

Another source of legal woes for real estate managers is what the legal community refers to as negligent hiring, retention, and supervision. If you hire or retain an employee whom you know, or should have known, is trouble, and someone gets hurt as a result, *you pay*. Similarly, if you supervise someone, and do so inadequately, with a result that someone is injured, *you pay*. This is where the good judgment mentioned earlier enters the picture. Some specific cases provide examples.

Negligent Hiring.   In one case, an ex-convict was hired as an apartment manager. He had access to all of the units with his pass key, of course, and it only took a couple of weeks before he entered a unit and raped the resident at knifepoint.[2] The Minnesota Supreme Court held that those hiring such a person could be liable:

> If they employed someone with known propensities (toward wrongdoing), or
>
> If such propensities should have been discovered through reasonable inquiry (i.e., background checks), and
>
> If, because of the circumstances of the employment, it should have been foreseeable that the hired individual posed a threat of injury to others.[3]

The duty imposed by law here is to not hire a person whom you know, or should have known, could reasonably be expected to injure someone.

Negligent Retention.   Negligent retention is failing to terminate someone who has proven to be a problem. This is the old concept that "where
there's smoke, there's fire." An example is a case in which a railroad passenger was able to sue the railroad depot after the passenger was injured as a
result of a beating received at the hands of a baggage handler who had
beaten others "savagely" on the property over the previous six years.[4] The
Court said that the depot had "no more right" to permit continued employment of a dangerous person than it would have to permit dangerous physical conditions on the property.

The rationale derives from a simple question: Did the railroad have any
reason to think that if this individual had beaten others, then he might do
the same thing again? The answer is: Yes. Therefore, the railroad was negligent for retaining him.

If you have a problem employee, you should consider terminating his
or her employment. However, I would offer these words of caution: If
premises liability does not scare you, *wrongful termination* should. (Be
sure to consult your legal advisor before firing anyone!)

Negligent Supervision.   The essence of negligent supervision is that, if
the owner of a property supervises someone, that supervision had better be
adequate. People who are hired should not be allowed to "do their own
thing"—i.e., with no training and no supervision. This does not mean that
every single employee has to be watched every minute of the day. What it
does mean is that you will bear some responsibility for directing your employees, setting guidelines, and responding if they are not behaving accordingly. If failure to supervise adequately could result in foreseeable injury,
you could be legally responsible. The point is made directly in an article by
Ellen Sampson and Daniel Oberdorfer,[5] in which they provide these practical tips:

> When hiring new employees or moving employees into new posi-
> tions, employers should make a careful assessment of the risks of
> violence or other wrongful conduct that could be associated with
> the job.
>
> Thorough background investigations are warranted when the
> employee has authority over others, perhaps by virtue of a uniform
> or gun necessary for the job; is working closely with children; or
> has access to private quarters . . . . Background checks may include
> calling references and prior employers, as well as checking appro-
> priate public records for criminal history.
>
> While working diligently to reduce negligent hiring and reten-
> tion, employers must also be cautious not to expose themselves to
> liability on the other end—for discrimination against prospective
> or current employees. Background checks should be enforced

uniformly. Overly rigid prehiring criteria may be discriminatory in themselves.

Sampson and Daniel conclude by stating: "The threat of liability from both sides demonstrates how this area of employment law, like many others, is colored in shades of gray and is fraught with potential pitfalls for employers."[6]

Literally everything anyone does, whether at home or at work, involves some degree of risk. An extreme fear of legal liability would result in a kind of paralysis—an inability to take action because of fear of the consequences. The law should not make one helpless. In fact, it is the law that helps people understand that they have certain responsibilities to others, and that responsibility is to do what they can to prevent foreseeable injury to others. After all, that is exactly what they expect everyone else to do.

Being Prepared

The old Boy Scout motto, "Be Prepared," should be the real estate manager's guide as well.

- Prepare yourself and your property to be safe.
- Use the resources available to you, including the crime prevention division of your local police, or hire a security consultant.
- If your geographic area has a property managers' association, much can be learned by becoming actively involved in such an organization.
- Take advantage of periodicals and trade journals that relate to your business—inevitably there will be articles on legal actions taken against those in similar positions, along with recommendations about what to do to prevent problems that could result in lawsuits.
- Be aware of problems that are occurring on or around the properties you manage (or own), and every time an incident occurs, ask yourself if there is something that you could have done differently.
- Take the time and the opportunity to survey the properties you manage, including the people who work for or with you, and be willing to ask what you can do to make things *safe and secure.*

There is an all too common attitude about negligence and liability that "it can never happen to me"—but it can happen to you, and you need to be prepared.

Notes

1. Crime Free Multi-Housing Program—Program and Instructor's Guidebook.
2. *Ponticas v. KMS Investments,* 331 N.W.2d 907 (Minn. 1983).

3. *Id.* at 911 (relying on Restatement (Second) Agency 213 (1958)).

4. *Dean v. St. Paul Union Depot,* 43 N.W. 54 (Minn. 1889).

5. Sampson, Ellen G., and Oberdorfer, Daniel: "Negligent Hiring, Retention and Supervision: An Update," *The Hennepin Lawyer* March-April 1995 (pp. 4–32).

6. *Id.* at 6.

Civil Law: A Foundation in Torts

The majority of security-related lawsuits are civil tort actions. A *tort* is wrongful conduct, either an act or failure to act, by one party which violates the common law or statutory personal or property rights of another and for which the victim may elect to bring a civil suit (distinct from a contract or criminal action) to obtain judicial relief.

Categories of Torts

There are two major categories of torts: *Intentional torts* are purposeful acts (e.g., assault, battery, false imprisonment, and defamation), whereas *negligent torts* are breaches of the legal duty to act reasonably (e.g., negligent operation of a vehicle, negligent hiring, and negligent security).

In order to prevail at trial, the injured party *(plaintiff)* must prove all the elements of each alleged tort against the entity believed to be responsible for the injury *(defendant)*. Elements of an intentional tort are:

Intent
Act
Cause in fact (i.e., actual cause)—
—"But for" test
—"Substantial factor" test
Injury

Elements of a negligent tort, on the other hand, are:

Duty owed
Breach of duty (i.e., failure to act reasonably)
Cause in fact

Foreseeable cause based on—
—Actual notice (i.e., prior similar incidents)
—Constructive notice (i.e., knowledge of reasonable person or professional in the same situation as defendant)
Injury

The following examples illustrate the difference.

CASE 1. If a youth threw an egg at a passing car, and the egg hit a passenger in the eye and caused permanent vision impairment, are the elements of an *intentional tort* present to hold the youth responsible—i.e., did the defendant have the intent to commit the act, did he commit the act, and was the act the cause in fact of the injury?[1]

In this case, the answer would be yes. The youth would likely be charged with the crime of assault and battery with a dangerous weapon (the egg), and the civil issues would be addressed separately. (Assault and battery is a tort as well as a crime.)

CASE 2. If a janitor mopping a floor with a soapy solution put out a warning sign, and a woman slipped in an area where the sign was not located and injured her back, are the elements of a *negligent tort* present—i.e., did the defendant have a legal duty owed, did the defendant breach this duty by failing to act reasonably, and was this breach of duty the cause in fact and foreseeable cause of the injury?[2]

In this case, the answer would also be yes because the wet floor contributed to the victim's injury. There should have been a procedure for mopping that included the area of floor to be wet at one time and to ensure that the wet area could be reasonably identified by placement of signage.

Determination of Damages

Damages may be categorized as nominal, compensatory, or punitive. The focus in this section is on how the courts determine the amount of damages a defendant must pay if the verdict is rendered in favor of the plaintiff.

Nominal Damages are awarded when a plaintiff's actual injury or loss was very slight. The judgment may be as small as one dollar. *Compensatory or actual damages* are awarded to compensate financially for the loss sustained by the plaintiff. Compensatory damages are further differentiated. *General damages* are for injuries which are a natural result of the act and common to all victims—e.g., "pain and suffering" and medical expenses. *Special damages* cover those injuries which are unique to the victim—e.g., lost past and future wages (if the victim was employed or employable), loss of affection (if the victim was married), and child care (if the victim had children who need to be cared for). *Punitive or exemplary damages* are awarded in addition to compensatory damages to punish defendants for conduct which showed a "conscious disregard" for the rights of others or was "outrageous," "willful," "wanton," or "malicious" in nature. Punitive damages may be awarded individually against the employee and the employer. The amount of the damages may be based upon such factors as:

1. The outrageousness of the defendant's conduct,
2. The extent of injury to the plaintiff,
3. The cost of litigation, and
4. The wealth of the defendant.

The amount of insurance available is also a consideration.

The following examples illustrate an escalating situation and its potential consequences:

- If a security officer, without verbal warning, pushed a peaceful male demonstrator to move him behind the court-ordered protest line, and the demonstrator was deeply upset emotionally and sued, what type of damages, if any, will the demonstrator receive?
- In the same situation, will the type of damages be any different if the officer shoved the demonstrator, and the demonstrator tripped and smashed his head on the sidewalk?
- Also in the same situation, will the type of damages be any different if the officer hit the demonstrator with a nightstick several times over the head?

In the first instance, the injured party might receive only nominal damages or nothing; the injury in the second instance could possibly require payment of compensatory damages; in the third instance, the willfulness of the officer's behavior coupled with the use of excessive force could warrant payment of punitive damages. Additional examples arise out of specific cases:

CASE 1. Suppose a mall employed one officer, instead of two officers (as recommended by its contract security agency), to patrol its parking lot, and plaintiff was abducted from the parking lot, assaulted, run over by a car, and left with her hair pinned under the car which was set on fire by the assailants. Was the conduct of the mall sufficient to sustain punitive damages?[3]

In this case, the answer would be yes, based in particular on the inadequacy of security because the mall did not follow the staffing recommendation of the agency it hired.

CASE 2. Suppose a store loss prevention manager detained two employees in order to verbally coerce them into confessions and threatened them with arrest if they did not confess, had them arrested in order to make an example of them for the other employees, and failed to appear at their criminal trial. Was the manager's conduct sufficient to justify punitive damages?[4]

In this case, the answer would again be yes. The manager, having filed an initial complaint, would be obligated to follow through and appear at trial. If the employees were found innocent, the manager's failure to appear could lead to a lawsuit accusing the manager of false arrest.

Notes

1. *Flynn v. Burnett,* Arizona, Maricopa County Superior Court, No. CV 872057, reported in 32 ATLA L. Rep. 258 (Aug. 1989).

2. *Williams v. ARA Food Services,* N.Y., New York County Supreme Court, No. 27135/86, reported in 32 ATLA L. Rep. 410 (November 1989).

3. *Jardel Co. Inc. v. Hughes,* 523 A.2d 518 (Del. 1987).

4. *Redican v. KMart Corp.,* 734 S.W.2d 864 (Mo.App. 1987) and 885 S.W.2d 578 (1990).

Giving a Deposition

As a result of a civil lawsuit, a property manager may be called upon to give testimony relative to certain facts that he or she is aware of regarding overall operations and/or the employees of the property. You should go to this *deposition* fully prepared—review related documents and discuss the case with your counsel beforehand—and respond truthfully when asked a question.

Depositions are usually taken at an attorney's office; in a lawsuit, they are taken at the office of the plaintiff's attorney. Both plaintiff and defense attorneys will be present along with one or more members of their staffs. The entire proceeding will be recorded by a court reporter. While the setting is less dramatic than a courtroom trial, the seriousness of the intent should not be underestimated. [NOTE: If you were asked to serve as an expert witness, you would be deposed by the attorney who invited you to serve in this capacity, and you would be expected to comment on the situation at another managed property. Also, while videotape recording holds out the possibility of giving testimony *in absentia* (for example, if you would be out of state at the time of trial), the technology is used only rarely because of its limitations: Attorneys prefer to have witnesses appear in court to respond to questions directly.]

Before the court reporter swears you in, the lawyers may joke among themselves—about other trials, their colleagues, a judge—but once you are sworn, there are no more jokes or games. In fact, it is stressful for all involved. Taking of depositions is a preliminary, evidence-gathering step. While a lawsuit may not actually go to trial, giving a deposition will not relieve you of an obligation to testify if the suit does go before a judge and/or a jury. Since it is likely that at some time an incident on a property you manage will lead to a lawsuit, the following are some things to keep in mind as you prepare to give a deposition.

- While the process is informal, you are not conversing with a personal friend. Anything you say may—can, will—be asked of you again in court.

- Your statements will be reviewed very closely by opposing counsel's staff and experts.

- The scheduled time for a deposition can affect your responses and reactions. Early in the day and early in the work week are optimal times: Studies have shown that 2:00 P.M. on a Friday afternoon is least desirable—and productive—because people are fatigued and their blood sugar levels may be low. Monday or Tuesday at 9:00 A.M. is generally a better time. (Tell counsel *when you are available,* and choose the best possible time for you.)

- When you enter the room where you are going to be deposed, relax and make yourself comfortable. You are going to be there for a few hours, at least. Take off your coat or jacket; men can loosen their neckties. Ask for a cup of coffee, a soft drink (preferably *not* sugar free), or a glass of water.

- There should be opportunities to take a break
  —When the reporter changes the tape in the machine,
  —In the event you need to go to the bathroom, or
  —At least once every hour.
  Take advantage of the first or request the second as necessary.

- Assuming that plaintiff's counsel is deposing you, he or she is going to attempt to do the following:
  —Find out what you know about the case;
  —Find out what facts and evidence you are prepared to present;
  —Find out what your defense may be;
  —Create conflicts between your testimony and that of other personnel on your staff; and
  —Back you into a corner (in the vernacular, try to "put you in a box").

This is why it is important to *sit down with your counsel and discuss in detail* what you know, what the facts are, and what you are expected to testify about specifically. (Some additional tips for handling yourself during a deposition appear in the accompanying box.)

Because the stakes are high—both professionally and monetarily—for a real estate manager involved in a lawsuit, it is critical to prove there was no negligence and therefore no liability. Care and attention to documentation before, during, and after the fact are vital to defending a lawsuit—all the more reason to avoid having to defend a lawsuit by preventing problems that can give rise to one.

The purpose of a deposition is to discover what you know about a spe-

Some Tips on Giving a Deposition

- Always tell the truth.
- Always make sure you understand the question. If you don't, ask the lawyer to repeat it.
- Take your time, and think about your answer.
- Never guess at a response. If you don't know, say "I don't know"; don't speculate about an answer.
- Never volunteer any information. The attorney must ask the question. Don't open up an additional area for exploration.
- Stay focused.
- Be clear and consistent in your presentation—a deposition is not a leisurely conversation.
- Always be polite and patient; never lose your temper. Speak slowly—in a calm and controlled voice—and keep your answers short.
- Usually the attorney will frame the question so there is no need for a detailed or descriptive response. Most questions can be answered simply:
  —Yes, Sir.
  —No, Sir.
  —That's correct.
  —I don't know.
  —I don't recall.
- You can correct your answers at any time. If you recall some additional facts as the questions are being asked, don't hesitate to correct an earlier misstatement.
- You have the right to complete your answer, although the attorney may cut off your answer if it is not what he or she wanted to hear. Don't let the deposing attorney upset you.
- Pay close attention to the way questions are asked: Attorneys tend to phrase questions: "Mr. Manager, you will agree with me that . . . ." Be very careful if this line of questioning is introduced. Slow down; listen carefully and don't be rushed into a response.
- The attorneys will object to various questions being asked; listen carefully to these objections before answering. Your attorney will tell you if you can answer.
- Finally, giving a deposition is not a game; it is serious business. No one will ever tell you what your rights are or what you should or shouldn't do. Remember, your goal is to tell the truth—clearly, concisely, and completely.

cific case and to learn about your background, education, and training. You need not feel intimidated, and you should not think you have to discuss your entire knowledge with every question asked. You will not be penalized for being honest and truthful if you have nothing to say in response to a question or if you do not understand the lawyer's question and ask to have it repeated.

Crime and Criminal Law

Real estate managers should have a basic understanding of the different types of crimes that can be perpetrated at managed properties. Crimes are classified according to their punishment as a *felony* (punishable by death or imprisonment in a state prison for more than one year) or a *misdemeanor* (punishable by fine, penalty, or other lesser means such as imprisonment in a county facility for less than one year). According to federal law and most state laws, any offense other than a felony is classified as a misdemeanor. Crimes are also distinguished on the basis of their objectives as *crimes against people* and *crimes against property.*

In the discussion that follows, each crime is described in common language to facilitate understanding; the specific criminal classifications are from the Criminal Code of the Commonwealth of Massachusetts. (Because the fine points vary somewhat from one state to another, only broad concepts are addressed here. Legal definitions and the manner of punishment for specific crimes may be found in your state's criminal code or penal code.)

Crimes Against the Person

Assault is an attempt or threat to inflict injury or a display of force that creates fear or apprehension of injury. An assault can exist without any actual injury resulting. Simple assault is usually classified as a misdemeanor while aggravated assault, including assault with a deadly weapon, is a felony.

The intentional and unjustified touching of another person is *battery;* it requires some physical contact or resulting injury. Because the threat (assault) is inherent in the actual use of force (battery), the two are commonly classified together as *assault and battery,* which is considered a misdemeanor.

If a person is killed, regardless of whether another crime has been committed concurrently, the death may be ruled as *manslaughter* (committed without malice) or *murder* (committed with malicious intent). These crimes are usually further differentiated by degree, and all are punishable as felonies. (An unintended homicide that occurs during the commission of a felony is a *felony murder* punishable by life imprisonment or death; however, the law of felony murder varies throughout the United States.)

Possession of a dangerous weapon increases the severity of lesser criminal acts from misdemeanors to felonies. Courts have classified dangerous weapons into two categories—those that are *dangerous per se* and those that are *dangerous as used.* The first are inherently dangerous because of the ability to inflict injury without human intervention—explosives are an example. The latter constitute a danger under certain circumstances because of the manner in which they are used—a rolling pin used to commit a battery becomes a dangerous weapon. Laws often prohibit the carrying or use of *concealed* or *deadly* weapons, and such unlawful possession is usually punished as a felony.

Rape is unlawful sexual intercourse against a person's will or under threat of bodily injury. It is classified as a felony. Assault with the intent to commit rape is likewise a felony. Failure to report a rape, which is a violent crime, is a misdemeanor.

Robbery is the taking of money or property from another person by force or violence against that person's will. Robbery involves bodily injury or the threat of injury and is classified as a felony because of that.

Crimes Against Property

Starting a fire or causing an explosion for the purpose of damaging property or destroying a building or occupied structure is classified as *arson* and is punishable as a felony. *Attempted arson* is also a felony; so is *aggravated arson* in which there is danger to human life as well as property damage or destruction.

At common law, *burglary* consisted of breaking and entering the dwelling of another in the nighttime with intent to commit a felony and was itself classified as a *felony.* Modern statutes are less restrictive, encompassing entry of all kinds of structures at all times. Such entry with intent to commit a misdemeanor is classified as a misdemeanor. Burglary is often classified into degrees (first, second, and third) and may be related to other specific statutes regarding breaking and entering, all of which are classified separately as to punishments, most often as felonies.

The fraudulent appropriation of money or personal property by a person to whom it was lawfully entrusted either by or for the owner is the crime of *embezzlement.* In Massachusetts, if the property is a firearm or if the value exceeds $250, the crime is a felony. However, if the value of the property does not exceed $250, the crime is a misdemeanor. Embezzlement is a form of theft distinguished in common law by the unlawful possession having come about by virtue of the relationship or employment. This is particularly relevant to real estate managers because of the *agency relationship* established by a management agreement that empowers the manager to act as a fiduciary of the owner.

Larceny, on the other hand, is unlawful taking and carrying away of the property of another with the intent to deprive the rightful owner permanently of its use. In Massachusetts, if the value of the property does not exceed $250 dollars, the crime is a misdemeanor; but if the property is a firearm or the value exceeds $250, the crime is a felony.

Many state statutes no longer differentiate between embezzlement, larceny, and obtaining money under false pretenses—i.e., by *fraud*—grouping all such crimes under the heading of larceny. Some states differentiate *grand larceny* from *petty larceny* based on a dollar amount also set by statute. The crime defined as larceny is more commonly known as *theft.*

Any person who intentionally takes possession of merchandise offered for sale without paying for it is guilty of *shoplifting,* which is classified as a misdemeanor. The Massachusetts Criminal Code includes refinements related to concealment, alteration of labeling, removal of price tags, and similar acts.

The crime of *receiving stolen goods* is typically defined as receiving stolen property with the knowledge that it has been stolen or otherwise acquired illegally. In Massachusetts, the crime is a misdemeanor if the value of the property does not exceed $250; if the value exceeds $250, the crime is a felony.

The crime of *injury or damage to property* occurs when personal property or a building belonging to another is damaged or destroyed in any manner or by any means not previously described or mentioned. In other words, such crime relates to damage only and does *not* include conversion or taking by eminent domain. In Massachusetts, willful and malicious (i.e., intentional) damage to property where the value exceeds $250 is a felony while wanton or reckless damage is a misdemeanor.

Other Considerations

There are many other types of crimes real estate managers should be aware of, including trespassing, disorderly conduct, vandalism, malicious mischief, counterfeiting, and crimes involving controlled substances.

Trespass (including criminal trespass) and disorderly conduct are perhaps more likely to be encountered in real estate management in general, and they are also very difficult to define here because the terms cover a

Types of Crimes and Categories of Crime

Following is an abbreviated listing of different types of crimes against people and property, differentiated by their punishment.

Crimes Against People
Assault (M)
—aggravated assault (F)
Assault and battery (M)
Manslaughter (F)
Murder (F)
Possession of dangerous weapon (F)
Rape (F)
Robbery (F)

Crimes Against Property
Arson (F)
Burglary (F)
Embezzlement*
Larceny*
Shoplifting (M)
Receiving stolen goods*
Injury to property
—willful and malicious (F)
—wanton (M)

F = felony; M = misdemeanor.

A *felony* is a crime punishable by death or imprisonment in a state prison; all other crimes are *misdemeanors*.

*Punishment is often differentiated in state statutes by the value of the goods involved, and a second offense (e.g., of receiving stolen goods) or use of a weapon (e.g., in larceny) may upgrade a misdemeanor to a felony.

Source: Criminal Code of the Commonwealth of Massachusetts.

variety of behaviors and situations, and definitions among state statutes vary. In general, *trespass* can be considered an unauthorized entry of private property of another with no apparent intent to commit a separate crime (otherwise such entry to commit a crime would be burglary). *Loitering* may be considered a form of trespass. If the trespasser remains on the property knowing such presence is unauthorized, or in defiance of an order to leave, the offense would be a form of *criminal trespass.* Any behavior that is contrary to law and, in particular, such behavior as disturbs the public peace or safety is categorizable as *disorderly conduct.*

Any willful or malicious act intended to damage or destroy property without regard for the rights of others is considered *vandalism;* this is differentiated from *malicious mischief,* which is intentional destruction of another's property based on ill will or resentment toward the owner. Graffiti and other defacement of property can fall into these categories of crime.

Counterfeiting and crimes involving controlled substances—i.e., drug dealing and use—are addressed in federal laws as well as by state statutes, but these types of crimes are outside the scope of this book.

Regardless of the type of crime, if it is committed on or near a property you manage, you may very well have some responsibility after the fact. In particular, you need to understand what takes place at a *crime scene* and be prepared to establish a more defensive posture against potential future crime *(target hardening).*

Crime Scene. As a real estate manager, there are several things you should be aware of after a crime has been committed. Law enforcement officials will want to rope off the area where a crime has taken place until their investigation is completed. They will want to check for fingerprints, blood stains, clothing, or indications of forced entry (jimmy marks). These are components of the *physical evidence,* which may be defined as materials or articles that are found in connection with the crime and that aid in identifying the perpetrator.

While the police are conducting their investigation, management should be reviewing the steps they should be taking to prevent this type of incident from occurring again.

Target Hardening. Steps taken by management to prevent future criminal activity constitute so-called target hardening—making the property a less-desirable, less-accessible target for criminals.

Consider having a *security survey* performed. This can be done by the crime prevention officer of the local police department or by a security consultant. In addition to a security survey of the property, you should request a *crime demographic survey* of the area within a radius of one mile from your site. (CAP Index, Inc., of King of Prussia, Pennsylvania, is one source for such data. They generate very accurate reports on crime statistics based on coordinates provided by the client. The service may be costly, but in the long run it may provide more meaningful information more quickly than police raw data.) These types of efforts are important as a demonstration that management is taking a proactive approach to security.

Examine local law enforcement crime records, which will give you a listing of all calls for police services. Combining this neighborhood information with in-house security reports will allow you to assess potential risks at your property and identify security measures which should be implemented in order to reduce future losses.

Approaches to target hardening will be described throughout the remainder of this book.

Notes

The definitions of specific crimes presented here are supplemented with assignments of punishment from the Criminal Code of the Commonwealth of Massachusetts, which is a common law state, as it read in 1996. Because the fine points of specific crimes and their assigned punishments vary from state to state, real estate managers should consult their state penal code or criminal code to determine the implications if a particular crime is committed on a property they manage.

The Issue of Foreseeability

Property managers sometimes consider their liability to end at their property line. This is possible if a court favors the *"prior similar acts rule"*—i.e., no similar crime having occurred on the managed residential or commercial premises, the manager could not have predicted that a criminal act would have occurred. It is possible to have a property that is considered low crime in a high-crime area and just as possible to have a high-crime property within a low-crime area. However, no one can predict crime or how it will impact the property you manage. All you can do is anticipate and try to minimize losses in regard to people, property, and profits. *Foreseeability* of possible crimes based on prior similar acts is a crucial concept.

Unlike the "prior similar acts rule," the *"totality of the circumstances rule"* focuses on all the circumstances of a particular case rather than on any one factor (i.e., the fact that there were no prior similar crimes perpetrated on the premises does not preclude the foreseeability of criminal activity occurring). For example, beyond "prior similars," "totality of the circumstances" asks what kind of neighborhood surrounds the property. Is there gang activity, drug dealing, or other unlawful activities at your property or in the general area near, but not on, your property? This question is meant only to increase your security awareness. Remember what you have learned from preceding discussions in this book:

Civil law is different from criminal law.

Testifying in a deposition or at trial is not a friendly conversation you are having with a lawyer.

Good security is not a loss of profits; it is meant to reduce losses, not only of profits, but of assets—people and property. (Consider, too, that

---

"Prior Similar Acts" and "Totality of Circumstances" Tests

The "Prior Similar Acts" Test
- Type of prior criminal activity on your premises.
  - —Crimes against people.
  - —Crimes against property.
  - —Crimes involving controlled substances/narcotics.
- Frequency of prior criminal activity.
- Date of prior criminal activity.
- Location of prior criminal activity.

"Totality of the Circumstances" Test
- Prior similar crimes not essential.
- *All relevant information is admissible.*
  - —Prior crimes on or off your property.
  - —Local crime statistics.
  - —Industry crime statistics.
  - —Management company crime statistics and/or incident reports.
  - —Type of neighborhood.
  - —Proximity of major roads, intersections, etc.
  - —Employee complaints.
  - —Tenant and/or other invitee complaints.
  - —Use of security officers.
  - —Security awareness programs for residents/tenants and employees.

Admissible statistics include data on crimes that occurred within a one-mile radius of your property (local) as well as crimes committed at or against similar properties (real estate industry information).

---

beyond the economic losses are the negative impact of criminal incidents and lawsuits on a property's reputation and the loss of good will.)

"Prior similars" and "totality of the circumstances" are elements of negligence that will be considered in determining foreseeability—i.e., whether *Plaintiff's* injuries were foreseeable by the *Defendant*. (Elements of the two tests are listed in the accompanying box.)

There are several things you should know in comparing and contrasting the two rules. The "totality of the circumstances" test may be admissible under the "prior similar acts rule," provided the plaintiff first introduces evidence of prior similar crimes on the premises. *Specific foreseeability* pertains to crimes on your premises (i.e., prior similars). *General foreseeability* considers crimes in your environment or vicinity. The property manager should be aware of *"imminent danger"* and "(t)ake immediate steps if you are aware of any criminal activity on your property that implies a breach of security."[1]

The concept of *imminent danger* implies that the defendant (property manager) knew or should have known that:

- A specific person is *dangerous* at a time and/or place.
- A specific person is *in danger* at a time and/or place.

- A particular aspect of security on the property not only *does not reduce* the opportunity for risk or crime, but *actually generates* the opportunity for risk or crime (i.e., having one or more security guards stationed at one post without random patrols).

With this in mind, consider the following, which are some of the factors utilized in establishing general and specific foreseeability:

- Newspaper advertisements that mention security.

- If there is a rank ordering of most-reported crimes versus least-reported crimes in an area. (Does such ranking mean that *security awareness* is higher or lower, or that *crime* is higher or lower, in these neighborhoods than in other areas?)

- Area demographics, including population density, age groups, income levels, and general stability of the neighborhood.

- Potential problems or areas of concern.
  —Bars or establishments that dispense alcoholic beverages
  —Specific residential uses of properties under government or privately sponsored programs
  —Highways, major streets; intersections
  —Bowling alleys, skating rinks
  —Parks—recreational or industrial
  —Cemeteries
  —Schools
  —New construction
  —Shopping centers, malls
  —Video arcades and/or game rooms
  —Stores open 24 hours a day
  —Abandoned buildings
  —Golf courses
  —Drug houses, "crack" houses, houses of prostitution
  —Local police opinion about your property and the surrounding area

- Local area organizations addressing security.
  —Police crime prevention units
  —Neighborhood associations
  —City council
  —Churches
  —Community colleges and high schools offering continuing education workshops
  —Real estate housing associations offering training
  —Security associations such as the American Society for Industrial Security
  —Chambers of commerce, Rotary Clubs, etc. (guest speakers on crime, security, crime prevention)

Security Documentation

Administration and Organization
- Mission statement on security
  —Goals, objectives
  —Chain of command
  —Organizational chart
- Standards of conduct and dress for security
- Policies and procedures
- Security director
- Communications to residents/tenants, police, security, etc.

Fiscal Management
- Security's participation in budget expenditures
- Appropriations for security

Personnel
- Personnel selection (background checks)
- Performance standards
  —Employee conduct
  —Disciplinary actions
- Performance evaluations
- Supervision policy
- Security deployment—number of officers; days, hours; coverage changes

Training and Staff Development
- Training requirements—new staff orientation; reorientation for security and non-security personnel
- Training records—in-house; outside training (police, experts, consultants, local associations, etc.)
- Post orders—by whom; based on what; how often changed and amended
- Changes in security staff—when; why

- City newspaper versus neighborhood newspaper statements regarding area crime and/or programs for assistance (victims, welfare, crime statistics).

- State or other governmental requirements for security (security guards, lighting, etc.).

- Pattern and practice of similarly situated properties in your vicinity.
  —Signage (warning, no trespassing, etc.)
  —Alarms
  —Contract security, off-duty police, etc.
  —Security services offered (private and public)

- Vacancy and turnover rates of your property versus other similarly situated properties in your vicinity.

- Modes of transportation in the area (automobile; bus, train, rapid transit).

Security Documentation *(concluded)*

Records
- Incident recording and data management
  —Company records
  —Official police reports
- Daily security log reports
- Security officer notebook
- Security surveys—why or why not; when; conducted by whom; frequency of audits (annually, etc.)
- Security recommendations (based on complaints, surveys, etc.)
- Evaluation mechanisms
- Correspondence with residents/tenants, police, security resources, etc.
- Lease requirements
  —Restrict number of permanent occupants per unit
  —Define security requirements and expectations

Physical Facilities
- Preventive maintenance program—lighting, locks, etc.
- How key control is maintained
- How and when locks are changed
- Any security devices or information distributed to residents/tenants (e.g., Charley bars, personal security precautions) or secondary locks put in place

Safety and Emergencies
- Fire safety and evacuation plans
- Fire prevention procedures and equipment
- Monitoring emergency procedures

Security Operations
- Control center operations
- Equipment control
- Security lighting
- Closed-circuit television
- Patrolling of facility
- Entrance controls and alarms
- Parking lot escorts
- Parking lot security assignments—shifts; numbers of security officers, off-duty police, etc.
- History of property's security
  —Changes in security
  —Periods of security interruption (reasons for interruption)
  —Reasons for security and/or its cancellation
- Police officers as residents in an apartment complex

- Screening of job applicants and prospective residents or tenants.
  —Criminal background checks
  —Credentials
- Proper security documentation. (You should not only collect documentation, but be sure to utilize the information as a management tool; see accompanying box.)

Still another potential problem area may derive from poor construction and poor landscaping reducing defensible space (the natural defense provided by the environment), natural surveillance, and/or territoriality (a feeling of belonging or ownership created by the environmental design of the premises).[2]

In dealing with the issue of foreseeability, consider the consequences of, among other things:

- Ignoring residents' or tenants' complaints.
- Discounting the benefits of free or inexpensive advice from local crime prevention specialists, such as the police department.
- Landscaping with shrubs that prevent surveillance of the property.
- Offering unsubstantiated opinions at a deposition.
- Assuming that a property has no security problems and not understanding why others think it does.

"Complacency about security measures provides greater opportunities for crime. Regular inspections and thorough preventive measures are the best defenses against crime at a property."[3]

Disregard for the security of property assets creates the impression that no one cares about maintaining the property. The majority of criminals, wanting to expend the least effort, are attracted to a property that looks as though it is not taken care of and controlled. Negligence is either failing to do something that is reasonable or doing something that is unreasonable. Setting up a "dummy" security operation to fool a criminal will not fool the smart ones, but your residents or tenants could face increased risks or experience actual harm. On the other hand, the extra money spent on security will be more than recouped in the reduction in the loss of profits.

Notes

1. As stated by Edward N. Kelley in *Practical Apartment Management,* Third Edition (Chicago: Institute of Real Estate Management, 1990), p. 88.

2. Defensible space and territoriality are concepts defined by C. Ray Jeffery in *Crime Prevention Through Environmental Design* (Beverly Hills, Calif.: Sage Publications, 1977).

3. As stated in *Principles of Real Estate Management,* Thirteenth Edition (Chicago: Institute of Real Estate Management, 1991), p. 167.

Strategizing Proactivity: The Predatory Prevention Matrix

The Predatory Prevention Matrix is a tool to assist you in reducing your liability regarding your assets—people and property. If followed properly, it will allow you to document your preventive efforts and demonstrate proactivity.

If you are sued, improper documentation of your attempts to reduce crime can easily indicate that you put property before people, or consider property first and people not at all. This is not what you want presented to a jury in a courtroom. Instead, your goal should be an equal ranking of people and property or, ideally, people first and property second. While equality is difficult to achieve quantitatively, the real estate manager can approach it qualitatively by use of the matrix. This is important because if you do not document your interest in people (e.g., your residents and/or tenants and your employees), you may be perceived as short-sighted or caring only for money and property. You do not want to be thought of as someone who considers it a reasonable management practice to sacrifice people for the sake of property.

The less crime and violence on your property, the more profitable the property will be. You may not prevent as much loss as you would like, but if you do not properly attempt to reduce losses, you will reap less profit than you imagined. This is particularly true if you do not document your efforts.

First, you must communicate to and with your organization so that the problem is correctly defined in the first place. Successful communication is not a function of information transmission; rather, it is a function of thought transmission. The mind is *reactive,* "it does not think of what you said, it thinks of something else *because of what you said.*"[1]

Proactivity

Proactivity is *anticipation* of types of problems or incidents (e.g., potential for unauthorized access to a building and potential for people or property to be endangered by such a breach), *planning* ways to deal with them and *implementing* preventive measures (e.g., initiating access controls and training staff members and tenants to safeguard themselves and their personal property at all times) to avert incidents or deal with them appropriately when they occur. It is the difference between the general and the particular—planning that encompasses a wide range of possibilities compared to predicting (ineffectively) specific possibilities.

There are also terms to avoid—"predict" and "common sense" in particular. Predicting implies foreknowledge; it will only cause problems, and you will not be able to explain it to a jury or anyone else. Also, what is common sense to you will not be common sense to another person, particularly if he or she is not as well trained as you are.

The question is: How can you, as a real estate manager, reduce criminal opportunity on the premises you manage if you have no "common sense" and cannot communicate consistently? The answer is *teamwork,* and that is your challenge. You have to proactively build a *performance ethic.* Groups become teams through disciplined action—you have to shape the team's purpose by getting your employees to *agree on performance goals.* In order to do this, you have to define common working goals, and each person has to be held accountable. Although this may seem complex, or even impossible, it is neither; but it will need organizational commitment to communicating with employees so that:

They know WHAT they are supposed to do;

They know WHY they are supposed to do it; and

They know HOW they are supposed to do it.

The Predatory Prevention Matrix is a tool for analyzing new information and allowing employees at different levels and locations to participate in strategy development. The focus of preventing loss as a concept similar to sales increasing profits can ensure market-driven operational goals. Finally, the matrix provides a simple, new, agreed-upon language that can be used by property managers working in environments that are less stable than in the past. For example, two managers in different parts of the United States—one in Portland, Maine, the other in Portland, Oregon—can utilize the matrix in discussing a variety of problems related to security. The managers may never have met, and they may be at different levels of their respective organizations, but they will have a common ground for communication based on a very small matrix vocabulary in which they have been trained.

The matrix is primarily a model for information development and communication. It can be used as a starting point in developing policy on security as well as a host of security-related applications such as:

A common vocabulary for training employees at different levels of the organization and in different geographic locations, analyzing new information input, and deployment of personnel.

In conjunction with feasibility studies, needs assessments, security audits, critical incident evaluations to facilitate case preparation, deposition and trial testimony preparation, and other authority and responsibility analysis and/or allocation.

An analytical tool for identifying new issues, trends, threats, and opportunities regarding security and evaluating responsiveness of the corporate leadership, management, and supervisory personnel (action planned and/or taken).

Implementing the Matrix

The Predatory Prevention Matrix is comprised of four key factors—policy, control, risk, and phases of an attack—which are addressed in rank order with policy first. Each factor has three key elements which are also rank ordered—primary, secondary, and tertiary. To maximize predatory prevention, primary must exist before secondary and tertiary, and secondary must exist before tertiary (see box on page 40).

Policy as a key factor is a static definition of the problem. Its primary element (policy) is *what* the problem is believed to be—an awareness that a problem exists and the rules that apply; its secondary element (objectives) is the reasons *why* the organization's employees need to follow the policy; and its third element (procedures) spells out *how* the employees are to carry out the policy—what to do, who to contact. Policy, in general, may be established practice rather than documented policies and procedures. However, policies should be formally documented (paper).

While policy is static initially, it becomes dynamic via the implementation of *control*—resolutions proposed in response to specific problems. Following rank order, control itself is primary; it requires paper documentation to determine its consistency, certainty, and stability. (Security surveys and audits, employment background checks, performance evaluations, records of proactive attempts at problem definition and corresponding resolution are all examples of control documentation.)

Documented control lends *credibility* to static policies. In a lawsuit, a defense based on *patrol* (secondary) will be short-lived without a survey, incident reports, or other documented justification of the need for the patrol components (number of security officers, post orders, etc.). Similarly, providing a parking lot escort (tertiary) without secondary patrol and primary

The Predatory Prevention Matrix

BENCHMARK CELLS

(rank order, across rows and down columns)

Key Factors	Primary	Secondary	Tertiary
POLICY (static definition of problem)	Policy (what)	Objectives (why)	Procedures (how)
CONTROL (necessary documentation of proposed resolution of defined problem)	Control	Patrol	Escort, etc.
RISK (random or non-random choice of person or premises)	Intent —to take risk —to commit crime	Capacity —to take risk —to commit crime	Opportunity —to take risk —to commit crime
PHASES of an ATTACK (spontaneous or non-spontaneous; against person or premises)	Invitation —to attack	Confrontation —acceptance (or) —rejection	Attack —implemented —no attempt —incomplete —complete

CELL STAGES DEFINED

Primary: The goal or major role of the organization is to show that security awareness is a constant presence. An important first step in the accepted concept that "security is everybody's business" is to educate people as to the consequences of their decisions to act or not to act.

Secondary: The goal is to intervene before an incident. It is different from Primary in that it anticipates why employees need to follow the policy. It is different from Tertiary in that Secondary precedes actual crimes being attempted and/or perpetrated.

Tertiary: The goal is to reduce the probability of a perpetrator attempting and/or completing a criminal act as long as the perpetrator and premises are controlled.

control will not be considered an adequate defense in court. In other words, documentation of follow-through is just as important as statement of intent (secondary); an integrated, cohesive program is more important than isolated actions (tertiary).

The primary, secondary, and tertiary elements of *risk* are intent, capacity, and opportunity to commit crime and/or violence. *Intent* is the desire to commit a criminal act. Intent may be deliberate, or its consequences may have been presumed or determined not to be harmful. (Intent cannot be known before an attack—it is seldom proved by direct evidence; rather, it is inferred from the circumstances of the criminal act.) *Capacity* is competence—having the (mental) ability to take the risk, to commit the crime, to understand the consequences of one's actions. The property manager may not know the intent and capacity of the person posing a threat. However, *the manager's documented intent and capacity becomes the control* by attempting to reduce the opportunity—only documentation can effectively indicate proactivity toward *reducing the opportunity* to commit a criminal act.

Risk may be random (no opportunity) or non-random (targeted opportunity or deliberate). For the sake of discussion, assume a property manager is a defendant in a civil lawsuit in which the plaintiff is a resident or tenant or other injured person who claims negligence (or otherwise) on the part of the property manager. In order to prevail in court, the plaintiff must prove the risk was non-random. Because violence in itself is not predictable, random risk involves little thought being given to the choice of person or premises to attack and consequently leaving an inadequate time frame to prevent the attack. (It is possible for a perpetrator to choose a random person on a non-random premises or vice-versa). If opportunity is effectively reduced, there is a higher probability that unknown intent and capacity may also be reduced, displaced, or prevented.

Another consideration is whether the attack on the plaintiff was spontaneous (against *any* person or location) or non-spontaneous (against a particular person or location). The *phases of an attack* are invitation to attack (primary), confrontation—i.e., acceptance or rejection of the invitation (secondary), and the attack itself (tertiary). Analysis of these phases can indicate foreseeability and notice. *Foreseeability* is the reasonable anticipation or expectation that harm or injury can result from certain acts or a failure to act. That is why documentation is so important. Similarly, *notice* means communicating the knowledge of an existing fact. *Actual notice* is communicated by a person in authority—to be affected by a particular fact, there must be conscious knowledge of the fact. *Constructive notice* is written warning or advice intended to make the property manager aware that his or her interests are involved in the information imparted—information the property manager could have obtained proactively. *A property manager has notice of a fact— if he or she:*

Knows the fact,

Has reason to know the fact,

Should know the fact, or

Has been notified of the fact.[2]

If all three phases of an attack occur at the same time, the attack was *spontaneous*—i.e., it could not have been prevented.

Some Ways to Avoid Losses

- Define the security problem.
- Write down some simple policy statements so you can benchmark your attempts at identifying problems and educating your employees about your expectations.
- Consult local law enforcement agencies, crime commissions, and professional associations for security recommendations.
- Ask your insurance agent for advice (insurance companies can perform a risk audit).
- Check with local community colleges or other educational institutions for workshops, seminars, or courses related to your problem areas.
- Document your efforts at prevention.
- Treat good security as an economic consideration—like good sales, it is a source of profits.
- Obtain feedback from your residents and/or tenants and your employees—ask about their concerns and invite their suggestions for addressing security issues.
- Provide security orientations for employees, residents, and/or tenants—use the Predatory Prevention Matrix to develop a common vocabulary regarding security issues.
- Invite the crime prevention officer from your local police or sheriff's department to come to your property and discuss security—invite all residents, tenants, employees, and others on the property to attend and participate in the discussion.
- Let your staff and your residents and tenants know their opinions and suggestions are being considered and included in continuous realignment of your security policy.
- Make sure your staff and your residents and/or tenants observe you supporting any policy you establish.
- Use whatever you document as a management tool—incident reports can tell you what, where, who, why, and when security breaches happened; unused plans are neither dynamic nor responsive.
- Be prepared to take advice if you ask for it—you may be on notice because of having asked for advice.
- Respond positively to staff and resident and/or tenant requests for information concerning your security program. (Don't try to avoid the issue: If you get sued, it is due to somebody making damaging allegations.)
- Foster awareness among your employees, residents, and/or tenants—distribute flyers, ask their opinions, and warn them when you receive information about criminal incidents (from police and other sources).
- Talk to other property managers—find out if they have similar problems, whether the problems have been solved, and how they were solved.
- Seek out formal and informal associations that address general and specific real estate problems.

Following are some of the questions to be asked in assessing security liability:

- Given that violence is unpredictable and there is adequate documented control—e.g., through policy, survey, evaluation, police liaison—could the property manager still have had foreseeable knowledge of an attack?

- Is there a time lag between invitation and confrontation and/or attack?

- Is it reasonable that an attack was invited because there was a reasonable length of time before the confrontation and/or attack? Was there time to change the situation before the actual attack?

- Was the invitation presented seconds, minutes, hours, days, weeks, months, years, or another measurable amount of time beforehand? What form did the invitation take—e.g., screams, prior attacks, official or unofficial documented notification?

- Has the property manager kept accurate records of inspections and repairs (e.g., of doors, windows, locks).

- Are there incident reports on file?

- Has the property manager used the control documentation as a management tool for planning (remember the difference between the plan and the act of planning—static versus dynamic and/or responsive)?

- Has the property manager been proactive or reactive?

Property managers should try to make their apartment (and other) properties as unattractive to potential perpetrators as possible. (Some steps real estate owners and managers can take to avoid liability and high-dollar losses are listed in the accompanying box.)

Security is good business. Prevention is good management. However, prevention does not work when the internal apparatus of the organization is unresponsive and shuts down. For each new employee, resident, and/or tenant who learns about the concepts in the Predatory Prevention Matrix, you have two more eyes potentially looking out to protect your assets: Open communication creates security awareness.

Notes

1. Fournies, F. F.: *Coaching For Improved Work Performance* (Blue Ridge Summit, Penna.: Liberty Hall Press/McGraw-Hill, Inc., 1987).

2. Black, Henry Campbell: *Black's Law Dictionary,* Sixth Edition (St. Paul, Minn.: West Publishing, 1990). (Emphasis added.)

Spotlight
on
Security Needs

Identifying Security Needs

A variety of tools is available to real estate managers for assessing security risks at managed properties. Although the terms security survey and security audit tend to be used interchangeably—as they are within this book—a *security survey* is a critical examination and analysis of a property to ascertain the present security status, identify vulnerabilities, and make recommendations to improve overall security. It is most often an inspection of a facility using a checklist or series of questions to be answered. Like a maintenance inspection report form, the contents of a security checklist should be tailored to the property because it will be used repeatedly. A *security audit,* on the other hand, is larger in scope and includes not only a security survey but also other components of a comprehensive risk assessment (e.g., life-safety compliance issues, recommendations of specific security measures, a cost-benefit analysis) and risk management program. A security survey may be restricted to current shortcomings while a security audit is usually more comprehensive, looking to the future from a "big picture" perspective. The differences are represented in the chapters that follow.

First, Randall I. Atlas, an architect as well as a criminologist, discusses the relationship between "The Security Audit and Premises Liability." Included in this chapter is a list of questions managers should ask themselves about security preparedness. The questions are generally applicable to all types of properties with a few added items that are specific to one or another property type. There are also discussions of risk analysis and factors that encourage premises liability litigation.

Among the issues mentioned by Atlas (and explored in more detail by other authors in other chapters) is that of pre-employment screening. A concern about data privacy can make things like criminal and credit checks a sensitive issue. However, real estate managers who employ others for jobs that include accessing the leased premises of residents and tenants have a particular obligation in this regard. Incidents used as examples in other chapters point out ways in which residents, in particular, may be victimized by employees at a property. In Minnesota, concern over this issue has led to a state statute mandating that apartment managers prescreen their employees. Other states may have established similar requirements.

Audit questions for managed properties may also include questions about security representations in advertising or other marketing efforts. This can be an especially sensitive issue because prospective residents and tenants usually want assurances (read: guarantees), and in most situations there are none. This does not mean a manager or leasing agent cannot state the types of security measures that are in place and how they work; however, so much depends on individuals taking responsibility for themselves that it is usually inappropriate to try to define what a particular security measure will do for a given individual. There is always a possibility that some well-meaning employee could overstate the level or capabilities of a security program. This then raises a question of intentional misrepresentation or unintentional negligence, either of which might have to be explained in court.

Next, "The Security Survey" discusses the survey as a risk-assessment tool. In addition to a focus on vulnerability, this chapter includes a list of general security considerations and a sample checklist that addresses the particular security needs of businesses and office building tenants. The checklist is applicable to commercial properties in general. For retailers and shopping centers, however, it may be desirable or necessary to add questions related to shoplifting, interior and exterior common areas that often have unique features not found in other types of properties, and the property being open to the general public. Obviously, the types of businesses at a particular retail property would also need to be addressed. The security concerns of video arcades, movie theaters, and restaurants are different from those of large and small merchandisers. For an industrial property, one would need to address safety and security of manufacturing facilities (heavy equipment, vehicles operated indoors); safeguarding of raw materials, finished goods, and packaging supplies; and the peculiarities of shipping and receiving facilities and/or warehouse space. Perimeter security is usually extensive and different from that provided at other types of properties (e.g., fencing, gates, a guard house, etc.).

One point in the office security survey warrants additional comment. While it is important for valuable or confidential records and papers to be kept in locked files, there is no need to lock file cabinets as a general practice. If papers are valuable enough to keep under lock and key, perhaps they should be stored in a separate secured room, and files containing non-confidential records that are generally accessible to company personnel can be left unlocked. This will deter a burglar from destroying a cabinet just to see what is inside.

To close this exploration of security needs identification, Dana Perrin has allowed us to adapt a comprehensive checklist form used to evaluate campus security at the University of Rochester (New York). In addition to specific questions, "A General Security Checklist" includes some grid forms for noting responses, with spaces for explanations or comments.

The variety of checklists and questionnaires included here demonstrates the different approaches that can be taken to the conduct of security surveys. Tailoring the forms to the property being surveyed is critical. You will need to review the devices in place and the personnel and procedures that work with them. If your property has a particular access control system, questions should be specific to its operations. Similarly, if contract guards are used, the form should include questions related to their duties and whether the guard company is performing as specified in the contract. A checklist for the management office might include business-specific questions regarding high-tech equipment (e.g., cellular phones, computers) and protection of business information (computerized records and data bases).

The importance of knowing what security measures are in place, how effective they are, and whether additional or different measures need to be implemented cannot be overemphasized. Security needs change over time, and the overall effectiveness of in-place devices and strategies may be diminished as new security problems and challenges arise. Among other things, technology is driving both the need for security and the means of providing it—for example, while typewriters could be anchored to a desk and the documents produced on them could be locked in files, computers are vulnerable not only for their hardware, but for the software and, in particular, for the data they contain. Often the latter is of much more value to a business than the hardware and software, which can readily be replaced. Conducting surveys periodically helps assure that security measures continue to be appropriate and identify new security needs. Because the surveys document security needs and implementation efforts, they are valuable business records. However, they are also a source of information that can be useful in litigation, so their retention needs special consideration (see box on page 50).

Assessment of a property's or a company's security status is at the owner's or operator's discretion, although this situation may be changing. In Alexandria, Virginia, for example, there is now a requirement for new busi-

Security Surveys and Record Keeping

The conduct of security surveys is one more area of real estate management that warrants specific policies and procedures. One such policy might be to require use of a standardized form or checklist to document security surveys or inspections. The relevant procedure might require all questions on the form to be answered or all blanks to be filled in—if something does not apply, the person conducting the survey should say so. (The rationale for such a requirement is that the absence of any specific note or comment on a checklist point might be considered a mere oversight in the conduct of the survey, or it could be interpreted as a lapse in the implementation of a specific security measure.) It may also be appropriate for the written analysis or report of findings to be based on areas that the survey or checklist indicated as potential problems—and that management will take action to remedy—rather than rely exclusively on a checklist form that may not provide sufficient space to record detailed observations.

While it is very important to document the security status of a property, it is also important to minimize the potential for these records to open the door to other problems—e.g., through accidental discovery by a plaintiff's attorney—in the event of a lawsuit. The thinking at some organizations is that records of security surveys should not be retained for longer than the statute of limitations for filing a lawsuit. In Texas, for example, the statute of limitations is two years, and therefore records need only be retained for the past two calendar years in addition to the current year. (The retention period varies from state to state.) Each year, the oldest set of records should be destroyed. It is also prudent to keep security survey information—especially comments and recommendations—separate from the records of general property inspections and routine maintenance records.

Given the potential for liability and the current litigious climate, it may be appropriate to limit the dissemination of security reports and records within the organization. Keeping to a minimum the number of people who can provide information to a plaintiff's attorney is a sound risk management strategy. As an added safeguard, some firms that perform extensive security surveys or utilize outside consultants have the resulting reports sent direct to their corporate counsel. (They may even have their attorneys make the arrangements for the surveys.) The information can then be discussed with the firm's senior officers and decisions made while the written report is held in the realm of attorney-client privilege. This strategy can be particularly beneficial in the event an outside expert's observations were not implemented, for whatever reason.

Because security is a sensitive issue with wide-ranging potential opportunities for litigation, advice of legal counsel should be sought regarding specific security policies and procedures, conduct of security surveys, the distribution of survey results, and the retention of these records.

nesses to undergo a security survey conducted by the Alexandria Police Department crime prevention unit. (Businesses that refuse a survey can be denied a permit to open a new business or change an existing one, but no business has challenged the requirement.) The survey results yield general advice to the business on how to handle things like shoplifting, robbery, and credit card fraud along with recommendations for making it more difficult to steal valuable items. Although there have been some "spot checks" of businesses that had been previously surveyed, there is no systematic follow-up to see what security measures have actually been implemented.

While security surveys and risk assessments can be conducted by professional consultants for a fee or by local law enforcement crime prevention officers—often at no charge—qualified management company personnel can often conduct an appropriately competent survey while also keeping in mind the specifics of the property and its ownership and management. Another possibility is to contact your insurance agent. Often the insurance company that writes the policies for a property will conduct a risk analysis or survey in conjunction with an assessment of insurance needs. (Safety and security measures in place can lead to lower insurance premiums.) There may or may not be a specific fee for this service, or it may be included in the property's insurance premiums.

The Security Audit and Premises Liability

Randall I. Atlas

Criminologists have studied criminal behavior for the last three hundred years, and they have usually associated crime with urban centers. However, the flight from the cities to the suburbs since the 1960s has created lucrative crime magnets in the suburbs as well. Office parks, apartment complexes, industrial sites, and strip centers and shopping malls have all become targets, and the courts are finding owners liable for criminal acts that occur on their property.

The Security Audit

The most important steps that can be undertaken to prevent premises liability are:

1. Identify the level of criminal activity at the site and in the neighborhood. The evaluation should include a three-year history, with periodic annual reviews. The radius or area to be reviewed will vary from site to site. Consult a security expert for a site-specific recommendation for your property.

2. Conduct a security survey or audit that identifies the *assets* to be protected, *threats* and/or *vulnerabilities* (i.e., risks), and *recommendations* for security improvement. Results of the survey should be submitted in the form of a written report and used as the basis for a plan of action.

3. Look at the big picture. Security is more than the guard gate, perimeter fence, wall construction, closed-circuit television (CCTV), security patrol, or detection technology. A security delivery system is an

integrated approach for the protection of people, information, and property using access control, surveillance, management, and territorial strategies.

4. Do as you say, say as you do. If you start a security program, complete it. Installation of CCTV but having no one watching the monitors, or having broken equipment and not repairing it, or not having trained staff to respond to emergencies creates an illusion or false sense of security. Apart from the real-world consequences in the event of a criminal incident, the illusion can be very damaging in court.

In order to determine the level of preparedness of your facility, you should ask yourself the following questions:

- Do you maintain good relations with the local law enforcement agency?

- Do you maintain active membership in associations that have strong national standards for their members such as the Institute of Real Estate Management (IREM), the Building Owners and Managers Association International (BOMA), or the American Society for Industrial Security (ASIS)?

- Have you established policies and procedures for notifying residents and/or tenants about the development of crime and security problems?

- Do you document all security or criminal incidents and keep these records on file for the duration of the statute of limitations for negligence in your local jurisdictions?

- Do you have a clearly stated security mission that includes job descriptions, shift descriptions, and essential functions?

- Is sufficient training on proper security practices at the site given to both security personnel and non-security staff members?

- Do you review, update, and document all policies and procedures at least once a year?

- Are all employees issued their own copy of the policies and procedures manual and required to sign an acknowledgment of having received and reviewed it?

- Can you ensure that all locks and locking devices are sufficient in quality and number to protect residents and/or tenants from an unauthorized entry?

- Are locks on doors and windows inspected at least once a year and again whenever a resident or tenant vacates the space and a new occupant moves in?

- Are intercom, security alarm, fire safety, CCTV, and other systems tested, inspected and documented periodically—at least once a year?

- Are lighting levels even and consistent in all exterior parking areas, walkways, and entries?

- Is all perimeter fencing maintained intact and in good condition generally?

- Do residential units have viewers (peepholes) installed in all entry doors?

- Are all vacant building spaces and units kept secured at all times to prevent unwanted criminal activity?

- Are all keys properly and continuously controlled in their distribution? Is an inventory of all keys kept in a secure location? Is there a key control policy and procedure that is followed?

- Is foliage around the grounds and building perimeter trimmed to eliminate hiding places and allow exterior light fixtures to illuminate the area adequately?

- Are all roof, basement, utility space, and mechanical room doors secured to prevent unlawful entry?

- Are installed security bars, grilles, or screens designed to allow fire egress in the event of an emergency?

- Is the building entry designed to screen visitors and other persons who do not belong on the property?

- Are all utilities, power supplies, telephones, air conditioners, generators, and gas containers located and installed in as secure a manner as possible?

- Do all advertising and marketing materials that represent the level and type of security at the site do so accurately and adequately?

- Do rental agents, managers, or staff misrepresent the level of security or history of crime at the site?

- Are disclaimers and warnings included in lease agreements and contracts and appropriate warning signs posted in areas of risk, such as swimming pools, parking areas, mall areas?

- Are all residents and tenants kept informed of changes in security and criminal events that require warning?

- Are all employees screened and tested, and their backgrounds checked, prior to employment?

These will be the first questions asked by a security expert in the event of a personal injury or premises liability lawsuit. How many of these questions were you able to answer YES?

Security Risks and Vulnerabilities

Security in a managed property is often easily breached or compromised. A man is robbed in an apartment lobby left unguarded in the afternoon. A woman is attacked in a parking lot of a design showroom. A door with a broken lock allows a rapist to enter an apartment building and assault a resident. An elderly visitor at a condominium is seriously injured because of a faulty stairway design. A secretary walks through a sliding glass door in an office—the door had no caution markings on it. An entry rug in a bank buckles when the door jamb hits the edge of the carpet and an elderly client trips over it. In an apartment walkway, a child is shot accidentally by a stray bullet from a drug deal gone bad. These are just a few examples of cases that are being litigated under premises liability.

To initiate protection for yourself, your property, or your client against potential lawsuits, a security or safety professional should look for vulnerabilities in the building and conduct a risk analysis. The expert can check municipal codes for specifications and fire-safety regulations and advise you of the property's compliance status. By helping to identify foreseeable crimes and accidents, the expert can recommend strategies for reducing your liability for their consequences. A security expert can work for you in an analytical role or against you in court if there is litigation. You should take the initiative.

The expert can serve a crime-preventive role, and a critical role in litigation prevention, by conducting a risk analysis or study of the crime and safety threats on the premises and building. Concerns about rape, robbery, burglary, thefts, and safety are addressed in a risk analysis and security audit. An audit gives the owner direction as to the challenges that need to be addressed and what is a *reasonable* standard of care. A risk analysis also serves to put the owner on notice regarding defects in the building or problems with or inadequacies of the staff. Subsequently, being able to show that reasonable steps were taken to correct such defects will greatly enhance defensibility in a lawsuit.

Premises Liability

A key issue in security and safety liability cases is the "foreseeability" of a crime or accident at a given location. If one or more persons have been robbed or attacked in a parking lot or building lobby, further criminal incidents may be considered foreseeable and, thus, preventable. Legal liability increases dramatically if no action is taken to correct the defect that permitted the incidents to occur in the first place.

An expert in security and safety can provide a risk analysis or security threat analysis to assess vulnerability, foreseeability, and the precedent of crime or accident incidents. The landlord—i.e., building management and/or the property owner—has certain duties that have been established in court decisions. These duties include:

Reasonable care (in general);

A contractual duty based on an implied warranty of habitability (under landlord-tenant law); and

The exercise of reasonable care to protect a guest or invited party from third party acts (similar to that of an innkeeper).

A review of cases from around the United States indicates that the courts have examined many different facts and issues, and the following factors seem to be most frequently cited as encouraging premises liability litigation.

1. Prior crime on the premises (i.e., foreseeability).

2. Prior crime in the neighborhood, or being in a "high crime area," thus having increased awareness.

3. Similar properties in the area having a standard of care better than the subject property, and which took reasonable measures and were aware of or had precedent experience.

4. Physical maintenance and upkeep of existing conditions in the building. Were the conditions in the building up to the standard of care? Survey items might include the working order of lights, doors, locks, fences, closed-circuit television, and intercoms.

5. The adequacy of security measures to detect, delay, or deter criminals. Adequacy is the overall measure on which legal cases based on security issues are usually judged.

6. The availability and performance of security personnel. Key factors considered are employee screening, training, policy and procedures, response time, and qualifications.

7. The actual or constructive notice that ownership has (or should have) of prior crime or defective condition. Did the landlord have notice of prior criminal incidents or defective conditions? (Did the landlord have notice of a broken door, faulty stairway, burned out light, or past crimes?)

8. The lack of warnings to the occupants (residents, tenants) of dangerous conditions. Were the occupants warned of an activity so as to be put on notice and take responsibility for their own safety (e.g, cautioned about slippery conditions, advised to ask for an escort to their car)?

9. Violation of statutes, codes, or regulations. A breach of a building code or ordinance provides strong support for negligence and liability claims.

10. Decreased measures of safety and security below a prior level of reliance and expectations. Were services cut back due to finances

or management changes and the occupants (residents, tenants) not notified of the cutback in services?

The security or safety professional can play a vital role in determining and establishing these ten conditions. Whether the expert is operating in a preventive nonlitigation situation, or working for the defense or plaintiff in a legal case, these key issues must be addressed to determine the standard of care, foreseeability, precedent, liability, and the most appropriate response for correction and prevention.

Many crime and accident sites have an architectural or environmental contributory factor that may or may not be attributable to the landlord. Architecture impacts the safety and security of a building in its many different features, including stairway and ramp designs; handrails; interior and exterior lighting; floor materials; parking lot design; blind spots; appliances; doors, windows, and access-control systems; building circulation patterns (internal traffic flow); elevators; etc.

In litigation, the security or safety expert can assist the attorney by looking at the scene of a crime or accident and determining what variables led to the cause of the incident. A risk analysis of a property might ask some of the following questions:

- Could someone be struck by any item?
- Could someone be blinded by changes in lighting or surprised by floor surface changes?
- Are there any potholes or trenches not covered or marked that someone could fall into?
- Does the design make provisions for avoiding excessive demands on persons with respect to their height, build, ability to reach, ability to balance, walking gait, strength, or grip?
- Is the risk of injury increased for someone walking barefoot or wearing high heels, long sleeves, loose clothes, or a necktie?
- Is there sufficient lighting for surveillance of exterior grounds and interior common spaces?
- Are there guards or other personnel assigned to patrol the grounds or challenge a stranger's entry?
- Are windows on the ground floor secured?
- Are doors sturdy, with secure hinges and dead-bolt locks?
- Are lobbies and elevators equipped with mirrors in their corners to allow visibility and assist in preventing assaults (rape; robbery)?
- Are fire escape doors locked from the outside to prevent unauthorized entry?
- Are employees screened before hiring and provided with written security rules, regulations, and policies?

Most security professionals and lawyers say the best way to determine "adequacy," and at the same time protect building owners from lawsuits, is through inspection of the premises by an independent non-vested consultant. From a legal standpoint, independent inspections (such as a threat analysis) can be used in court to support the building management's security decisions in the event of a lawsuit.

A Perspective on Security Audits

The advantage of a security audit by an independent expert is that the fee for services pays in part for the expert's assumption of (some) legal liability. The cost incurred for the expert's services yields a qualified opinion *before* litigation. That is proactive and the best prevention. If litigation is imminent, the expert can assist by assessing vulnerabilities or the defensibility of the property. Alternatively, the property owner or manager can pay for the expert to defend him or her in court *after* a suit has been filed.

The Security Survey

A *security survey* is a critical examination of a property for the purpose of making recommendations that will reduce crime risks. It is generally conducted by a security consultant or a local crime prevention officer, although in-house staff may also be qualified to do this work. The purpose of the survey is to define the parameters of the security problems at a particular managed property.

The process should include interaction with residents or tenants of the property. Scheduling some time for a local crime prevention officer to visit your apartment complex, regardless of size, is generally a good idea and is within the jurisdiction of the local law enforcement agency. For a commercial property, it may be more appropriate to bring in a private consultant or to encourage individual tenants to make their own arrangements. Having someone in authority speak to residents and tenants about crime prevention accomplishes several basic goals:

- It expresses your concern for your residents and/or tenants.
- It allows the officer or consultant to distribute information about identification of valuables and other personal property plus other adjunct materials such as labels and window stickers that signal participation in a "crime watch" or similar program.
- It gives the real estate manager an opportunity to learn residents' and tenants' concerns and complaints that may not have been stated previously.
- It affords residents and tenants the perception that they are taking part in the creation of security and provides valuable information for the security survey.
- It underscores the fact that "security is everybody's business."

The following discussions offer guidelines that will help you conduct your own security survey and allow you to better understand your premises and your responsibility.

The Premises

The location of a property, how its improvements (e.g., buildings) are constructed, and particulars regarding the contents of the premises are important points to consider. If the premises are in an area where vacancy is high, there is ready access from the rear, lighting is poor, and there is a history of past offenses, an improvement in existing physical and electronic protection or notification may be necessary. If these do not exist now, they should be among the security measures considered for the immediate future.

Construction of the building should also be considered. Unfortunately, the modern offender is equipped with the knowledge and the means to enter most premises. In past years, bars, solid-core doors, and locks may have been sufficient to deter or deny entry. The less-sophisticated alarm system may have advised of unlawful entry or frightened an offender away. Additionally, the safe which may have been with the business or in the residence for years was strong enough to defeat cutting tools available at the time it was purchased. Existing doors, locks, alarms, and safes should be evaluated in terms of whether they provide the level of security needed currently.

The nature of the contents of the premises also partially determines risk. The degree of security necessary will be greater for items that are small, easily disposable, readily removed from the site, and have a high value (intrinsic to the item or as a marketable commodity) than if the opposite is true. Large items that are difficult to remove or dispose of because they have manufacturer's model and serial numbers as well as identifiable physical characteristics are less likely targets but not wholly without risk.

The security survey is your opportunity to review all aspects of security on site, including cash handling, locking of individual leased premises (as well as the building itself), and other procedures relevant to the storage of property or valuables. The greater the number of obstacles placed between an offender and the target, the more difficult it will be for the offender to succeed—more time will be needed to gain access and accomplish the mission. *Defense in depth* embraces:

- Perimeter security
- Physical features of the building, as well as fittings
- Intruder detection
- Work practices and procedures

Assessing Vulnerability

A vulnerability analysis should identify possible targets, define potential threats to them, and determine the relative efficacy of security measures in place. Measures of security effectiveness include numerous probabilities:

- The likelihood of detecting and announcing intrusion and/or criminal activity *before* it is completed (effectiveness of surveillance equipment, alarm systems, etc.).

- The likelihood of an intruder or criminal perpetrator being interrupted *during* the commission of the act (law enforcement or security personnel arriving while the intrusion or crime is taking place).

- The likelihood of the intruder or criminal perpetrator being apprehended quickly (effectiveness of follow-up; potential for confrontation or capture by personnel responding to the scene).

All of these factors can be assigned numerical values that allow for a mathematical expression of risk as low, moderate, or high, similar to insurance actuarial calculations. Used with cost data, a vulnerability assessment can be a basis for a cost-benefit analysis of existing security measures or proposed new, additional, or replacement systems. The goal is to maximize risk reduction while controlling costs.

The survey should look at the premises from the perspective of someone trying to gain entry illegally, i.e.:

Without using a key;
With no regard to damage that may result; and
With no real worry about noise or being seen by others.

To arrive at a decision as to whether a particular premises is to be considered "at risk," it is important to answer the following questions:

- What is the reason for the request?
  —General security survey
  —One or more incidents on site
  —One or more incidents nearby
  —A particular type of incident has occurred locally or is occurring with increasing frequency

- What areas are in need of protection?
  —Cash flow
  —Payroll
  —Transportation of goods

- Protection against what type of activity?
  —Burglary
  —Staff pilferage
  —Industrial espionage

- What is the level of security needed?
  - —Personal protection, in general
  - —After hours protection for staff and/or premises
  - —Added protection for goods manufactured or stored
- What is the nature of the premises and/or its occupants?
  - —Apartment complex
  - —Office building
  - —Hotel
  - —Factories or premises with a large payroll
  - —General retail stores
  - —Cash-handling institutions, e.g., credit unions
  - —Service stations, particularly a 24-hour operation
  - —Hospital pharmacy (drug cabinets)
  - —Drug store
  - —Gun dealers
  - —Gun collectors, especially those holding concealable handguns
  - —Jewelry store
  - —Art gallery
  - —High-rise building

Any evaluation of risk must take into consideration a variety of factors that, grouped together, weigh differently in different circumstances. The type of business or trade is a factor—businesses that have large amounts of cash on hand or valuables have a high degree of security risk, as do those where drugs or weapons are present. In fact, the nature and value of the stock (merchandise) held are key considerations. "Costume" jewelry has less intrinsic value than that containing real gemstones (e.g., diamonds, emeralds); the same distinction applies to personal jewelry.

Vacant apartments and stores—even those that only appear unoccupied—are particularly vulnerable. There are "markets" for stolen fixtures (lighting, plumbing) as well as personal items and electronic gadgets. The fact that leasable premises are unoccupied should not also mean they are unattended or unprotected. Even occupied stores run the risk of having HVAC and other mechanical equipment stolen, usually at night, because these items are typically installed on the roof or at the back of the building and therefore exposed and accessible.

A properly conducted security survey will include preliminary research regarding:

- Locality—Is the area residential? Commercial? Industrial?
- History of offenses—What types of criminal incidents have been reported at the property? In the neighborhood? In the surrounding area?
- Nature of the premises and present security precautions—Does existing security adequately protect the property now? For the future?

What has to be done to upgrade it for current needs? If there is no security presently, what is needed?

Residential and commercial properties have different security needs, and a residential complex that includes retail tenants poses different risks than a property that is exclusively residential or retail. Some premises will belong in the "low risk" classification while others will be considered "high risk." Naturally, the latter will require a sophisticated type of alarm detection and notification system. However, when considering the various aspects of security, all premises have one common factor—the proven principle of "defense in depth."

The following pages provide first a listing of general considerations followed by a checklist of questions that can be the basis of a security survey for an office building. Most of the checklist questions are broadly applicable to any type of property, but the list is not all-inclusive. Ideally, you should consider unique features of your property's location, construction, and tenancy and include questions about security issues that affect people and property at the site.

Some General Security Considerations

1. *Keys* should be kept in a secure location and not be readily available if an intruder does gain entry to the premises.

2. High risk property (e.g., *valuables*) can be placed in a vault or an appropriately constructed, lockable cage.

3. *Patrols* can visit the interiors of leased premises to verify that offenders are not present and that offending residents are not actively offending other residents.

4. Property should be marked for *identification;* property that cannot be marked should be photographed. An inventory of all property (to include serial numbers, descriptions, and identifying characteristics) should be maintained and regularly updated.

5. For *retail in a residential property,* a door isolating the shop from the residential area, with appropriate locks and fittings, should be considered. If access is available from the first floor of the residential area, it may be necessary to provide adequate physical security supported by alarm activation devices at this level (depending on the situation).

6. In some small businesses, a *secure room* to store valuable items is installed. One room is nominated and additional security provided. Glass areas are eliminated, the door is reinforced, locking devices are improved, and the ceiling is protected. An alarm may also be provided.

7. *Lock cylinders* should be changed when each subsequent resident or tenant takes occupancy.

8. Exterior and interior *lighting* should be adequate—it should illuminate without casting shadows that create hiding places.

9. On-site personnel need to be informed. *Staff awareness* of security measures is essential, regardless of the size of a complex. Well-informed, alert employees will assist in preventing crime.

10. Staff should be *trained* in how to cope with armed robberies or similar situations which they are likely to face.

11. *Emergency procedures* and phone numbers of contacts should be known by all staff.

12. After hours' *contact numbers* for staff members of your organization should be provided to police.

Sample Office Security Checklist

1. Do you have electronic access control? If so, where?
2. Do you have an employee entrance and a policy regarding its use? If so, do you enforce this policy?
3. Are other doors restricted to use as emergency exits? If so, do you enforce this policy?
4. Do you have closed-circuit television (CCTV)? If so, where?
5. Do all locked office doors have security locks?
6. Do you restrict keys to those who actually need them?
7. Do you keep complete, up-to-date records of all keys issued?
8. Do you have a procedure for collecting keys when employees are terminated?
9. Do you control duplication of keys?
10. Do you mark all keys "Do Not Duplicate"?
11. Do you require all file cabinets to have locks?
12. Do you require all file cabinets to be locked at night?
13. Do you have a person in charge of key control?
14. Do you secure all office equipment with anti-theft devices?
15. Do you have and enforce an inventory control policy for all office equipment?
16. Do you record all serial and model numbers?
17. Do you require all desks to be cleared of important papers each night?
18. Are all important papers shredded before they are placed in waste containers?
19. Do you have a supervisor inspect all trash before it is removed from the building (to deter internal theft)?
20. Do you control unauthorized use of phones by programming them for limited usage?
21. Do you require your employees to wear badges or carry photo identification cards?
22. Do you provide lockable desk drawers for secure storage of employees' personal items?
23. Do you have a policy about employees bringing personal property to their work stations? If so, are they advised that the employer is not liable if the property is stolen?
24. Do you have a policy regarding inspection of employees' packages?
25. Do you have a policy regarding employees using office equipment for personal projects? If yes, do you enforce this policy?
26. Can employees take home equipment such as computers from the office?
27. Do you require employees who work late to notify someone?

Sample Office Security Checklist *(concluded)*

28. Do you have an emergency procedures manual? Does it tell what to do in case of fire? Natural disasters? Bomb threats?

29. Is the building inspected each night for safety and security?

30. Do security or night personnel keep a log of their own activities? Of the comings and goings of other (non-security) personnel?

31. Do you have a policy limiting entrance to the building after normal business hours and on weekends? If so, must employees log in and out?

32. Do you have a policy for inspecting visitors' packages?

33. Do visitors have to register when entering the building?

34. Are visitors escorted within the building?

35. Are restricted areas (those not open to the public) properly identified with "Employees Only" signs?

36. Are all ground-level windows that open secured with security locks?

37. Are the parking lot and entrances to the building properly illuminated for safety?

38. Has there been a lighting audit conducted by the local utility company or a lighting engineer?

39. Is the building protected by a burglar alarm system? Is the system tested once a month?

40. Is there a fire alarm system for the building? Is the system tested once a month and checked out completely once a year?

41. Do you have a system that allows employees to report security problems or theft?

42. Are employees aware of all security policies?

43. Do you conduct security awareness training for employees?

44. Do you have an annual security audit of the building?

In conducting a security survey, remember:
Every door and window must be checked.
Every alarm point (fire and intrusion) must be checked.
Internal procedures and controls must be checked.

Based on the results obtained using the survey shown here or any other comparable questionnaire that addresses security issues and particulars at your managed property, security recommendations can be designed to reduce overall risk and hazards.

A General Security Checklist

Dana Perrin

The purpose of this checklist is simple: To be a reference for you, the property manager, in identifying problems—both real and potential—and finding ways to better protect the property you manage. Like a building maintenance inspection form, the security checklist that follows indicates both items to be reviewed and related considerations. While it is intended to be comprehensive, it is not all-inclusive. Adaptation for different types of properties and, more importantly, higher levels of in-place security measures will assure that security at a particular property is appropriately reviewed.

Sample Security Checklist

General Checklist

	Not Chkd	Daily	Weekly	Monthly	6 Months	Annually	N/A
How often are doors checked to be certain they are secure?							
How often are windows checked to be certain they are secure?							
How often are other areas or storage buildings checked to be certain they are secure?							
How often are fences and gates checked to be certain they are secure?							
How often are lights checked to be certain they are working properly?							
How often is the general condition of the building checked?							

Door Survey

All *exterior* and *interior* doors should be checked for the following:

- Locking hardware is in proper working order.
- Framework is strong and door fits properly.
- Strike plate is strong and securely affixed to frame.
- No breakable glass within 40 inches of locking mechanism or panic bar.
- Door cannot be bypassed through drop ceiling or transom.
- Panic bar operates properly.
- Exposed hinge pins cannot be easily removed.
- The inactive (stationary) side of double doors can be secured at both top and bottom.
- Overhead doors can be secured with an auxiliary locking device.
- Portals and hatches are secured with heavy duty hasp and padlock.
- Key numbers have been removed from all padlocks.
- Outside handles are removed from "egress only" (exit) doors.
- All areas are in compliance with ADA standards.

For the questions below and in subsequent sections, if a NO is checked, please explain in the space provided at right.

	YES	NO	
Can all outside entrances be secured?			
Can all inside doors be secured?			
Can any overhead door be secured?			
Can any portals or hatches be secured?			

Sample Security Checklist *(continued)*
Window Survey

All ground floor windows, as well as accessible areas above ground level, should be checked for the following:

- Locking hardware is in proper working order.
- Additional measures are provided for windows with air-conditioning units.
- Any basement windows are protected with security grille or well cover.

	YES	NO	
Are all ground floor or other accessible windows secure?			

Miscellaneous Openings and Outbuildings

All openings and exterior barriers should be checked for adequate security. Particular attention should be given to roof hatches, cornices above protective overhangs, and sheds or outbuildings containing materials or equipment.

	YES	NO	
Are all openings accessible from the outside able to be secured?			
Are all outbuildings and storage sheds able to be secured?			

Key Control

Optimum security is contingent upon a proper key control system, such as:

- The responsibility for lock and key control is assigned to one individual.
- All file keys and duplicates are kept in a key cabinet, under lock and key.
- All keys are maintained and issued with strict supervision, including the requirement that each key issued must be signed for (using key receipt tags).
- Master keys are kept to a minimum and are retained by top administrative personnel only.
- Penalties are enforced when a key is lost.
- Employees are not permitted to make duplicate keys on their own.
- Keys are collected (and logged) from employees who are terminated or leave employment and from residents/tenants who move out.
- Lock cylinders are able to be replaced.

	YES	NO	
Is the key control system adequate?			
Is the key cabinet adequate?			

Sample Security Checklist *(continued)*

Lighting

	YES	NO	Required Foot Candles	Foot Candle Reading
Is the perimeter of the building protected by adequate lighting?				
Is there sufficient light to provide marginal coverage when a lighting fixture needs replacement?				
Is additional lighting provided at entrances or other points of access?				
Are corridors and stairwells properly lighted for safety?				
Are exterior lights aimed at or away from the building?				

	YES	NO	
Are lighting repairs able to be made immediately?			
Are photocells used?			
Are accessible lenses protected by unbreakable material?			
Is the wiring for lighting protected?			
Are switches and controls properly located and protected?			
Is the lighting system designed and fixture locations recorded so that repairs can be easily made?			
Are materials and equipment in storage areas arranged properly to allow for lighting?			
Are mechanical rooms/electrical panels and hazardous areas locked?			

Sample Security Checklist *(continued)*

Perimeter and Grounds Fencing

	YES	NO	
Is there fencing?			
Can the fence be violated?			

Visibility and Access

	YES	NO	
Are all areas of the building and grounds accessible to patrol cars?			
Are buildings visible to passing patrol cars?			

Vandalism and Theft Prevention

Grounds should be checked for the following:

- Grounds are kept mowed and shrubs and trees are kept trimmed.
- Areas are kept free of graffiti.
- Broken glass in doors or windows is replaced promptly.

	YES	NO	
Are facilities generally kept neat and in good repair?			
Are sections of the building able to be locked when not in use?			
Are there protective screens or guards installed on windows?			
Are vital records maintained in a secure location?			
Is there a record kept of areas that require maintenance?			

Property Identification and Inventory Control

	YES	NO	
Has all property belonging to the building residents and/or commercial tenants been marked with an ID number?			
Has all property belonging to the building owner and/or management company been marked with an ID number?			
Is there an up-to-date inventory of all such property?			
Is there a specifically designated area for valuable items? Is access to it monitored?			
Have special measures been taken for high-target items (computers, etc.)?			
Is cash deposited daily?			

Sample Security Checklist *(continued)*

Access Control Procedures

	YES	NO	
Are there policies in place regarding access by occupants of the building (residents; tenants' employees)?			
Is there a designated entrance for tenants' employees?			

Visitors

	YES	NO	
Are there policies in place regarding visitors to the building?			
Are there signs indicating a visitor policy?			
Is there an entrance designated for visitors?			
Are there signs on other entrances requesting visitors to use only the designated entrance?			
Are visitors required to sign in and out?			
Are visitors issued ID cards or badges?			
Is proper ID required of vendors, salespersons, or repairpersons?			
Are deliveries required to be made to a specific area?			
Are delivery persons accompanied by a staff person from the building?			
Are staff members aware of how to report a suspicious person(s)?			

Management Staff

	YES	NO	
Are staff required to wear ID cards?			
Are there policies in place for after-hours entry?			

Is there a person assigned to perform the following duties at the end of the day?

	YES	NO	
—Check that business tenants' premises are properly secured?			
—Check exterior entrances to make sure they have been secured?			
—Make sure alarms have been set and are functioning properly?			
Is there a person designated as an emergency contact for after-hours problems or situations?			

Sample Security Checklist *(concluded)*

Alarms

	YES	NO	
Is the building protected by an alarm system?			
Is there a regular schedule for testing and/or maintenance of the system?			
Are there fewer than four false alarms per year?			
Are there policies in place for the arming and/or disarming of the system?			
Are high-risk areas inside also protected?			
Can portions of the building or area be accessed while other alarms remain armed?			
If power fails, is there backup?			
Are staff trained to use the system?			
Do staff know their responsibilities when responding to an alarm?			
Is the alarm UL-listed?			
Is UL-listed equipment being used?			
Is there line supervision?			

Closed-Circuit Television (CCTV)

	YES	NO	
Are there CCTV systems in use?			
Do you record from your cameras with time-lapse recorders?			
Did you remove dummy cameras?			
Do you monitor 24 hours a day?			
Do you rotate personnel?			
—If yes, how often?			
Do you use domes to shield cameras?			

Spotlight
on
Crime Prevention

Proactive Prevention

High-profile crimes are treated sensationally in the news media. Large metropolitan areas report record numbers of crimes each year. According to a 1993 Gallup Poll, Americans are taking action—43 percent have installed special locks on their doors and 18 percent have burglar alarms. Fear of crime hurts businesses as well as residential areas. Downtown retail areas continue to lose shoppers to suburban malls because urban areas are perceived as unsafe (i.e., crime-ridden), but even the suburban malls are not immune to crime.

Although most Americans feel safe at home and in their immediate neighborhoods, they feel insecure in the community at large and when traveling outside of it. Americans' fear of crime is likely only to increase in the future because crime *appears to be increasing* and because the age group most concerned about personal safety and security—i.e., the middle-aged segment of the population—is growing. (The large generation of baby boomers born between 1950 and 1965 will be 35–50 years old in the year 2000.) Preventing crime is important for today and for the future.

Crime prevention requires first an acknowledgment that crime exists. It also requires acknowledgment that, no matter who they are or where they live or work, everyone is a potential victim of crime. Proactive prevention requires taking precautions to minimize the likelihood of becoming a victim. The chapters that follow identify strategies that can be adopted and adapted to meet the needs of the properties you manage—within the limits of available funding.

First, "Crime Prevention Concepts" by Patrick J. Lenaghan presents a general overview of prevention strategies with an emphasis on planning. After defining the basic elements that must be present for a crime to be committed, Lenaghan describes many of the physical measures that can be employed to limit access to a property by criminals or other unauthorized personnel. Special considerations in providing security in high-rise buildings and shopping centers are also outlined along with strategies for establishing a security program. (Many of the issues and security measures introduced by Lenaghan will be discussed in more detail in later chapters.)

Planning is a key concept in prevention. One of the planning tools available to real estate managers is *Before Disaster Strikes: Developing an Emergency Procedures Manual,* an IREM publication that addresses security issues as well as natural and man-made disasters.

Moving from the general to the particular, "Crime Prevention Through Environmental Design" by Timothy D. Crowe focuses on design strategies that influence people's behavior in a particular setting. The concept of crime prevention through environmental design—CPTED—has been around for many years, and while the discussion by Crowe is focused on its application to shopping centers, the same principles can be applied in office buildings and at apartment communities.

Both residential and commercial properties typically have multiple entrances, and parking lots or garages are common adjuncts to all types of properties. All are subject to the same types of problems—unauthorized access (including piggy-backing on access codes), unrestricted vehicular movement, and real and potential criminal activities (theft, vandalism) that can lead to injuries to people, damage to property, and liability for the owners and managers of the real estate. Moreover, the potential for criminal incidents as well as any actual occurrences tends to engender fear in the people who are the authorized users of the facilities. Fear will drive away residents and customers, both from personal experience and negative word of mouth—the fearful resident or business customer will not hesitate to tell others of his or her concerns.

Shopping centers present unique challenges in establishing and maintaining security. People come there to meet and to shop but do not always buy. Customers of individual retailers are automatically customers of the mall because all but major anchor stores are accessible only through the mall. In this environment, it can be difficult to differentiate "customers" from "loiterers" because people's behavior may not always clearly indicate their reasons for being in the mall. Crowe points out the kinds of problems that some malls and shopping centers have experienced with young people. However, real estate managers should also keep in mind that teenagers and young adults do have money to spend and represent a large percentage of retail sales for some retailers, among them music and video stores and specialty clothing shops.

Also, even though they are private property, shopping centers and malls are often perceived to be public places simply because they are open

Shopping Security Features

Real estate managers routinely employ surrogate shoppers to find out about their competitors or to monitor the properties they manage. Posing as prospective apartment renters, for example, shoppers can determine unit sizes and rents as well as marketing and leasing strategies in use at competing properties. In addition, a property may be shopped to find out how management company personnel treat prospective residents—employees' attitudes and actions in showing apartments, touring the property, and completing rental applications. Shopping has also been employed to ensure that apartment leasing practices, in particular, are nondiscriminatory—a necessary countermeasure when "testers" are also shopping apartment properties looking for opportunities to sue for discrimination.

Retailers sometimes employ "shoppers" to observe how sales personnel and other employees conduct the company's business. Usually they are testing cash handling procedures (e.g., whether the full amount of a sale is rung up properly and deposited in the cash register) or the observation skills of the sales—and/or security—personnel (e.g., a demonstration of how easy or difficult it is for a shoplifter to succeed).

The same principle can be utilized to determine management employees' effectiveness and professionalism (quality control) as well as observe any illegal activities or unauthorized practices. Potential problems that can arise because of the physical layout of a property can also be detected. Usually this type of surrogate shopper is a security professional who is qualified to comment on his or her specific observations.

to the public. This has sometimes created problems related to rights of "free speech" when an individual or group harasses legitimate mall customers— e.g., by distributing handbills or soliciting contributions or by blocking access to a customer's intended destination. Such behaviors can be controlled by establishing a policy that requires permission from the management for anyone other than tenants to use the mall premises for a defined activity. Enforcement of such a policy can include calling upon the police to deal with offenders, especially if their behavior is disorderly.

Efforts to improve visibility of building entrances and of vehicles and activities in parking facilities, coupled with implementation of specific security measures, will not only help deter offenders, but also improve "customer relations" through positive perceptions of the property having a measure of safety and security. For example, speed bumps or pavement-level spike devices can be installed to control the direction of traffic flow and, thus, regulate movement within a garage or parking lot. (Operational aspects of providing security in parking lots and garages are presented in a later chapter in the context of assets protection.)

Whether designing a building to incorporate safety and security features in the first place, or rehabilitating (retrofitting) an existing building to

Designing for Security

In order for CPTED to be used effectively, a thorough risk and threat assessment is needed. Crime is not the only issue to be addressed. Some risks are inherent in certain types of businesses or facilities. For a bank, armed robbery is a risk. For a manufacturer, industrial accidents and air, water, and soil pollution are potential risks. Employee negligence is a risk for any business. Other risks are site specific—location on a flood plain or a fault line poses a risk of flooding or earthquakes, respectively.

A *risk assessment* not only identifies potential risks, it should also determine vulnerability to those risks, the likelihood of their occurrence, and suitable countermeasures to minimize damage or loss. The latter often include an array of options, from minimal to comprehensive, and their respective costs. The level of acceptable risk for the company or the property and the availability of funding will determine whether the security measures to be implemented are the minimum needed, the maximum possible, or something in between.

When such risk assessment is conducted before a site is selected, site selection criteria can be included in it. The intended use—the types of businesses or residents who will occupy the building—will establish parameters for or impose limits on site selection, as will the physical and other characteristics of specific sites. Environmental concerns (potential flooding, pollution of soil or water by operations at adjacent properties) as well as the potential for criminal activity (high crime versus low crime, urban versus suburban locale) are as important in site selection as are aesthetics and intended use.

The project design should incorporate security measures from the very beginning, or it should be modified as necessary to include appropriate security features based on the risk assessment. If a site has been pre-selected, the assessment should incorporate security measures needed to compensate for site deficiencies. Commercial properties that are partially leased before construction begins can incorporate security features specific to the needs of the major space users as part of the build out of their leased space.

Economics also need to be considered. Real estate managers perform cost-benefit analyses in anticipating operational changes or comparing approaches to a building rehab. Security measures and their implementation should receive the same scrutiny. Over time, real estate improvements—buildings and their component systems—wear out and diminish in value.

add these types of features, the security systems and devices should be integrated aesthetically with the building design. Security should not appear to be an afterthought.

The other major crime prevention strategy is the neighborhood or community watch, also sometimes called a block watch. The neighborhood watch concept is usually applied in a small defined geographic area. Where there are single-family homes and small (two- to ten-unit) multiple dwellings, the "neighborhood" may be defined as a single block along both sides of the street, including the houses on each corner at the ends of the block

---

Designing for Security *(concluded)*

Likewise, neighborhoods change over time as populations move in and out of them and there is extensive new development or no development at all. Adjacent land uses also affect the value of a property. In a situation where commercial tenants are struggling to remain in business and meet their obligations under the lease (rent and pass-through operating expenses), it may be difficult to implement security measures because of the added cost.

Among the factors that need to be considered in developing a security plan are:

- The size of the property
- The age of the property
- The economic strength of commercial tenants
- Neighborhood conditions
- Costs of specific security measures
- Funds available for security, now and into the future

A cost-benefit analysis should look at what security measures are needed *and* what can be accomplished within the budget allocated for security.

In real estate, location is critical. However, the land cannot be moved. When their leases expire, tenants can and do relocate if the property or its surrounding neighborhood has declined over the period of a long-term lease. If vacant stores or offices cannot be re-leased, the tenants who remain will not yield sufficient revenue in the form of rents or prorated pass-through expense payments to support an elaborate security program, even though the decline in the property and adjacent premises may have created a need for more or different security measures.

Even at a fully leased property, it is important to look at the bottom line. The cost of providing security at a typical neighborhood shopping center can be the largest expense line item of common area maintenance (CAM) costs after taxes. Starting a program where none existed previously can double the basic CAM pass-through. (Because CAM costs are usually prorated based on gross leasable area, the cost for security is likely to be lower per square foot at larger centers.) Comparison data on the costs of security are compiled in *Income/Expense Analysis®: Shopping Centers* published by the Institute of Real Estate Management, *Dollars and Cents of Shopping Centers* published by ULI—The Urban Land Institute, and *The Score* published by the International Council of Shopping Centers.

---

and the houses behind them. In an urban setting, the neighborhood might be the two or three large multiple dwellings that face each other across a street or a single apartment building or property. Regardless of how the neighborhood is defined, if area residents do not know the other people living on their own street or in their building, they cannot distinguish a resident from a visitor or guest or someone who has no business being in the area. Overcoming this particular hurdle is a key crime prevention strategy outlined in "Neighborhood and Community Watch Programs."

Although neighborhood watch programs are commonly perceived as an activity of homeowners or apartment residents, the principle applies as

Mall Watch

Too often citizens expect their local police departments to do everything in the fight against crime, but citizens need to become involved if crime prevention efforts are to be successful. Mall Watch is a program designed to enhance security in shopping centers; modeled after the neighborhood watch concept, it is a self-help program that can lighten the burden on law enforcement agencies.

Mall watch is a proactive program that allows customers, mall merchants, mall security, and law enforcement agencies to work together to fight crime and control store losses. It works in much the same way as a neighborhood watch, combining awareness with educational seminars and a telephone alert network. A mall watch can be effective in curtailing all kinds of undesirable activity at a retail site, including shoplifting, the passing of bad checks, and credit card fraud. In a pilot mall watch program, the number of shoplifting incidents was reduced by 35% in its first year of operation.

Customers are an important component of a mall watch. They can participate actively by reporting any suspicious behavior they might observe in the parking lot or inside the mall to the nearest mall security guard or store employee who can contact the appropriate persons in the mall watch network.

A mall watch program also benefits customers. For example, the losses incurred because of fraud and theft typically are passed along to the customer—i.e., as higher prices—and these losses can amount to billions of dollars annually across the United States. Car theft happens in mall parking lots, or cars are broken into to steal their contents. Customers are sometimes assaulted or robbed—or both—as they go to their cars. Even frequent patrols by security personnel do not always catch the would-be criminals. The fears and negative perceptions generated as a result of actual or attempted criminal incidents drive customers away. By being observant and reporting suspicious activities—by helping make the shopping mall property unfriendly to criminals—customers make their own shopping experiences more enjoyable and profitable and make the mall more inviting to other shoppers.

well at office buildings and shopping centers. Business tenants and their employees have just as great a need to know who does and does not belong on a property and how to recognize suspicious, potentially criminal activities as do residents. Sometimes it may be necessary or desirable to enlist the aid of local politicians (city aldermen, county board members) in support of watch programs or to obtain zoning variances that will facilitate implementation of crime-preventive design strategies.

The application of the community watch concept in commercial as well as residential properties has been addressed by the Institute of Real Estate Management (IREM) in its SMART Partners® publications and seminars. [SMART is an acronym; it stands for Safety Management Alliance of Residents and Tenants. Both the acronym and the slogan are registered service

Operation Shop Safe

Non-mall shopping centers have their own unique challenges when dealing with crime issues. The comparatively small size of these neighborhood and community shopping centers (in the range of 75,000–250,000 square feet) means they typically do not have on-site management, yet the retailers— and their customers—expect shopping to be a safe activity.

Weingarten Realty Management Company, an operator of 175 non-mall shopping centers in ten states, has developed a unique crime-prevention program for its properties that makes partners of Weingarten Realty Management Company, the shopping center merchants, and the community in the effort to reduce crime-related losses. With a focus on crime reduction and community education, Operation Shop Safe features signs that offer safety tips for shoppers and rewards for information leading to arrest and conviction of those who commit crimes at the participating properties. Decals in store windows and brochures for retailers to distribute to their customers augment the prominent signage.

The program is co-sponsored by the local Crime Stoppers organization and the National Crime Prevention Council (NCPC). This arrangement has enhanced public awareness of the Operation Shop Safe program through the use of the McGruff logo—"take a bite out of crime"—and the Crime Stoppers program for obtaining information from the public. The program has generated interest among tenants at retail properties in other cities and fostered development of a network of security and risk management professionals from among Houston area shopping center management personnel. Operation Shop Safe has established a partnership between Weingarten Realty Management Company, the shopping center merchants, and the community, all working together in an effort to reduce crime. In addition, Weingarten Realty Management Company was presented with a Resolution from the City of Houston commending them for their responsible leadership in the area of crime prevention.

Source: *The REIT Report* August 1995 (Operation Shop Safe: A Security Partnership Tool by Joseph W. Karp). Operation Shop Safe is a service mark of Weingarten Realty Management Company. Published by permission of Weingarten Realty Management Company.

marks of IREM.] *IREM SMART Partners Program: Better Properties through Stronger Communities* outlines strategies for enhancing resistance to crime in apartment properties, office buildings, and shopping centers. Two supplements are also available: *Sustaining SMART Partners: A Community Approach to a Community Watch* addresses specialty niches that a crime watch program can enhance, and *Working Out SMART Partners: Practical Concerns for Every Property* provides insight into some realistic aspects of crime prevention and security management, especially at commercial properties. A "starter packet" of materials for initiating a SMART Partners watch augments the written materials. In addition to logos, labels, and stand-up cards, there are "SMART Tips" safety awareness and crime reduction flyers for distribution plus *A Guide for Organizing an IREM SMART Partners Watch: Establishing and Maintaining a Strong Community Watch at Your*

Other Joint Efforts at Crime Prevention

Joint efforts at crime prevention are not limited to residential neighborhoods. The deterioration of downtown business districts in many major metropolitan areas has made these city centers targets for crime, and the downtown centers are starting to fight back. Many of the department stores, specialty shops, movie theaters, restaurants, and other businesses that once attracted residents from the entire metropolitan area to the downtown center and enticed workers to remain downtown after their workday ended have shifted their activities to suburban malls or gone out of business.

With the establishment of ever larger shopping centers and enclosed malls anchored by the same major retailers as are downtown, suburbanites who commute downtown to work can do their shopping close to home. Cinemas adjacent to or inside malls mean entertainment is available close to home as well. As people abandon the city centers for shopping and entertainments closer to home, downtown stores have tended to keep shorter hours and some have closed their doors altogether. The ancillary businesses that depend on crowds of shoppers and workers—restaurants, theaters—are following a similar path. Vacant stores and often poorly maintained streets and sidewalks create an impression of abandonment and desolation, and such areas breed crime. City centers that once were bustling with crowds on weekdays and weekends, and into the late evening hours, are becoming places no one wants to be in the evening and sometimes even during the day.

Deployment of police with arrest powers and weapons to provide security in public buildings or at public functions is obviously not an appropriate use of resources. (Public police have no legal duty to attempt to provide security services with on-duty police officers.) Furthermore, police departments seem always to suffer manpower shortages, and these become more acute as the incidence of crime increases. However, law enforcement partnerships with private security forces are allowing cities to take back their downtowns. Many U.S. cities have created business improvement districts (BIDs) in which private security officers supplement police patrols and perform other services—some 1,000 BIDs exist in the United States and Canada. ("Storefront" police substations established in some urban neighborhood retail enclaves and at suburban shopping centers and malls are examples of similar partnering efforts outside the downtown area.)

Philadelphia, for example, created the Center City District (CCD) in 1991. Administered by a nonprofit entity, the district includes the city's highest concentration of office buildings, stores, and hotels and is funded by a real estate tax surcharge paid by property owners in the CCD. Supplementing the police are foot patrols of community service representatives (CSRs) who receive special training that addresses customer service and hospitality as well as teaching team-building and problem-solving skills.

Property. (The "Tips" and the guide book are also available in Spanish.) The intent is for real estate managers to use these materials to help their residents and tenants establish watch programs.

Crime prevention also includes more active involvement of the police in the community or neighborhood, a step that has been supported by anti-

Other Joint Efforts *(concluded)*

Community service representatives also learn first aid and CPR (cardiopulmonary resuscitation) in addition to police policies and procedures regarding the use of force. (Police officers assigned to the CCD also receive special training for interacting with visitors.) Community service representatives function as public concierges and a paid neighborhood watch; they wear uniforms but are unarmed and are not allowed to use force. Although they share facilities in the CCD police substation, the community service representatives are not auxiliary police. In addition to foot patrols deployed on two shifts, their duties include reporting crimes and helping citizens and visitors—they and the police officers also serve as city ambassadors. Crime has been significantly reduced in the CCD since this program was launched, and the public perception of the safety of the CCD is generally positive.

St. Louis has also supplemented the police force in the downtown area with private security patrols. The patrols wear uniforms and are not armed, but they do have the authority to make arrests. Although the supplementary security force has been in existence for some ten years, the district was actually created in the late 1950s and is funded by a real estate surtax paid by district property owners. Patrols cover assigned beats whose size and schedules are varied to allocate manpower effectively for activities as needed—e.g., sporting events, conventions, and the Christmas shopping season. These patrols were launched in response to public demand for more security, and as the downtown is revitalized it is being perceived as safer.

The impact of these types of efforts has been substantial. Crime has been effectively reduced, and as crime is reduced, downtowns are once again attracting visitors and shoppers because people can feel safe there.

Suburban properties have also become crime targets, and the same types of strategies are being used effectively there as well. The manager of Northwest Plaza, a major mall outside of St. Louis with more than 200 tenants, was prompted to increase security after a shooting occurred at the mall. His first step was to switch from in-house to contract security personnel; later, off-duty police officers were employed as an added force to patrol on horseback—the high perch gave them a distinct advantage in visually monitoring the entrances and parking lots of the mall. Parking lot lighting was also improved: The original lights, though bright, gave everything a yellow cast; the metal-halide replacements emit a white light that is perceived by many shoppers as brighter. Ultimately, a police station was established at the mall—constructed and outfitted at mall expense. The combination of contract security and the police presence along with anchor stores' own loss-prevention officers and the improved lighting is helping keep this suburban mall crime-free: Car theft—a major problem—has been drastically reduced, as has the total number of criminal incidents.

crime legislation—and some funding—at the federal level. David R. Struckhoff briefly describes some of these activities in "Community-Oriented Policing."

Belief in the "broken windows" theory, which argues that minor violations can create a disorderly environment that generates more serious crime, is a crucial component of the philosophy behind community-oriented policing. In mid-1996, the Office of Community Oriented Policing Services (COPS) of the U.S. Department of Justice reported that more than 9,000 communities nationwide had received funding to put more than 34,000 additional police officers on the streets during the first 18 months following enactment of the 1994 Crime Act. Large cities (over 1 million population) that reported decreasing crime rates before 1994 have cited community-oriented policing as a contributing factor in the continuing precipitous drop in their crime statistics.

Crime Prevention Concepts

Patrick J. Lenaghan

The two major areas of security that have the greatest impact on the employer, building owner, or security manager of a building or complex are physical security and personnel security awareness and training. When planning for the physical security of a facility, certain basic principles need to be followed to help identify security shortcomings or deficiencies. The other major area of concern is deciding who will have access to and work within these buildings or facilities and what security precautions they are expected to take.

This will be a general discussion of some of these basic principles and how they apply to safeguarding separate buildings, businesses, shopping complexes, and high-rises. They can be applied to either commercial or residential properties.

The Crime Risk Triangle

The first consideration is, why does a crime take place? How can you prevent it from happening in your building or business? Three basic elements must be present for a crime to take place: desire, ability, and opportunity. This is referred to as "the crime risk triangle."

You have no control over what the criminal may *desire*, and you cannot ascertain the criminal's *ability* to commit a crime; but you can limit the *opportunity*. Simply stated, if you make it easy to steal from you, or to harm you, then someone will. What you need to do is make it *difficult, risky*, and *unrewarding* to do so.

To prevent a crime from taking place, you must first consider where the threat is. You as the owner or manager must be aware of it and pre-

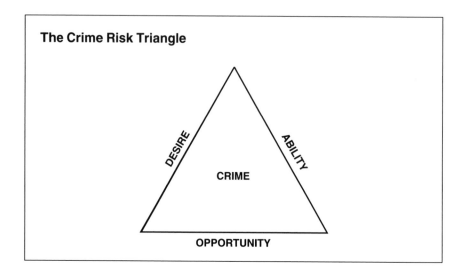

The Crime Risk Triangle

pare for it. There are two ways that crime enters a business, building, or facility.

1. External threats
2. Internal threats

External crime comes in the form of robbery, burglary, assault, or shoplifting. Internal crimes are basically the same but are perpetrated by your employees or building occupants (residents; employees of commercial tenants).

Internal crimes account for about 80 percent of all losses and increased liability for the owner. It is therefore critical to ensure that your prospective employees (or tenants) do not have criminal tendencies before you allow them inside your facility. This can be done as simply as verifying past job performance with their last employer—in the case of prospective tenants, checking with prior landlords—or it can be as sophisticated as background checks and personality and honesty testing conducted by security professionals. These methods go a long way in preventing internal crime and are worth the investment. Internal crime can be controlled, but to prevent external crimes you have to prepare for the unexpected. You need to be proactive and *prevent the crime from happening.*

Crime Prevention.   *Crime prevention* is the anticipation, recognition, and appraisal of a crime risk and the initiation of some action to remove or reduce it. In crime prevention, you need to be proactive. This begins with *physical security planning.*

Before you can develop your physical security plan, you need to analyze your present security posture and identify your deficiencies. The basic instrument used to determine vulnerability is called a security survey.

Security Survey.   The *security survey* is a critical on-site examination of a business or residence to ascertain its present security status, identify deficiencies, determine the protection needed, and implement changes to improve security. The survey should include:

1. Analysis of the overall environment (neighborhood, block area, etc.).
2. General vulnerability of the premises.
3. Specific points of vulnerability.
4. Recommendations focused on physical improvements, countermeasures, and security hardware to counter the threat.

When you conduct this survey—or contract for it with a security professional—consider what your end state should be. Remember "the crime risk triangle." The only element you can control or influence is the opportunity for a crime to take place.

To help you limit the opportunity for a crime to take place, and as you consider what you want your security posture to be, use the four Ds—deny, detect, deter, delay.

Physical Security Planning

If your physical security planning and precautions are adequate, you will be able to *deny* the criminal the opportunity to commit the crime altogether because the risk is too great. With sufficient countermeasures, barriers, deterrents, and hardware, you can *detect* the crime in progress and be able to react to it or stop it. If you cannot deny or detect the criminal, make entry more difficult and time consuming. This will either *deter* or *delay* the criminal, thus increasing the perpetrator's anxiety level as well as improving the likelihood of detection and apprehension.

Physical security is a system of tangible countermeasures designed to control or limit access. This includes barriers designed in concentric layers surrounding the target (the property), with security growing progressively tighter the closer you get to the center or objective. What you want to achieve is *protection in depth*. There are three layers to consider—outer, middle, and inner. These layers can also be considered lines of defense.

The Outer Protective Layer—The First Line of Defense.   The first line of defense is the perimeter of the property and surrounding areas. The security measures that are implemented in this area should be designed to deter and delay. The physical countermeasures that can be implemented are:

Fences
Gates
Crime-preventive landscaping

Signs
Lighting
Walls

These measures also delineate property lines and enforce controlled access, channel vehicles and people, and may discourage trespassers.

However, you should not place too much reliance on a fence as a barrier that will deny entry. A fence is often perceived by those inside its borders as a positive security measure. However, the U.S. Department of Defense has shown that a fence alone should not be considered a serious barrier—field tests have demonstrated that a chain link fence arranged in any configuration can be breached in 1.5–12 seconds.[1] The fence is only one of many protections in the concentric layers of physical security.

The following are some things to keep in mind when conducting an analysis of the outer perimeter—you need to attempt to keep the area as clear as possible to allow maximum observation.

- When landscaping the area, ensure that it has aesthetic value *and* does not allow a criminal a place to hide or permit observation of the building. Crime preventive landscaping should include such things as trimming tree limbs away from fences and roofs and keeping shrubbery trimmed low.

- Trash receptacles should be placed away from the fence so they cannot be used as a means of scaling the fence or as a place to hide.

- Lighting is the best deterrent. If properly installed, it will illuminate the area without creating deep shadows that could be used as avenues of approach to the building.

Lighting should be designed to serve as both physical barrier and psychological deterrent. Adequate lighting and security precautions for parking lots and structures need to be included in your security plans for the outer perimeter. Even though recent studies have shown that only a small portion of a community's violent crimes takes place in parking areas, they are still perceived as high-crime areas. Precautions need to be taken to allay the fears of employees, customers, and tenants. Random checks by security personnel, duress alarms in the parking areas, and closed-circuit television (CCTV) monitoring all go a long way to counter a perceived threat and prevent problems. This increased security posture will also deter automobile-related property crimes.[2]

The Middle Protective Layer—The Second Line of Defense.   The next layer or second line of defense is the exterior of the building. More conspicuous and positive controls will be needed here than on the perimeter of the property. The four major areas of concern are the entry points through the walls, roof, windows, and doors.

Whether your business or residence is a freestanding structure or part of a larger complex, mall, or high-rise building, you need to consider ease of access by the criminal through these areas. You want to be certain that a criminal cannot gain entrance by cutting a hole in the roof or walls or removing something like an air-conditioning unit, air intake or outflow vents, or a skylight.

- *Walls.* The best time to ensure that outer walls are adequately reinforced is when the building is under construction. If this ideal cannot be achieved, there are several ways to reinforce the walls in a decorative manner. Incorporating additional brick walls on the interior and installing metal plates under the plaster or sheet rock are examples.

- *Roof.* There are several techniques that can be used to "harden" or strengthen the roof so as to deny entrance. They range from adding metal plates and bolting them to the roof, then welding the nuts to the bolts, to using wire mesh or additional insulation to fill the space from the roof to the ceiling, or a combination of all of these. Ventilation ducts that are too narrow to be used as entrance points and skylights that are secured and have intrusion alarms in place also help deny entry.

- *Windows.* Windows can be "hardened" by installing shatterproof glass, reinforcing window frames, and adding wire mesh and window locks. Windows can also be sealed permanently. This can be done as simply as drilling a small hole through the window sash where the two portions of the window meet and filling the hole with a nail from which the head has been removed. When you do need to open the windows for maintenance or cleaning, a small magnet can be used to withdraw the nails.

- *Doors.* Exterior doors should be metal or solid wood—the latter can be reinforced with metal plates—and locks can be replaced with pick-resistant dead-bolt type locks that have a minimum 1-inch throw. Door frames can be reinforced (16-gauge steel is preferable for this).

Your goal should be to harden the existing vulnerable entry points so as to *deter* or *delay* the criminal. An example would be fitting all windows and doors with intrusion alarm devices (contact switches, glass breaks, etc.) tied into a central monitoring system. A system that can be monitored by security personnel on the premises increases your protection significantly. Additional measures to deter or deny entry are:

1. Lighting directed onto the exterior of the building, covering entrances and other vulnerable points.

2. Warning signs announcing the existence of alarms and/or that the area is patrolled regularly.

3. Bars on the outsides of windows.

4. Spot-welded hinge pins on doors.

5. Intrusion alarms.

6. Protected roof access points, such as access ladders and fire escapes—also consider barriers on the roof to deny access from adjoining buildings.

7. Additional landscaping that does not offer concealment—shrubs should not obscure windows.

The Inner Layer—The Third Line of Defense.   The inner layer—the objective or third line of defense—is the most critical. This area should also encompass several layers of protection. When properly planned, even if the other layers have been penetrated, the intruder will still be unable to find anything of value or have access to a victim. Components of this layering could include:

1. Motion detectors

2. Duress alarms in isolated common areas

3. Infrared detectors

4. Dead-bolt or cipher (numeric key pad) locks on all doors

5. Closed-circuit television with a recorder that is activated when the barriers are breached

6. All common areas (hallways, lobbies, utility rooms) kept illuminated and, if feasible, under surveillance

7. Security guards

8. Controlled access

All of these measures can be effective, especially if the building or complex is not occupied after normal working hours. Public buildings, apartment complexes, and other high-traffic facilities offer other unique challenges, especially high-rise buildings.

Special Considerations

High-rise buildings pose some unique security challenges. These structures, even to maintain a moderate level of security, must have additional countermeasures and safety devices in place. For buildings that are open to the public, access control is critical, and stringent measures are often required. However, in a mixed-occupancy building there might be resistance to stringent access controls, especially if some of the tenant businesses depend on walk-in customers. Strip shopping centers and malls also require specific consideration.

High-Rise and Public Access Buildings.   In physical security planning for a high-rise building, you need to consider the potential hazards to personal safety as well as the security of physical assets. The most critical threats to these structures, from a safety standpoint, are fire, explosions, or contamination of life-support systems (e.g., fresh air and potable water supplies). A critical event can be triggered intentionally or accidentally; but if not planned for, such an incident can have catastrophic results. Thus, safety considerations have a significant impact on your security posture and must be taken into account in your security planning.

This aspect of ownership responsibility should not be taken lightly. Not only in-depth planning, but implementation of the plan, is necessary to guarantee the safety of residents and tenants and your property. Some general safety considerations and ways to counter possible threats are outlined below:

1. Install early detection devices—know the precise location of potential hazards and monitor them.

2. Have a reliable communication system throughout the building. A redundant system (alternate backup) is recommended in the event of primary system failure.

3. Establish escape routes and be sure they are well-marked, illuminated, and easily accessible for evacuation. Make sure everyone knows where the escape routes are, and post diagrams of them prominently throughout the building. Tour the routes periodically to make sure the path is clear.

4. Ensure that all your countermeasures—fire extinguishers, sprinkler systems, smoke detectors, fire alarms, carbon monoxide (CO) monitors, shut-off valves for water and filtration systems, battery-powered auxiliary lighting, etc.—are in place and operational.

5. Work very closely with building and fire inspectors to ensure that you are in compliance with all municipal codes and OSHA rules. Then plan how you are going to ensure emergency egress and prevent unauthorized access to your building.

6. Brief all your tenants or residents on where and how to assemble for purposes of accountability in the event of an evacuation.

Access Control.   The most critical area of concern in public buildings or high-rise commercial and residential buildings is access control. For purposes of access control, you need to divide the structure into three classes of interior space:

1. *Public access or common areas* include street-level entrance lobbies, main elevator lobbies, and access routes to retail businesses—in newer buildings, mezzanines and promenades should be included.

2. *Rented or assigned occupancies* are leased or owner-occupied spaces on various floors. Depending on the occupant, such spaces may be open to the public during building "business" hours, or access may be restricted to identified and authorized persons.

3. *Maintenance spaces* include mechanical rooms and floors, communications and utility access points, elevator machine rooms, janitorial closets, and spaces with generally strict limited access.

Access control measures will be different for each class of space.[3]

The first step to consider in controlling access is to be certain that all persons entering the building pass more than one control point. This requires all access points that are not controlled to be locked or provided with intrusion alarm devices. To be even more effective, on-site security personnel should monitor these devices and be prepared to react to an attempted intrusion. All basement entrances should be locked or have alarms installed, except those that are the principal ingress or egress routes to the lobby level.

Security personnel or guards are most desirable in these situations. On first glance, the use of security personnel may appear expensive. However, when considering potential loss and possible civil liability if there is an incident, the cost is minimal.

Single-Occupancy Buildings.   In a single-occupancy building, such as a private business, all access to upper floors can be controlled by:

- Denying access to or from the fire stairs in the lobby or on the lower floors. Fire doors fitted with crash bars and a warning posted on the doors that an alarm will sound when the bar is activated will deny access to the stairways from the lobby or ground floor and keep employees from using the stairs except in a real emergency.

- A control point can be established at the passenger elevators. For this to be completely effective, all personnel using the elevators would have to show identification or be escorted.

- Stairways that are to remain open for movement from floor to floor should be illuminated; if practical, they should be monitored via CCTV and patrolled by security personnel at irregular times.

- Duress alarms may also be installed for greater security.

- Have positive control over employee break areas and smoking areas. Only authorized personnel who have been cleared through an access control point should be able to utilize these areas. If these areas are outside the building, they can be walled in to create a courtyard adjacent to the building. The goal is to ensure that no unauthorized persons can enter or leave the building from these areas.

- Employee badges and visitor sign-in/sign-out rosters are also effective.

- CCTV and duress alarms in elevators are also good safety precautions, especially in residential or commercial buildings that have heavy traffic.

- If cipher locks or punch codes (keypads) are to be used to gain entrance, users need to be instructed to not let anyone "piggy back" on their input or follow them into the building once they have gained access. What may appear to be a simple courtesy could allow a criminal to gain entry to the building and result in serious harm.

Mixed-Occupancy Buildings. If some of the tenant businesses depend on walk-in customers, there is likely to be resistance to such stringent security measures. However, pre-planning of space allocations and stacking arrangements to secure the access to more critical areas can overcome tenants' resistance. (Such planning should identify sensitive owner occupancies, isolate sensitive owner space, and impose strict access-control measures in the sectors with sensitive occupancy—and assure that controls cannot be bypassed.)

Maintenance Spaces. All building maintenance spaces should be considered sensitive areas, and access to them should be controlled. Even in a large building with multiple maintenance spaces, it is feasible to maintain access control. The limited population requiring access to maintenance spaces is easily identified. In newer buildings, automated systems using access cards can be installed; in older buildings, controlled key issuance, intrusion devices, and telephone contact with security personnel by an authorized key holder immediately before or after entry could be employed at low cost.

Tenants in Strip Shopping Centers or Malls. Some special security problems exist for the business or retailer that operates in a strip shopping center or mall setting. All the precautions previously listed apply in safeguarding one's leased premises; however, the nature of these retail properties means that access often cannot be specifically restricted, and additional (or different) precautions have to be taken. This is especially true if any business in the center is operated on a 24-hour basis.

For tenants, vigilance is key: Be aware of your surroundings and your neighbors. Find out who shares your interior walls and who is located above and below your premises. If you have a suspended ceiling, make sure the interior walls go all the way to the roof so no one can gain entrance

---

Security Tips for Retail Property Tenants

- Check out your neighbors.
- Check with local law enforcement and crime prevention officers.
- Leave interior lights on and be sure patrols and pedestrians have an unobstructed view through store windows.
- Leave empty cash register drawers open and in plain sight; treat safes the same way.
- Become educated about local gang activity and how to identify gangs.
- Verify that there is adequate lighting in the parking lot and direct lighting on the building exterior.
- Ask the property owner to provide security guards or establish an agreement among the tenants to share the cost of patrols.

---

through the ceiling from an adjacent office or business. Check out your neighbors—is their business and/or tenancy legitimate?

Before investing in or opening a business in a strip center or mall, it is a good idea to talk with the local police department, especially the crime control or prevention officer. Local law enforcement personnel will be able to tell you if there are problems in the area (e.g., shoplifting, gangs, drug sales, vandalism).

Make sure that security patrols or pedestrians will have an unobstructed view through store windows after closing. Keep some interior lights on to facilitate observation of the interior of the building by passing security patrols. Leave cash register drawers open, empty, and in plain view. If possible, do the same with any freestanding or floor safe if you use one. Posting emergency notification numbers on the front door will save time and confusion if the alarm system is activated.

Because gang violence is on the rise, in suburbs as well as urban areas, you should learn all you can about the local gangs—their colors, signs, graffiti (territory boundary markings), rivals, etc. Educate yourself and your employees so that you can anticipate the threat of violence—avoid groups that are loitering in or around the building or parking lot. If you feel threatened personally, notify security or the police. If gang activity is prevalent in your area, you should be alert for drive-by shootings and drug trafficking, and avoid those areas.

There should be adequate lighting in the parking lot and lighting directed onto the exterior of the building. This will help to discourage vandalism and graffiti. If graffiti is a problem, consider applying an exterior paint that breaks down the chemicals present in aerosol paints, allowing the graffiti to be cleaned off with water.

If security guards are not part of the protections established by the property ownership or management, you may want to consider hiring a security guard for your premises or entering into an agreement with the other business owners to defray this expense for the whole property.

Establishing a Security Program

The preceding discussion has provided some general guidelines on what to look for when evaluating your current physical security posture and identifying areas that need to be improved. However, any security program or upgrade is only as good as the people who have to implement and enforce it. The property manager needs to be certain that the people who are responsible for building security understand its importance and are going to enhance the security posture rather than take advantage of it.

To have a fully operational and successful security program, everyone must understand and believe in it. This is achieved through:

- Security awareness
- Security training
- Establishing policies and procedures and good employment practices

Security Awareness.   "Security awareness may be defined as a state of mind through which an individual is conscious of the existence of a security program and is persuaded that the program is relevant to his or her own behavior."[4]

Technically speaking, awareness differs from education and training, the distinctions being that *awareness* seeks to solicit conscious attention, *education* seeks to impart knowledge, and *training* seeks to develop skills. This discussion will take a more general approach in that all three of these subject areas will be considered as interrelated and important for a successful security program. Once security awareness is achieved, security education and training should be implemented or continued to enhance your security posture.

Before security awareness can be promoted, the owner or management at the highest level has to understand its significance and support the effort. This program needs to be driven from the top down. If the owners and/or high-level management place the proper emphasis on security and security awareness, the mid-level to lower-level management and employees are more likely to implement it.

Policies and Procedures.   Once employees realize that security awareness is everyone's responsibility, they need to be provided with set policies and procedures to be executed. The first step in this process is establishing what your overall security goals and objectives are. This will become your *policy statement*. The policy statement should be concise and specific so all employees will read and understand it and can refer to it when they have a question. It should also have a cover letter from the owner or top executive reminding the staff at all levels of the importance of the security program. You will need to emphasize that the policy will be audited and enforced, otherwise it will serve no purpose.

Once the policy statement is published, it is necessary to consider the practical aspects of how it should be implemented. These are the *procedures*. To be effective, all procedures have to be followed and enforced. Simply stated, these are "rules and regulations" for the employees on how to execute the security program. The complexity of these procedures will vary from organization to organization and depend on the level of security required to meet the needs of the facility or complex.

Security Training.   The final step in this process is the continuing education and training program. All procedures and information are perishable if not reinforced periodically with remedial or additional training. This training should involve everyone in the company.

Security training should be the responsibility of supervisors at all levels. It should be conducted at least semi-annually but preferably monthly. Making security training the responsibility of all staff members will require them to remain current on policies, procedures, and upgraded security measures. This also fosters a feeling of increased responsibility, encourages team building, and provides a vehicle for response from all levels of the organization on how to improve security.

Semi-annual training for all employees should cover, at a minimum, policies and procedures and any changes or security upgrades. A record of who attended, what information was covered, and when the training sessions were held should be reviewed by management and kept on file.

Points to Remember

The two major areas of security that have the greatest impact on the property owner, employer, or manager are *physical security* and *security awareness and training*. The two are interdependent.

To fully understand the threat, one must have an understanding of what crime is and what needs to be present for it to take place. This is called "the crime risk triangle," which consists of desire, ability, and opportunity. To prevent crime from taking place, you need to make it risky, difficult, and unrewarding for the criminal. This is achieved through *crime prevention*—anticipation, recognition, and appraisal of the crime risk and initiation of some action to remove or reduce the risk. To assist in preventing crime, you should conduct a thorough analysis of your present security posture and identify shortcomings or deficiencies. A useful technique for doing this is a *security survey,* which identifies deficiencies and corrective actions or countermeasures that are required to correct them. The next step in the process is physical security planning.

Physical security is the tangible countermeasures designed to limit access. This is achieved by planning for security in depth. The plan should encompass three layers of security or lines of defense—outer, middle, and inner. All of these countermeasures are designed to limit access to the building by unauthorized or undesirable persons. Access control is especially critical in high-rise and public buildings.

All the protective countermeasures in the world are still *only as effective as the people who implement them.* All personnel in the organization have to be security conscious or understand the need for security awareness. They should also be given a set of policies and procedures to follow—i.e., rules and regulations that will ensure the security measures are used and enforced. As with any desired level of awareness or behavior, all affected parties need to be trained to implement these policies, and such training has to be repeated and reinforced.

Physical security is more than chain-link fences and alarm systems, and personnel security awareness is more than signs in the employees' locker rooms. Both are integral parts of a continual process or program of countermeasures requiring diligence, training, and implementation. Physical security and personnel security awareness training, if done properly and in concert with each other, will deny the criminal the opportunity to steal your property and harm you or your residents or tenants.

Notes

1. Walsh, Timothy J.: *Protection of Assets* (Vol III; Santa Monica, Calif.: The Merritt Company, 1991), pp. 19–25.
2. Rykert, Wilbur: *Public Crime—Civil Justice: A Study of Crime and Liability Issues in Parking Facilities 1990* (Dissertation; East Lansing, Mich.: Michigan State University, 1990).
3. Walsh, pp. 19–22.
4. Walsh, pp. 34–41.

Selected Bibliography

High Rise Buildings, A Review of the Problem (Report; New York: American Insurance Association, 1972).

Hopf, Peter S.: *Handbook of Building Security Planning and Design* (New York: McGraw-Hill Book Company, 1979).

Rykert, Wilbur: *Public Crime—Civil Justice: A Study of Crime and Liability Issues in Parking Facilities 1990* (Dissertation; East Lansing, Mich.: Michigan State University, 1990).

Walsh, Timothy J.: *Protection of Assets* (Vol III; Santa Monica, Calif.: The Merritt Company, 1991).

Crime Prevention Through Environmental Design

Timothy D. Crowe

Crime prevention through environmental design (CPTED) is based on the theory that proper design and effective use of the built environment can lead to a reduction in the fear of crime and its incidence, as well as improvement in the quality of life. CPTED concepts have been applied to all types of environments from an individual structure to entire neighborhoods. However, this discussion will focus on commercial property applications and, more specifically, on malls and shopping centers.

CPTED Fundamentals

CPTED principles are based on historical and scientific observations about the interactions between people and the physical environment. Observations and analyses of human behavior, crime, and crime prevention have demonstrated that the following hierarchy of behavioral effects occurs:

The *design* and *use* of the physical environment
Directly affects *human behavior,*
Which impacts *productivity* and *quality of life,*
Leading to an increase or decrease in exposure to *crime and loss.*

CPTED concepts emphasize natural surveillance, natural access control, and territorial behavior. It is important for CPTED planners to classify security strategies into the following three categories:

1. *Organized*—labor-intensive security in which the cost is extrinsic to the normal functions and requirements of human space (e.g., guards, police).

Key Concepts of CPTED

• Natural surveillance
• Natural access control
• Territorial behavior

---

2. *Mechanical*—capital- or hardware-intensive security in which the cost is, once again, extrinsic to the normal functions and requirements of space (e.g., fences, alarms, cameras).

3. *Natural*—integration of security and behavior management in which both human and physical resources are used (e.g., spatial definition, placement of workstations, location of windows).

The emphasis on natural approaches to security reflects the desire to integrate behavior management concepts into the plans for the use of human and physical resources that are required to carry out human functions and activities. These natural approaches are then supplemented with organized and mechanical methods of security which include use of guards and security systems.

Safe Versus Unsafe Activities and Locations.   It is necessary in planning for the use of CPTED concepts to rate human activities and locations with regard to their inherent vulnerability to victimization and risk. Activities and locations are rated as safe or unsafe in direct relation to the presence or absence of the three key concepts of CPTED—natural surveillance, natural access control, and territorial behavior.

For example, customer and employee parking is often considered an unsafe activity. Vehicles are vulnerable to criminal acts, and their owners are potential victims because of the low level of activity and movement in parking lots. The location of parking is likewise considered unsafe because it is generally isolated from buildings and accessible from many entry points. Malls, for instance, have traditionally "turned their backs on parking" by facing all business activity inward.

Safe locations are often found adjacent to high-activity areas, especially if they are visible from windows that provide an overview of the setting. Parking that is located in front of a building on a frequently used street is considered safer than parking that may be hidden behind buildings or outside the line of sight from activities. Safe activities are usually associated with organized functions such as an administrative office or some type of concession stand or sales booth. These safe activities provide the perception of access control and surveillance that make the normal user of space feel safer and the abnormal user of space feel at greater risk of exposure.

Some Space Management and Design Goals

- Defined spaces and transitional areas
- Strategic staging of events and activities
- Strategic location of gathering places
- Natural barriers between conflicting activities
- Perception of natural surveillance—high visibility

Space Users. The application of CPTED concepts to planning also requires that potential users of space be classified according to their role in and relationship to meeting the objectives of the human functions and activities. CPTED planners usually classify users of space among three types—normal users, abnormal users, and observers.

Normal users of space are those persons whose presence in a location at a particular time is desired (e.g., business clients, customers). *Abnormal* users of space are those persons whose presence in a location at a particular time is unwanted (e.g., loiterers, criminals). *Observers* are generally those persons who are required to be in a particular space because they live there, work there, or are hired to be there to protect the space (e.g., residents, employees, security personnel). The interaction between the various users of space is an important aspect of the behavior management and control concepts of CPTED. The following are some of the space management and design strategies used by CPTED planners.

- Clearly defining the boundaries of controlled space.
- Clearly indicating areas of transition between public, semi-public, and private space.
- Locating areas for people to congregate in places with natural surveillance and access control, away from the view of potential offenders.
- Placing safe activities in unsafe locations.
- Placing unsafe activities in safe locations.
- Providing for natural barriers between conflicting activities.
- Improving scheduling of space to provide for effective use.
- Designing space to increase the perception of natural surveillance.
- Overcoming distance and isolation through improved communications and design efficiencies.

CPTED Site Surveys. A CPTED site survey can be the most cost-beneficial service that may be obtained by a mall manager or owner. The best CPTED specialist is an employee of the management firm who has received training in the use of CPTED concepts. (Designers, planners, and

---

> **CPTED Reviews—the Three Ds**
>
> • Designation of purpose
> • Definition of identity
> • Design

security specialists from shopping center management companies have participated in CPTED training programs, which generally last about five days.) A CPTED site survey will contribute to a number of activities; marketing, risk reduction, security, and cost control are among the many benefits. Most surveys result in recommendations for savings in building maintenance and operations costs, as well as savings in security hardware and personnel costs.

A CPTED site survey differs from the traditional security review. Planners trained in CPTED emphasize the connection between the functional objectives of space utilization and behavior management. The planner is trained to differentiate between *designation* of the purpose of a space, its *definition* in terms of management and identity, and its *design,* which relates to the dimensions of (1) physiological support for human activities (function) and (2) the psychological element (behavior management). Designation, definition, and design are the three Ds of CPTED reviews.

Applying CPTED in Commercial Areas

CPTED is an age-old concept that has been renewed and expanded over the past 20 years. Its operating hypothesis—that proper design and effective use of space can reduce fear and the incidence of crime and improve the quality of life—translates into increased profits and reduced losses in the business environment.

CPTED helps to integrate good marketing with good security instead of security procedures conflicting with customer satisfaction and employee morale. New store designs and management techniques are increasing sales, reducing losses, and increasing employee productivity. CPTED concepts may be applied in any setting, and the shopping center is an especially appropriate environment for their use. The good news is that implementing CPTED strategies costs little or nothing.

While malls, shopping centers, and small businesses are experiencing higher crime rates, greater economic losses, and more liability problems, CPTED reviews and site plan assessments are producing excellent results for retail centers and their immediate neighborhoods. The following discussions provide an overview of the historical antecedents of retail centers; crime, loss, and liability; emerging responses to retail center crime, and common design and management problems.

Historical Antecedents.   The first shopping centers were the crossroads or core areas of towns. American cities and towns grew up and out from centers of commercial and retail activity. After World War II, however, there was an explosion of suburban development, with single-family homes and two-car families supplanting the high-density housing and public transportation of the city center. This signaled an end to traditional commercial and retail activities being centralized in downtowns exclusively. Business had to follow the customer to the suburbs, which were geographically removed from downtowns and from each other. The automobile became the primary means of transportation, and as shoppers became highly mobile, business responded with a proliferation of small shopping centers.

The old concept of the neighborhood store, with loyal repeat customers who protected their local businesses, ended after World War II. People used to live in apartments above retail businesses, thus providing the perception of surveillance at night and on weekends. However, stores and shopping centers now stand as islands within mixed land use areas that are constantly changing and often volatile, both financially and socially.

The growth of shopping centers as the primary method of reaching the customers who were moving away from the cities presented many logistical and financial challenges. Stores had to be smaller, inventories had to be spread among many locations, and transportation of goods and supervision of a diversity of operations had to be considered. However, the economy was booming by the middle 1950s, and business was expanding more rapidly than ever.

These new development activities also changed the social environment. People no longer recognized each other when they went shopping. Territorial identity and proprietary concerns for the old neighborhood store vanished. At the same time, criminals shifted their attention to the new shopping centers to take advantage of the large, undifferentiated environments. Later development of enclosed shopping malls, some with 100 or more different stores, only magnified the social changes and opened the door to increased potential for criminal activities, economic losses, and related liabilities that attend these risks.

Crime, Loss, and Liability.   Crime, customer and employee victimization, and civil liability are problems faced by every shopping center. Renewed urban violence may be added to the seemingly ever-growing list of their troubles. These problems cost more than money, in that the image and reputation of an individual store or group of stores directly affects the profitability of the center as a whole.

Shopping centers and malls became targets of crime and loss for many of the reasons that they were successful. Being located near freeways made them accessible to customers and offenders alike. Parking lots had to be

---

Shopping Centers as Crime Targets

What attracts customers also attracts criminals.

• Locations near freeways—easy access

• Large parking lots—easy for cruising

• Solid walls to screen backside of center from view—easy concealment of activities

• Overgrown landscaping—easy concealment of offenders

---

large to accommodate large numbers of customers; this also made them easy for an offender to cruise. As a means of appeasing the aesthetic concerns of local residents, walls were built to hide the backs of the centers, and these walls can be and are used by offenders as a means of concealment for their activities. Finally, landscaping was installed to improve the appearance of the site, but overgrown landscaped areas are often used for concealment by offenders.

It was popular a few years ago for young people in cars to "cruise" mall parking lots and "hang out" in certain areas at night. Territories within mall parking lots were "colonized," or pre-empted, by informal gangs or loose associations of youths. Now the young people are bold enough to move inside the malls in large numbers and colonize seating areas and other spaces that are near concessions and theaters. They call it "malling," but it is actually a form of harassment of legitimate customers.

Parking lot cruising outside and malling inside hurt retailers' business. Moreover, these problems hurt the surrounding neighborhoods. Some say that young people need a place to go at night, and that malls are the best place for them to congregate. There is no research or literature in youth development and delinquency prevention that supports this contention. However, the business community has avoided the issue of dealing with juveniles officially. Fear of liability and violation of confidentiality laws has paralyzed the private sector until recently.

Emerging Responses to Retail Center Crime.   History and urban planning have demonstrated many times that what is good for the shopping center is good for the neighborhood, and vice versa. A shopping center that is in trouble depresses local property values. A neighborhood that is in trouble hurts the shopping center.

In *Discouraging Crime Through City Planning* (Berkeley, Calif: University of California, 1969), Shlomo Angel presented research findings from the Oakland, California, area which indicated that neighborhoods and shopping centers should be planned to achieve "critical intensity." Too few or too many stores clustered together in any given area will not be profitable or defensible. A balance is required to achieve the perception of natural surveillance and territorial concern. Urban planning research and experience are continually demonstrating that:

- Malls, shopping centers, and small retail developments should be planned in relation to the values, priorities, and problems that are unique to the neighborhood and area.
- Traffic planning and control are important for mall/retail safety and profitability.
- Numbers of police calls for service and crime reports are higher per capita (in many places) at malls than in downtowns.

Criminal justice research and development activities have produced two major programs that can provide relief for malls, shopping centers, and other retail establishments. First is the development of new interagency programs to control delinquency and youth crime. The private sector is now involved in these programs because many of the real and perceived legal impediments have been removed through legislation, blanket court orders, or interagency agreements. The second program is "crime prevention through environmental design" (CPTED). CPTED planners are taking advantage of new interagency and interdisciplinary programs to improve on public and private cooperation in dealing with community physical planning.

Common Design and Management Issues

Many factors challenge the design function as well as the management of retail sites. Efforts to control or limit access must be balanced against concerns about accessibility for customers. Types of tenants and their locations are aesthetic as well as management concerns. Perceptions of safety are important to attracting repeat business as well as new customers. Parking is perhaps the greatest single challenge. The following discussion outlines some of the specific problems and suggests approaches to overcoming them.

Parking.   Parking lot access is usually designed with multiple ingress/ egress points to facilitate access during busy times. However, these access points also reinforce the perception of parking lots as public spaces, which increases the range of excuses for people who are cruising the lots or looking for opportunities to commit criminal acts. Barricades, gates, and landscaped islands may be used to channel traffic and control it when stores are closed or during off-peak shopping periods.

Internal vehicle flow is often unrestricted, making it easy for potential offenders to move about without any concern about being trapped by security guards or police. The unrestricted flow also creates a safety hazard for pedestrians who may be struck by vehicles that cross lanes. Parking bumpers, curb lanes, and landscaped islands can be installed to channel traffic and to break the parking areas into separate enclaves that may be closed with barricades during off-hours.

Parking structures are frequently designed as fortresses, which helps the abnormal space user avoid scrutiny. Customers are afraid to use these buildings at night and during slow business hours. When customers do use these facilities, they exhibit "avoidance behavior," which says to abnormal users that they are not being watched and to normal users that they are literally on their own. Vendor carts and, in some instances, permanent sales activities are being installed in parking structures to improve profitability and increase the perception of natural surveillance.

Perceptions of Safety.   Landscaping is essential for aesthetic and environmental purposes. However, many landscape ordinances mandate continuous shrubbery around parking areas, fences around trash receptacles, and walls to separate the mall from contiguous residential land uses—all features that produce surveillance hazards. Variances from local ordinances should be requested so that shrubbery and transparent fencing may be used to provide psychological screening rather than physically obscure vulnerable sites.

Incentives are important for prospective lessees as well as customers. Bakeries are advisable tenants for new or recovering malls because of the appealing aroma of fresh baked goods. Lease incentives can be offered for bake shops to cook during business hours. The smell of fresh baked bread is a masking odor, and it elicits psychological responses that remind people of home. Vendor carts and other visible activities are also advisable attractions—they provide a safe activity in unsafe areas. The best locations for many of these activities is at the entrances to the interior space of the mall. This helps to celebrate the arrival of the shopper as well as signify that the place is safe. The vendors can notify security of potential problems as they naturally observe people entering the mall.

The so-called 24-hour environment is a return to the tradition of people living where they work and where they shop. One of the best development strategies is to plan for high-density housing near the mall—or in the case of a vertical mall, above it. (Mixed-use developments in downtown areas are examples of this.) The residential use contributes to mall security during off-hours and is itself protected by businesses during high-activity periods in which many residents are at work or away from their homes.

Major events can be very profitable for malls, attracting shoppers who do not ordinarily patronize them. Locating such events in parking lots will attract the attention of passersby as well as present an impression of safety—safe activities may be scheduled for the most remote areas of

---

Some Solutions to Shopping Center and Mall Design Problems

- Limiting the number of points of direct access to parking (and the mall).
- Establishing physical barriers to restrict traffic flow in parking lots and structures and allow portions to be closed off when not needed.
- Locating vendors, events, and activities in parking lots to create a perception of natural surveillance.
- Requesting variances from local landscaping ordinances which mandate landscaping features that preclude adequate surveillance.
- Positioning vendor carts and other attractions near entrances to welcome shoppers.
- Using colors, lighting, and displays to create a perception of activity and safety.
- Avoiding tenancies and activities that make the mall attractive as a "hang out" or encourage "cruising" in the parking lot.

---

parking lots. Entrances may be controlled to route traffic past the temporary marketing activities. Portable furnishings can be used to create support for the desired activities. One of the best attractions is the street vendor of snack food (e.g., popcorn). Incentives may be offered to existing tenants to support these temporary functions—although all tenants theoretically benefit from traffic generated by such events, some may be concerned about competition. This can be a sensitive issue for mall management to deal with, but combining desirable marketing events with efforts to promote an image of safety at the site has potential long-term benefits for individual tenants as well as for the mall.

These safe activities should be conducted in prominent locations and in problem areas. Portability is an important factor, so that they may be positioned strategically. Publishing announcements of major events and holiday season promotional activities is an excellent strategy for convincing the impulse shopper to come to the mall and should be part of an ongoing advertising program.

Displays can be used to overcome the negative effect of the fortress-type walls that are common to the designs of major discount anchor stores. Wall-mounted displays can advertise merchandise and diminish the perception of a lack of natural surveillance. Lighting, bright colors, and active displays may be used effectively to create the perception of activity and, therefore, of safety.

CPTED Surveys of Malls and Shopping Centers

Successful malls and shopping centers all share some common features, which include the following.

- Clearly marked vehicle access.

- Parking lots designed to reduce pedestrian and vehicle conflict (e.g., using landscaped islands and other barriers to free flow of vehicles).

- Reduced confusion through architecturally celebrated pedestrian entrances to buildings.

- Visual accessibility of parking and concourses—a clear line of sight for ease of monitoring.

- Restrooms conveniently located near safe activities.

- Attractions that allow family groups and adults to dominate and control space.

- Absence of activities and amenities that encourage "hanging out" at a mall rather than being a shopper or user of services.

A number of issues are important to consider in planning and developing a shopping center or mall. Existing and planned land uses in the immediate area will be affected by the commercial development and, conversely, will affect the future of the shopping center or mall. Hours of operation are important because there is a legal right of access to commercial and retail properties during business hours. Public transportation can be an asset, as well as a detractor, depending on schedules and where bus stops are located. Many other variables must also be considered in planning.

Neighborhood and Community Watch Programs

The concept of the "neighborhood watch" group originated in the late 1960s. Since then, more than 20 million Americans have become involved in this type of program, whether it was called College Watch or Campus Crime Watch, Mall Watch, Apartment Watch, Neighborhood/Community Watch, or something else. Program participants learn how to identify suspicious activity and suspicious persons and steps they can take to make their homes and workplaces safe and unattractive to criminals. Consider the following scenarios.

- Your neighbor is a drug dealer, and you have seen dozens of people coming and going.
- The elevator operator in your building is dealing drugs and doing a great business.
- You see a scruffy-looking man climbing in through a neighbor's window.
- The janitor in the building where you work is seen carrying a piece of equipment out of an office from which a computer is reported missing the next day.

As a member of the community you have a choice to make. You can report these incidents to the police or building security personnel and reduce crime or stop continuing criminal activity, or you can do nothing and let it continue (and probably increase). People today are fed up with crime and the cancer that it causes. They are becoming more willing to involve themselves in reporting criminal activity and in preventing crime. The neighborhood watch concept provides a format for doing this, and it works—very effectively.

Basic Civility

Part of the rationale for establishing a formal community watch is to help overcome a general lack of civility. Especially in urban high-rise buildings, people live and work in increasing isolation—what technology has not created or nurtured, a generalized fear of the unknown has overtaken. Lobby attendants scrutinize identification cards for people they see—and often chat with—on a daily basis. People entering elevators face forward and stare at the doors or the floor-selection buttons. If the elevator is crowded, they hunch into themselves, their body language shouting, "Don't look at me!" and "Don't touch me!"

In the not so distant past, people knew their neighbors and their co-workers, if only to exchange pleasantries. Yet there was an unspoken acknowledgment that, in an emergency, they could count on each other. Neighbors willingly took in each other's mail or parcels if no one was home to receive them. Cups of sugar borrowed across the back fence and occasional cups of coffee shared in each other's kitchens established bonds of nominal obligation to assist one another in times of crisis.

In such an environment, simple civility—pleasant greetings, good wishes, inquiries about each other's families and jobs—came naturally. In the 1990s, a stranger who says, "Hello," or "Good morning," often receives a quizzical stare in return, perhaps reflecting the mental question, "What does this person want from me?"

A community watch program sets up a framework for mere civility to build into mutual interest and interdependence. By becoming aware of the environment beyond one's self, participants learn to reach out—to help and be helped. Knowing a danger exists means understanding that the danger is not exclusive to one person or one property. Assistance offered and information given encourages recipients to respond in kind. From small things—simple civilities, shared knowledge and experiences—grow opportunities to develop friendships and loyalties as well as a sense of personal security that comes from being able to rely on someone else's caring and consideration.

The primary purpose of a neighborhood watch is awareness of the following on the part of all the residents:

Who lives in the neighborhood,

Where they can be reached in case of an emergency,

What to do if an emergency arises, and

How to reduce the chances of crime occurring in the neighborhood.

When you do not know the people living in your own building or on your own street, how can you possibly recognize that someone is a stranger or suspicious person who does not belong there? This applies to both building residents and management personnel. A community watch program helps people know and understand each other and fosters a willingness to watch out for and help others as much as they would like (or need) others to help them—an extension of the Golden Rule. In today's urban settings, the tendency is to isolate oneself from neighbors; people can live in a building for many years and not know or recognize any of the residents and only rarely encounter management personnel in person.

A neighborhood or community watch brings together all the people living within a small geographic area—for managed properties, this would most likely be a single apartment building or condominium, or the several buildings in an extended apartment complex or planned unit development. (The watch can be extended beyond the boundaries of the property as necessary or appropriate or practical to do so.)

Steps in Setting Up A Watch Program

Although the larger goal of a neighborhood or community watch program is to prevent crime, the more immediate goal is to establish communication links. People need to know what to look for and how to interpret what they observe—i.e., how to identify suspicious persons and activities—and what to do with this information. Involvement of local law enforcement is critical. The primary "watch" activity is a series of meetings that establish a forum for learning ways to prevent crime in the first place and establishing where and how to report criminal activity when it is observed. It is also important for participants to learn how to care for crime victims and what facilities are available in the community at large to assist those victims in healing their injuries and seeing the criminals brought to justice.

Community Watch Meetings.   Ideally, every person living in the "community" should be a member of the watch. Both husbands and wives should be invited to participate, along with any teenagers in the family or household. (Perhaps someone can act as a babysitter and care for the smaller children in a room near where the meeting is being held so both parents can attend.) Those who are starting the program should make it as easy as possible for everyone to participate.

Optimally, watch meetings should be held in a private home or apartment, where the host's gesture of hospitality is a step toward pulling the neighborhood together. Experience has shown that attendance at meetings in private residences is proportionately larger than when meetings are held in schools or neighborhood centers. However, the size of the group may make it impractical to use someone's home if the watch program is to cover a large apartment community.

Organize the First Meeting.   Because a community watch program needs to be led—and sustained—by the residents themselves, the launch of the program should be initiated by recognized leaders from among the property's residents. To begin, one person should be responsible for inviting

---

Watch Participant Sign-Up Information

- Resident's name and street address or apartment number
- Phone numbers at home and at work and fax numbers (if available)
- Names, ages, and sex of all children and where they go to school
- Any particular information that might help neighbors differentiate the residents (or their children) from strangers or others who do not belong on the property

---

each of the residents to a get-acquainted session. The time of the first meeting should be mutually acceptable to the majority of those invited—the schedule for later meetings will be agreed to by those in attendance. The watch organizer can either call everyone or go door to door and ask them to join—a personal invitation is recommended over a written one.

At the first meeting, each person should fill out a form that asks for names, addresses, and telephone numbers (home and work) of adults and information about residents' children and where they go to school. It may be appropriate to ask for additional information that will help identify residents and guests and distinguish them from strangers or suspicious-acting people. Everyone should be asked to tell the group something about themselves and, in general, get acquainted with each other. Open discussion should be encouraged. A watch captain should be elected at this meeting, even if the position is only temporary, and the next meeting should be scheduled within 30 days—the date, time, and place should be agreed upon before everyone leaves.

Everyone should receive a packet of handouts that address locks and identification of personal property and include phone stickers with police, fire department, and ambulance service numbers for emergencies, as well as any other material the group thinks is in their mutual interest. Police department crime prevention offices and fire department public service offices may have these types of handout materials available. Sometimes a local merchant may have printed phone stickers that list emergency numbers as a business promotional giveaway; this is another possible resource to consider.

In order for a watch program to be effective, everyone in the community should be involved. This is important so no one will be "left out" in the event of an emergency or criminal incident. Even beyond crime prevention, the watch group is an opportunity to develop mutual support and assistance. So, before the first meeting is adjourned, the leader should call for volunteers to contact those community residents who were not present and tell them about the meeting and its outcome. The absent residents should also be given copies of the forms and handouts and encouraged to attend the next meeting.

Establish Specific Objectives. A watch program should encompass all economic groups, ages, races, and political persuasions. It should emphasize what is universal or binding in the community, and families with problems should be sought out to participate in the program whenever possible.

Choose a name that is relevant to the context of the program; it might include the words "home alert" or "neighborhood watch" along with a more specific identifier—e.g., Mayville Apartments Neighborhood Watch; Main Street Home Alert.

To assure an average attendance of fifty percent of community residents at each meeting, personal contact will be required. The watch leadership should plan on investing the necessary time to explain the purpose of the watch and the meetings to each family. Schedule some meetings at night to allow working people and school-age children to attend. Those who are unable to attend meetings can be reached through those who do attend.

Follow a Meeting Agenda. Each meeting should be chaired by a watch member (the captain, if one has been elected) with an appropriate law enforcement officer in attendance. The meeting agenda typically includes:

- A social period to allow late-comers to arrive and new neighbors and new watch participants to get acquainted with the group. (This is important.)
- Brief opening remarks by the chairperson that set the tone for an informal discussion and encourage active participation by community residents; provide background information on the problems and the program; and present broad goals, especially neighborhood cooperation.
- Law enforcement officer's remarks addressing one or more of the following topics:
  —Definition of burglary and criminal penalties (many people confuse burglary and robbery)
  —Home protection against burglary (locks, alarms, vacation maintenance, lighting)
  —Neighborhood security, especially reporting suspicious activity and looking after each other's residences during absences
  —Assistance to law enforcement officers
  —Self-protection against any other crime that might be of special concern
  —Recent criminal activity in the local area and particular perpetrators known to the police

Police departments track criminal activity logging when and where reported incidents have taken place (though not the exact address) along

---

Tips for Organizing a Watch Program

- Keep meetings simple; interest wanes when meetings are complicated.
- Keep it fun; allow time for socializing—getting acquainted and chatting over coffee or punch.
- Select someone to lead the program, even if the appointment is only temporary. This person—the watch captain (or block chairman or group leader)
  —Is coordinator of the watch group.
  —Is *the* person to turn to in a crisis.
  —May act as the resource person, having all materials possible at hand and being the first person people in the community turn to in order to solve problems and work out new ideas.
  —Is the liaison with other watch groups.
  —Represents the local group to the surrounding neighborhood (community at large).
- Choose a recorder or secretary to make notes of suggestions and important decisions.
- Spend time sharing problems: Some people will join in right away; others may need more time.
- Spend time sharing solutions: No solution is absolute, BUT any one solution may help someone else deal with a problem or incident they encounter.
- Identify crime problems in the community at large and plan proper deterrent goals for the watch group.
- Create a member list: Ask participants to write down their names, addresses, and telephone numbers; keep track of office phone numbers and business hours.
- From the member list and other information, develop a ranked list—in descending order—of whom to call first in case of emergencies or to report a crime in progress.
- Record the names of volunteers and the special services they offer.
- Let people know their privacy will not be invaded but that all residents may find their neighborhood safer and friendlier.
- Announce the next meeting before adjourning: Ideally, each meeting should be in a different location, and meetings should not be set for the same time every time—schedule some during the day and some in the evening.
- Invite members from adjacent apartment communities or "blocks" to observe the meetings to encourage them to start their own watch groups.

---

with a brief description of the incident. These reports are unverified and may include only felonies (e.g., murders, sexual assaults, burglaries, and auto thefts) and not drug arrests or gang activities. They are used to analyze crime trends, assign police patrols, gauge the rate of crime in given areas, and gain better insight for responding to crime. Police incident reports can be useful to watch groups by helping members become aware if a robber, rapist, or car thief is working in their community or around their property. The reports can also help stop rumors that tend to exaggerate the frequency and seriousness of crimes.

Partner with Other Watch Programs.   In order for a community or neighborhood watch program to be effective and accomplish the larger goal of crime prevention, the program should extend beyond a single managed property or neighborhood as is necessary, appropriate, and practical. Set a goal to have at least one meeting in each "neighborhood" within one or two years. If the community is large, however, a program restricted to one geographic sector would be more attainable and more effective. Answers to the following questions should help with this decision.

How many meetings can be held in a year based on available law enforcement and citizen manpower?

How many families per meeting can be accommodated in typical residences? (Twice that number should be invited.)

Are there sufficient manpower resources to conduct several programs simultaneously in different sectors?

The goal should be to saturate each neighborhood or community. The advantage of watch programs is that burglary is discussed where it occurs— in a private home, in the presence of people in a position to help each other. For the program to be effective, however, *everyone in the neighborhood* must be drawn in to some degree.

Operation Identification.   Operation Identification (O.I., or Operation ID) is a nationwide program to reduce theft by engraving an identifying number on valuables and other possessions. The marking makes the item traceable and difficult to dispose. It has been largely accepted—in fact, is recommended—as a component of neighborhood and community watch programs. Often the watch captain or group leader is the custodian of an engraving tool, which is checked out by individual members for marking their own property. The benefits of such a program are summarized in the following story:

Lawrence J. Fennelly, CPO, one of the authors of this book, first heard about O.I. after attending the National Crime Prevention Institute. There had been a burglary at a nearby leased property. A survey of the property after the break-in resulted in a recommendation that the personal property left behind and the newly purchased replacement property should all be engraved. Six months later, there was another burglary, but this time the property that was stolen was discarded by the thieves in a trash can. Why? Because

Precautions Individuals Can Take

Since burglary is a frequent crime against residences—both houses and apartments—it is important to take action to prevent or reduce the likelihood of such thefts. Installing equipment to make access difficult or impossible for unauthorized individuals and being selective in granting access to visitors and others are among the precautions that can (and should) be taken to increase residential security. Automobile owners also need to take precautions regarding their vehicles.

Residence Security Precautions. Every member of the family, even children, must be security conscious. The aim is not to frighten, but rather to make them aware that they can help prevent criminal incidents. In general, no one seeking access to your home should be allowed to enter unless you or another family member is completely satisfied with the visitor's identity and purpose. Entries by repair people should always be by prior arrangements—call the service dispatcher if you have any doubts about someone who shows up at your door. Any inquiries about activities or whereabouts of family members should be dealt with in a cautious manner if the caller is not known. Following are some precautions homeowners can take:

- Install dead-bolt locks on doors and appropriate locks on all windows.

- Install a "peephole" or door viewer to allow identification of visitors without opening the door. (One innovative design can be adjusted to provide a 4-way view—left, right, and below as well as forward.)

- Have an unlisted telephone number if possible. Do not give out personal information over the phone, and do not give out your phone number to callers who say they dialed a "wrong number." (It is better to ask what number they were calling and simply confirm that, yes, they dialed it incorrectly.)

- Develop emergency plans and procedures for your family, and include emergency telephone numbers. Conduct drills periodically to test the procedures.

- Store ladders in a locked garage or basement; they should not be left outside.

- Maintain strict control of keys. Change locks when a key is lost, when moving into a new residence, and when household employees are terminated.

- Make special arrangements for locking glass patio doors or install Charley bars inside to prevent opening from the outside.

- Consider the following adjunct precautions:
  —Install a master control switch at your bedside to activate exterior lighting.
  —Install a fire and home security alarm system.
  —Keep a pet dog on the premises (this is subject to pet restrictions in rental apartments).

A determined burglar can break into just about any home or office. However, the criminal's job can be made much harder: By upgrading locks, adding lights around the perimeter of the property, and installing alarms,

---

Precautions Individuals Can Take *(concluded)*

you stand a good chance of reducing your risk and discouraging future break-ins. According to a recent survey of convicted criminals, burglars get discouraged if a break-in takes more than 60–90 seconds.

Security Precautions Regarding Automobiles. The prevalence of the automobile makes it an additional area for caution. Some late-model vehicles are especially desirable and subject to car theft or "car-jacking." More important, a car can offer a potential attacker a place to hide. The following should raise individuals' awareness regarding their relationship with their automobiles.

- Whenever possible, park in a well-lighted area.
- Always lock your car.
- Have your keys in your hand when leaving home or work and going to your car.
- If you work late, try to have a friend or co-worker or a security guard accompany you to your car.
- Before getting into the car, check the interior, especially the floor in the back seat area.
- When driving, keep car doors locked.
- If you think you are being followed, do not drive home. Drive to the nearest gas station or fire or police station or to the nearest well-lighted area where there are people.
- If you have car trouble on the road, raise the hood and then wait *inside* the car with the doors locked and the windows closed. If a motorist stops to help, open your window only a crack and ask the person to call the police.

There are other things to keep in mind regarding vehicles when you are on the road. If you want to help a disabled vehicle, it is better not to get out of your car, but to drive to the nearest well-lighted area where there is a telephone and call the police. You should not, under any circumstances, pick up a hitchhiker; nor should you pull over for flashing headlights. (An emergency vehicle or police car will have flashing red or blue lights on top— although highway patrol officers monitoring speed limits may be in unmarked vehicles—and the personnel carry appropriate identification.)

---

the property was engraved and because it was traceable, it could not be sold.

In Operation Identification, personal possessions are engraved with a unique code or number to identify the items as personal property of a particular individual and distinguish them from similarly engraved items belonging to someone else. A driving license or social security number would serve as a unique identifying number for an individual—the state license is usually easier to verify. Inclusion of a location indicator such as the two letter state abbreviation (e.g., MA for the state of Massachusetts) helps expedite return of items taken across state lines. Each piece of property should be identified the same way.

Company property can be engraved with the business name plus an identification number (e.g., the 10-digit phone number or a state tax number) and possibly a city and/or state name. The location indicator may be most desirable if a company does business in several states and equipment has to be transferred between locations. The location information not only identifies the owner of stolen property but where it belongs if it is recovered. An item's size and composition may limit what can be engraved on it and where, but labels—even seemingly permanently attached model or manufacturer identification tags—will not be sufficient.

The engraving must become a permanent part of the item. Expensive portable office equipment is especially tempting to thieves, so computers, cameras, VCRs, television sets, and similar items should all be engraved for identification. For small items, other technologies may provide a means of properly identifying an object without damaging it. Engraving tools can be obtained at most hardware and home-improvement chain stores for a modest investment (around $15.00).

Individuals and companies should check with their insurance carriers. Premiums may be lowered if items of personal property are engraved and inventoried. As each item is engraved, it should be described in a written list showing the item, manufacturer, model, serial number, value (price paid), and date purchased. Ideally, capital equipment belonging to a business will be similarly documented from the date of installation since these records form the basis for depreciation and its allied income tax deduction.

One of the first things police ask for in developing a crime report is the model and serial numbers of electronic equipment (televisions, VCRs, computers). An inventory containing this type of information not only verifies ownership of the property if and when it is recovered, but also provides precise information for a claim against your insurance.

Although jewelry cannot be engraved, it can be photographed (preferably in color and with some item for size comparison such as a coin). Pieces of jewelry can be weighed and appraised by a jeweler and the details included in the property inventory. This will not only facilitate identification if the jewelry is recovered after a theft, but also assist in filing a claim for the loss against homeowner's or renter's insurance if it is not.

You may also want to reconsider your value coverage, especially for depreciable items. *Replacement cost* coverage reimburses at today's prices for comparable items while *actual cash value* coverage takes into account depreciation (age and use). Deductibles and coinsurance requirements are other considerations. (Appropriate levels of insurance coverage are beyond the scope of this type of book. Your insurance agent or carrier should be consulted to evaluate your particular needs.)

How to Avoid Becoming an Attacker's Victim

Part of crime prevention is education of the community and awareness on the part of individuals in the community. The following are precautionary steps individuals can implement for themselves.

- Be alert for the unexpected—while you are walking around, keep your mind on what is going on around you.
- Do not take unnecessary chances—
  —Walk confidently; know where you are going.
  —Whenever possible, walk with another person.
  —Stay near people—walking in deserted areas only invites trouble.
  —Stay in well-lighted areas.
  —Avoid shortcuts.
- If you are followed—
  —Cross the street.
  —Reverse direction.
- If you are still followed—
  —Go to a business that is open and ask to call the police.
  —In a residential area, go to a home and ask for help.
  —Attract attention—yell, scream, flag down a passing car; carry a whistle and blow it to attract attention.
  —Act like you suspect something—keep looking back at the person following you to let that person know you cannot be taken by surprise BUT do not confront the individual.
- If you are attacked—
  —Yell and scream to attract attention and scare away the attacker.
  —Swing an umbrella or briefcase or anything you have in your hand at the attacker's head.
  —Make a scene; take your attacker by surprise.
  —Jab the attacker with your elbow.
  —Bite the attacker, hard.
  —Twist your body to break free from the attacker's hold.
  —Scratch at the attacker's face with your fingernails.
  —Bend the attacker's fingers back.
  —Kick the attacker in the shin area.
  —Knee the attacker in the groin.
  (Any of the above actions may cause the attacker to release you and give you a chance to get away.)

Watch Programs at Managed Properties

No matter what type of property you manage, you can encourage your residents and commercial tenants to become involved in their own protection through neighborhood or community watch activities. Local police departments are an invaluable resource. Usually they can provide basic information, often in the form of preprinted handouts or materials that are ready to copy. They can also speak to residents and tenants about crimes, criminal activity in the general area as well as near or at the property, and ways in-

How to Avoid Becoming a Victim *(concluded)*

- Get a description of your attacker—try to remember the following types of details:
  —Height
  —Weight
  —Approximate age
  —Skin tone
  —Hair color
  —Color of eyes
  —Color and type of clothing
  —Any jewelry the attacker may be wearing
  —Any scars or tattoos; any disabilities; whether the person is wearing glasses
  —Odors you may detect about the attacker's person (e.g., alcohol, drugs, cologne)
  —Anything that may have made you suspicious prior to the attack (e.g., a motor vehicle may have passed you several times or someone may have appeared to be watching you)
  —Anything the attacker may say to you, also if the person speaks with an accent
  —A description of any weapon used by the attacker

As regards weapons, we do not believe anyone should carry a weapon unless he or she is thoroughly trained in its use and, if applicable, licensed to carry it. Two thoughts to remember: (1) Anything you use as a weapon can be taken from you and used against you, and (2) you might be better off using the time needed to ready a weapon to get yourself out of the situation or attract attention. As far as self-defense training is concerned, courses in karate, judo, and other martial arts can improve your self-defense skills, but it takes years of practice to master these tactics.

If you are *not* being physically attacked, but instead are being robbed, and if you do not think you are in physical danger, we suggest you comply with the robber's demands. If you do, chances are the robber will leave the area without harming you.

dividuals can raise their personal awareness and protect (or defend) themselves in case they encounter a criminal act or are attacked. Although the real estate manager may participate at some level in any watch group formed at properties he or she manages, the key to watch program success is resident and tenant initiative and ongoing support.

Neighborhoods can develop a reputation: Some are tough, some are easy. Make yours a tough neighborhood for the would-be criminal—force criminals to go elsewhere. It takes three things for a crime to occur—desire, plus ability, plus opportunity. You cannot do anything about a criminal's desire or ability, but you can remove the opportunity for criminals to find easy victims by taking a stand against crime in your community.

Community-Oriented Policing

David R. Struckhoff

Community-oriented policing has been described by George Kelling of the John F. Kennedy School of Government at Harvard University as a "quiet revolution" sweeping American policing. In cities, metropolitan areas, villages, and counties, this concept of policing is gaining wide acceptance and support. Rising popularity does not mean this approach is problem-free, but it clearly is an idea whose time has come. Not only is such policing an exciting development within communities, but it has strong implications for the real estate industry.

The technical definition of community-oriented policing is "a philosophy, management style, and organizational strategy that promotes proactive problem-solving and police-community ownerships to address the causes of crime and fear as well as other community issues." [Attorney General's Office, California Department of Justice, "Community Oriented Policing and Problem Solving."]

A more practical definition is that it is a way police and security departments involve themselves in and assess their impact on the quality of neighborhoods. The observable behaviors involve:

1. Returning to foot patrol,

2. Meeting with and surveying citizens to learn what their concerns are regarding public order, safety, and community social problems; and

3. Finding ways of responding to calls for service that are more effective than in the past—i.e., problem solving.

Some Community-Oriented Policing Programs

COP—Community-Oriented Policing

COPS—Community-Oriented Policing Services

CAPS—Chicago Alternative Policing Strategies

HART—Hartford (Conn.) Areas Rally Together

NOP—Neighborhood Officer Program

NOPT—Neighborhood Oriented Police Team

A Little History

At one time, citizens worked closely with the constables, sheriffs, and marshals who patrolled their towns and cities, generally on foot. There was a personal relationship (though sometimes strained) between law enforcement personnel and citizens. However, the introduction of the police car and the development of mobile communication technologies effectively created a situation in which police officers were alone in their squad cars, separated by glass and steel from the street and isolated from the people they were hired to protect and serve.

Past research has demonstrated conclusively that policing in squad cars does little to diminish crime, does not help citizens conquer fear of crime, and certainly contributes only minimally to the satisfaction of either police or citizens with the interactions that do (not) occur. In many instances, police patrol is a low-paying, isolated, minimally desirable job.

Police and Community Today

Community-oriented policing has reintroduced needed human contact, but it is much more than that. Now the officer is a closely accountable community problem solver, a consultant, and a partner with citizens. With this change in philosophy, police and communities are moving away from merely reacting to crime and moving toward preventing crime. One reason for this change is that it is now very clear to the practitioners and researchers in the field that the community itself is the first line of defense against disorder and crime and the first source of strength for the preservation of the quality of life. Moreover, with police actively involved in the community, the job of the police has itself assumed greater potential for satisfaction.

For those who invest in real estate (i.e., landlords), community policing can be perceived as a major asset. Community policing holds as a central tenet that citizens have ownership, not only of the land where they have their homes, but also of the very processes that protect their investment—e.g., infrastructure and community services, and especially the police. Naturally, the greater a community's perception of its value or stake in its land and services, the more desirable it is to live in that community. Values increase with successful community policing, and this is not merely a matter of perceptions. As communities stabilize, property values rise, and property becomes more desirable—witness some of the "gentrification" in large urban centers and the continued desirability of locations where a sense of community exists and crime rates are being lowered.

A big part of the community-policing effort involves classes and training for the community residents in communication, law, legal procedure, police strategy, and other relevant topics. Police officers are simultaneously kept informed via update meetings, advisement sessions, community board meetings, and other forums.

Both the police and members of the community are learning, and this is an evolving process. Evidently, this is a worthy investment of time and energy, with handsome economic and social payoffs as the system begins working. For example, in one community, police helped make several properties more easily marketable by clearing up problems at an adjacent property. In another community, a neighborhood was stabilized by placing a small police substation there. The substation area has since become a magnet for families and individuals who want stable living conditions.

The Role of the Real Estate Industry

The training and mutual communication, which are integral to community-policing concepts, are geared to the ordinary citizen and enhanced by the participation of a large segment of the community in such vehicles as police advisory boards, neighborhood watch groups, neighborhood teams, and other locally based organizations that enhance communication and understanding. The real estate industry, with its knowledge of each community, its survey ability, its sense of patterns, can make a vital contribution at this level of activity and, in this writer's opinion, take a leadership role.

Community policing is a viable tool to be used to enhance the community and the quality of life there. Support of community-based policing is in the best interest, not only of the community, but also of the real estate industry that serves the community, because of the emerging stability and increased value of property in areas where the police and community effectively work together in this new, "quiet revolution." Community-oriented policing is an asset to property ownership.

Community-Oriented Policing Services (COPS)

Federal funding for COPS programs has contributed to reducing crime in major cities (Chicago, New York) as well as small towns. COPS grants support the hiring of additional police officers and encourage police departments to think in terms of community partnerships, problem-solving strategies, and organizational change.

Collaboration between police and the community empowers residents and effectively deters crime. Police actively patrolling neighborhoods, their physical presence, is preventative—they are not merely waiting to receive a call from a victim *after* a crime has been committed. The most effective programs have several components:

- Officers going door to door and speaking with residents, both to identify trouble makers and gain residents' trust.
- Meetings between community residents and police officers, often with guest speakers.
- Neighborhood rehabilitation—fixing curbs and sidewalks, installing or repairing street lights, repairing broken windows, removing trash and debris.

Variants of COPS programs abound. In Raleigh, North Carolina, police officers volunteer to live rent-free in city-owned housing in high-crime areas in return for which they provide scheduled hours of community service—organizing community watches, working with local youths, and helping citizens comply with ordinances (i.e., acting as liaisons between citizens and the government). In particular, officers' "walking patrols" of the neighborhood are visible evidence of their presence, and residents begin talking to the police and to each other.

Landlords are joining forces with police, too. Property owners and managers often hire security guards who offer protection for managed properties; but having no police powers, the guards cannot make arrests. Landlords can be encouraged to lease apartments to police officers at a discounted rent or rent-free in exchange for the officer parking a police vehicle on the property and walking around the area during off-duty hours (an approach used successfully in Washington, D.C., and Baltimore). Landlords can also be proactive in developing relationships with law enforcement and reporting all suspicious activities. In addition, they can ask trusted residents of their buildings to serve as extra "eyes and ears" around the property and keep the landlord advised of any suspicious activity.

A nonprofit organization in Houston, Texas, works with lenders under a Community Development Block Grant to link private lenders and police officers who are first-time home buyers. Officers must agree to live in a suburban community for a fixed period of time and provide community service, also for a stipulated period, in exchange for money toward a downpayment on a house. They receive community policing training as part of the program and are expected to organize community watches, improve community-police relations, and work with young people. Patterned after the Columbia, South Carolina, program, this is one of some 70 similar housing-for-policing programs operating in different cities across the United States.

Community-Oriented Policing Services *(concluded)*

In Boulder, Colorado, police have taken the initiative in organizing Boulder Citizens On Patrol. Six to 10 members of the patrol walk a designated high-crime area as a group on a rotating schedule; the walk takes two to three hours and includes a survey of the area, based on which they report crimes and serve as witnesses (and try to avoid altercations with criminals). Being in charge of the patrols, the police can set guidelines and control the activities—a citizen patrol independent of the police could become a vigilante group and create more problems than would be solved.

The American Association of Retired Persons (AARP), the International Association of Chiefs of Police, and the National Sheriffs' Association have combined forces in support of Triad programs that link sheriffs, police, and senior citizens to improve law enforcement service to the elderly, especially in small towns where the sheriff may be the only "police." In addition to specific crime prevention goals, Triad programs also provide much-needed human contact through visitation programs that also monitor senior citizens' general well-being. Each Triad program is tailored to the needs of the community it serves.

Some 26 states have agreed with AARP to form such partnerships, but the National Sheriff's Association believes that while state involvement facilitates training and coordination, the program is more effectively implemented at the local level. Triad programs are inexpensive to launch, and they engender trust in law enforcement among senior citizens who are then more likely to report suspicious activity where fear of retaliation may have kept them silent before.

Special training in community policing is also available. Maryland has established a new academy to train police in the art of "community policing." In one or two-day sessions, patrol officers, police administrators, and citizens learn how to put the philosophy of community policing into action. Community policing requires a different approach to law enforcement—a change from being reactive to being proactive. This change in direction means that police recruiting will also have to be approached differently— community policing requires people with more education who can bring to the job the problem-solving, mediation, and communication skills needed for following up with victims.

Spotlight
on
Protection of Assets

Protection of Assets

Foreseeability of risk requires the real estate manager to be able to recognize potential problems. A criminal act may injure one or more people or result in damage to property or both. Any crimes perpetrated on a property are prosecuted under criminal law. In an increasingly litigious society, real estate managers have to be continually on the alert for potential problems and ways to solve them. A criminal incident is not likely to end with prosecution of the criminals if they are caught (sometimes the perpetrator of a crime is not caught). In addition to the individual who is the victim of a crime, others may claim some "injury" as a result, and any or all of these people could initiate a civil lawsuit against the property and its owner and manager, claiming negligence in the provision of security. Recognizing potential problems and seeking solutions to them is not only being proactive but may prevent future crimes.

One of the critical challenges in establishing and maintaining security at managed properties is that of knowing when problems exist and what those problems are. Managed properties are an attractive target for many types of criminal incidents, and real estate managers are well-advised to be aware and take appropriate preventive action. The ability to recognize potential problems is critical to planning security strategies and implementing specific measures. In protecting assets, there are issues of both personal safety and security and property protection and preservation.

As pointed out in the earlier discussions of prevention, one of the three ingredients necessary for a crime to be committed is *opportunity*. The chapters that follow focus on strategies for limiting or eliminating the element of opportunity.

In "Recognizing Potential Problems: A Police Officer's Perspective,"

Michelle Richter, identifies practical strategies for making a property crime-resistant. The author is an officer with the Metropolitan Nashville Police Department. After exploring the potential vulnerabilities of commercial and residential properties, she presents some questions managers can ask themselves to heighten their powers of observation and help them evaluate what they observe.

"Security Issues in 'The Residents' Guidebook' " outlines the kinds of safety and security information apartment managers can provide to their residents. Writing from the perspective of a professional property manager, Steven J. Rizzuto addresses apartment security, personal safety, and safeguarding of residents' personal property in addition to general building security.

"Security in Parking Lots and Garages" discusses the security needs of various types of parking facilities in an operations context. It also identifies the unique needs of the garage operated as a business open to the public. Parking personnel need to know who is authorized to use the facilities and how to recognize vehicles that are unauthorized users. Also, security guards who patrol parking facilities that are part of a managed property and attendants at facilities that are open to the public can play an important role in crime prevention, reporting unauthorized users and vehicles that appear to be abandoned to the appropriate authorities (security at the property, the police).

Although "Security at Other Commercial Properties" looks at measures that can be implemented at an industrial site, in particular, portions of this chapter are more broadly applicable. For example, loading docks are common at retail properties and office buildings, and the need to limit access to the "heart" of a business operation applies to all types of commercial enterprises.

In these as in earlier chapters, reference is made to dead-bolt locks preferably having a minimum one-inch throw or extension. This type of lock is more typically used in residential applications. Locks with longer extensions (e.g., two inches) are also available, and they are more typical of commercial installations. The thickness of the solid-core door and the construction of the doorjamb and the wall area—the areas that need to be hollowed out to receive the bolt—will affect the acceptable bolt length and, therefore, the choice of lock.

Real estate managers face many challenges in providing security at different types of properties. The type of use and, therefore, the occupants of a property are major determinants of protections to be implemented. However, not all managed properties are occupied, and vacant spaces for lease—indeed, vacant buildings—require as much care in identifying potential problems and implementing security measures as do occupied premises. Clearly the primary goal would be to protect the vacant property and preserve its value. Here again, keeping unauthorized persons out of a vacant building and off the property altogether may require intrusion alarms, guard patrols, remote monitoring (e.g., CCTV), or other measures.

A vacant property becomes a magnet for all types of problems, including and especially crime; and if it is next door or around the corner, those problems can easily migrate to your managed property if you are not ceaselessly vigilant. Professional real estate managers usually fight deferred maintenance because it diminishes the market value of the managed property. As crime continues to increase, in general, maintenance must become an integral part of security, not only to protect the value of the property, but to protect the lives of the people on it.

Although there are many approaches one can take in providing security at a managed property, we must point out that there are no established minimum standards for premises security. There had been some movement in the direction of specific standards. American Insurance Services Group, Inc. (AISG), had been working with the National Fire Protection Association (NFPA) on such a venture because it was thought that the NFPA had the structure in place to develop national consensus standards. However, NFPA decided not to pursue the project for a variety of reasons, including opposition to its role by some organizations. Previously, the American Society for Testing and Materials (ASTM) tried to establish minimum security standards and met with similar opposition. Thus, the future of national standards is unclear as this book is being written. However, accepted practice within the community and requirements of local ordinances are a starting point for determining effective security measures for specific managed properties.

Recognizing Potential Problems: A Police Officer's Perspective

Michelle Richter

Nowadays everyone is concerned with learning new ways to deter crime. Crime has increased and people are taking more interest in protecting themselves and their properties. As a police officer, I have had several business owners and apartment managers inquire about ways to deter crime on their properties. Based on my job experience and information from the Nashville Crime Prevention Unit, I have responded as follows.

First of all, it is very important to remember *you can only make an area crime-resistant, not crime-proof.* Most criminals look for crimes of opportunity. If a building or a business looks like a quick and easy target, criminals will likely hit when they first spot it although they may also case a place for days. Owners' or managers' should want to make entry to their business or building as difficult as possible for an intruder. The goal is to take away the opportunity from the criminal.

Commercial Property Vulnerabilities

One area of concern for a business should be lighting. It is a major deterrent. Parking areas and garages, doorways, and entryways should all be well lighted. Exterior and interior lights should allow visibility into a store from the street. Exterior lights should be placed out of reach and have weatherproof (and vandalproof) covers. Placing some lights high above ground reduces the chances of bulbs being broken or loosened. Lighting should be bright; it should reach the surface and not cast shadows. (It is important to be able to see the surrounding area.) Good lighting takes away hiding places and makes employees and customers feel safe. It also allows the businessperson to watch for criminal activity from the inside of the building. Lights should be on even when your business is closed. Timer-controlled lights as well as motion-activated lights can be used as a deterrent. A criminal will be alarmed by a sudden burst of light that flashes on while your business is being approached. A well-lighted area helps to deter criminals from entering it and enables police and others in the area to spot suspicious activity.

Consider installing or upgrading to dead-bolt locks, heavy-duty doors, fire and intrusion alarm systems, closed-circuit television cameras, and security windows. You can install a one-inch dead-bolt lock with a rotating cylinder on all doors and avoid placing door locks where they can be accessed by breaking out glass or door panels to reach inside (35–40 inches away is the rule of thumb). Glass or panels near door locks can be covered with a grille or other protective material. Upgrading can include solid-core doors, at least one and one-half inches thick, with strong hinges that have nonremovable hidden pins. Roll-down or sliding gates or grilles can be installed in front of doorways for added protection. Sometimes a metal ornamental gate (e.g., in front of a revolving door) serves the same purpose.

An intrusion alarm is a good tool for detecting unauthorized entry or attempted entry. Such an alarm might ring a loud bell when it is tripped or send a silent signal to the alarm company to dispatch the police. Using prominently placed exterior and interior cameras (closed-circuit television) will allow you to observe activity in several areas of your business while helping to deter criminals who see them.

To make windows more secure, consider using unbreakable polycarbonate (plastic) instead of glass. A lot of burglars gain access to buildings by breaking windows. However, plastic windows are easily scratched and may discolor, becoming unsightly very quickly. The scratchability may attract vandals because gangs often mark their territory, and such windows retain the markings unless replaced. Windows should be kept locked. Sliding windows can be broken into easily by lifting them up and out of their tracks. They can be secured by drilling a hole through the top of the window frame and inserting a steel pin or nail into the hole. Anti-sliding steel or wooden blocks that attach to the bases of these windows from the inside are also available. Casement or crank windows can be secured in a closed position by using an L bracket screwed to the lower part of the window. A removable steel pin installed into the sill will keep the window from being pried open. (Retailers sometimes install security bars in front of their store windows and doorways, but this option, while keeping intruders out, is unattractive and can hinder rescue efforts in a fire or other emergency.) In construction of a new commercial building, consideration should be given to placing windows at a height where they cannot be accessed easily.

It is important, however, to allow clear visibility into the store. A police officer should be able to drive by your store or place of business and see clearly inside. For example, if the windows of a supermarket or convenience store are covered with advertisements that block the view, a robbery or burglary taking place inside would not be noticed by an officer driving by on routine patrol.

In addition, the interior layout of a store or office should be designed as open as possible. A burglar or robber should *not* be able to hide behind displays or other objects. The interior should also have good lighting. If possible, controls for lights should be in a secured area accessible only by employees; otherwise, installing covers with locking devices over the switches will prevent a criminal from turning them off.

The exterior of a business property should also be designed to prevent easy access. Potential hiding places should be identified and eliminated. This can be addressed by keeping shrubbery trimmed low (no more than three to four feet high) and clearing shrubs away from walkways, windows, and doors so no one can hide behind them. Otherwise, you can choose shrubs that have thorns. (Thorns are built-in protectors. Criminals prefer areas where they will not be injured.)

Bright exterior lighting can be installed and, if possible, several surveillance cameras. (If the goal is surveillance, you will need "live" cameras. *Do not install "dummy" cameras;* they can add to your liability in the event of a criminal incident.) Fencing, if used, should be at least eight feet high. In some areas, it may be desirable to put barbed wire on top of it or thorny bushes on both sides (e.g., at an industrial property). The additions will make climbing the fence more difficult. It is also important to check that there are no loose rocks or other objects in the area that can be used to break windows.

Residential Property Vulnerabilities

Apartment managers also need to concentrate on deterring crime because it is important for their residents to feel secure. As in a commercial environment, lighting is very important: Entrances, hallways, stairways, parking areas, and laundry rooms should have good lighting. Furthermore, all apartment doors should have dead-bolt locks and peepholes. If units have sliding glass doors that open onto balconies, the doors can be secured by inserting pins in the frame or placing a wooden rod in the track. Ground-floor windows can be secured by installing grates or grilles. (The preceding discussions about securing different types of windows and doors apply to residential properties as well as commercial properties.)

Gated communities are gaining popularity as people seek more secure places to live. This type of environment can be created by installing fencing around the property and an electrically controlled gate at the entrance. This would provide more control over who enters and leaves the property. Residents would have to use a code or card key to enter the grounds, and visitors would have to be admitted by a resident. Limiting access helps deter unwanted vehicles from cruising on the property, which also helps deter crime. Another way to eliminate cruising and loitering is to allow only one-way traffic on interior roads.

Another factor to consider is the location of mailboxes and doorbells. These should be in a well-traveled area to prevent residents from becoming victims of crimes against their persons. In addition, laundry and storage areas should be locked and accessible only by those who have keys. This also helps keep residents from being victims of crime.

Signs of Potential Problems

The basic information provided here could be used by anyone to make building areas more resistant to crime. However, one also needs to try to recognize possible criminal activity. You need to be alert to strange vehicles or persons in the neighborhood or on the property. Questions that can be asked in such a situation are:

Is the person acting in a suspicious manner?

Is the person wearing clothing that is not suited to the weather (e.g., a heavy overcoat in the heat of summer)?

Is the person driving slowly or repeatedly through the area?

Is the person driving without lights at night?

Is the vehicle loaded with merchandise?

Is the person loading what appear to be valuables into a vehicle parked in front of a closed business?

Is the person trying to force entry into a locked vehicle or business?

Is the person peering through windows of cars or businesses?

Is the person going door-to-door or coming to your door with questions that do not seem legitimate?

Is the person carrying what appear to be valuables while running away?

Criminals will try to sell stolen property out of their vehicles. Some burglars and robbers pretend to be salesmen or repairmen, but they are really casing the area or a property.

Another thing that should make you suspicious is a person who appears to be loitering. While the person is on the property, are other people seen approaching him or her? Does any kind of transaction seem to be taking place? It is important to watch for transactions—some criminals loiter on foot, on bicycles, and in cars to sell drugs or stolen items. If someone approaches and hands money to the stranger, try to see what the stranger

---

Signs of a Gang Presence

If a group of people appears to be loitering, try to observe their behavior. Look for any unusual body language—for example, if they appear to be giving unique hand signs, they might be members of a gang. Another indicator would be their clothing—e.g., wearing identical clothing or same-color bandanas on their heads. In any of these situations, it is important to notify the police and describe for them what you have seen.

---

gave that person. (If you see an envelope, foil, pill container, or plastic bag, it is likely that a drug deal just occurred.)

If you observe any of these types of occurrences, it is very important to get a good description of the person and the vehicle. In describing a person, things to note include age, race, sex, height, weight, clothing, and distinguishing marks (tattoos, facial hair). A vehicle description should note the make, model, and color, as well as the license plate number and issuing state, whether it has two or four doors, and any distinguishing features such as stickers, tinted windows, or dents.

You should also keep a record of the times and dates when you notice any suspicious activity. After you collect the information, it is important to notify the police and turn the information over to them.

Crime Prevention Measures

Joining or starting a Neighborhood Watch program is a great way to reduce crime in an area. By being alert and recording information about suspicious activity and reporting it to the police, neighbors watching out for each other can decrease loitering, burglary, and other crimes. Everyone in the area concentrating on securing their properties will deter criminals. Criminals want an area or building that is easy to enter, not one where they know they are being watched.

In spite of doing your best to secure your property, residents or others may still be victims of crime, so it is important to keep a record of valuable property. Taking photographs or videotaping valuables in place is an excellent means of recording specific items. It is also important to keep a list of all serial numbers. The picture record and serial numbers should be kept at a different location than the property where the valuables are located (e.g., a safety deposit box, with insurance papers). This information is very important for the recovery (and identification) of property in the event it is stolen. Criminals like to pawn valuables to obtain cash quickly. If the serial number of an item has been entered in the police department computer, the number will identify the item as stolen. The more information that can be provided, the easier it is for the police to identify stolen property and its ownership.

Remember, a property manager can only make an area or property crime-resistant. Properties that look as though no one cares attract crime and the criminal element. To help you identify problem areas at a property and correct them, the local police department can be asked for a professional opinion regarding security of a property, or a security consultant can be hired.

Security Issues in "The Residents' Guidebook"

Steven J. Rizzuto

A guidebook containing "house rules," emergency contacts, and other useful information is usually given to new residents—prior to move-in, if possible. Although the discussion that follows will touch on as many security-related issues as possible, the contents of a residents' guidebook should be customized to reflect the unique needs of each building's resident population. Additional or different precautionary measures may need to be stressed, depending on the location and features of the property and the security systems and devices that are in place.

Addressing security specifically in the guidebook will help to heighten residents' awareness of their surroundings and thus help them reduce their personal risk and lessen the potential for physical damage to the building.

Apartment Security

The following are some basic precautions regarding apartment security as they might be presented in a resident's guidebook.

- Before leaving your unit, be sure that all gas and electrical appliances and water taps are turned off and windows are closed and locked. (However, a radio playing and lights burning, which imply someone is at home, are a deterrent to a burglar.)

- When leaving your apartment for the day, always *double lock* all doors. (Bolt the door from the outside.)

- Always lock the door when you leave the apartment, even if you will only be gone a few minutes (e.g., to the laundry room).

- Mailboxes should *always* be kept locked. If you are unable to lock your mailbox properly, inform the resident manager so it can be repaired immediately.

- Unwanted literature or other waste material should not be discarded in the lobby or hallways. This not only creates an untidy appearance, but also implies a lack of maintenance and security.

- Halls should be kept clear at all times, for reasons of security as well as fire safety.

- If you are vacationing for a period of time, have a friend or neighbor take care of your mail or notify the post office to stop delivery until your return. (Accumulated mail is an indication that you are not at home and an easy target for a break-in.) It is also advisable to inform the resident manager that you plan to be away and to leave a phone number where you can be contacted in an emergency.

- If anyone else is to use your apartment during a time when you will be absent, the resident manager should approve the arrangement *in writing* beforehand. (An apartment may not be occupied by anyone other than the lessee without prior written approval.)

- If you notice any kind of irregular marks on the entrance doors—for example, a bent guard plate or deep scratches on the door edge— inform the resident manager *immediately*. This could be evidence of an attempt at forced entry.

Personal Safety

A residents' guidebook might also include precautions regarding personal safety, such as the following:

- Never admit anyone to the building unless you have confirmed the person's identity over the voice communicator.

- Never admit anyone into your apartment without first identifying the person through the door peephole or, if you have to open the door, by keeping the chain lock in place. If the person is a stranger and you feel it is necessary to contact the police, call 911. Also notify the resident manager.

- Never leave messages for a friend on your mailbox or door indicating when you will return because this also relays the same message to a burglar.

- Always double lock or chain latch your door at night.

- Keep an emergency phone number list next to your telephone. These should include 911 (or other emergency numbers if your locale does not have 911 service), non-emergency numbers for the local police and fire departments, plus numbers for the resident manager and any others you consider important. (Guests and babysitters should also be given this information.)

- Keep a flashlight in your apartment (with extra batteries) and carry a whistle with you when you go out.

- Avoid walking alone at night and try to stay in well-lighted areas. Do not take shortcuts through parks or alleys.

Safeguarding Personal Property

Safeguarding personal property might also be addressed in a residents' guidebook. Some suggested points follow.

- Expensive jewelry and large sums of money should not be left in your apartment. If it can be avoided, do not carry an excessive amount of money with you when you go out.

- It is advisable to have renter's insurance because the building owner's insurance on the property does not cover residents' possessions. (Fire and theft are especially important coverages.)

- Make a list describing your valuables along with the serial numbers of video equipment, stereo, television, and other items. Keep the list in a safe place so it can be used to assist the police in identifying your property in case of theft. You can also use an electric engraver to inscribe your name and social security or other identifying number on your property. (This is recommended by the police.)

- Get to know the locations of fire alarms, extinguishing equipment, and fire escapes in your building. Understand the operation of fire extinguishers, pull station alarms, and other equipment in case of emergency.

General Building Security

The most common method used by burglars to gain entrance into a building is simply to ring a bell and wait to be admitted by a resident or a friend of a resident. A burglar does not want to damage a door if that can be avoided because it only attracts attention to the fact that someone has gained entry illegally. Professional and even amateur burglars have absolutely no qualms about the methods they use. They often pose as police officers, fire inspectors, census takers, meter readers, building inspectors, or delivery or service personnel.

Residents should be encouraged, even admonished, to get to know their neighbors and other people living in the building. Management can hold meetings to explain security measures and the importance of fire prevention. The following are the types of items that can be included in a residents' guidebook to address general building security.

- It is important for everyone to always remember that the main entrance doors should be kept locked at all times. These doors are never to be propped open or left unattended while moving supplies and furniture into or out of the building. (It takes less than a minute for a stranger to enter a building unobserved.)

- When entering or leaving the building, never under any circumstance allow a stranger to enter. This includes salespeople, service personnel (maintenance workers, cleaners, painters), and prospective residents. However, if your phone is to be removed, you need to be at home to admit the telephone service person into your apartment. For security reasons, the person should also be escorted from the building. Visitors are to be admitted only by the residents who are expecting them. Also, a guest should never admit a stranger into the building.

- Never admit a repair worker or other service person who is *not* someone you have contacted yourself to work in your apartment—for example, telephone installation, appliance repairs. Whenever residents admit someone, they become completely responsible for building security. For example, when doors are propped open during move-in or move-out, you are responsible for maintaining security and for being certain that a stranger does not enter the building during this time. (Moving time is a peak period for breaking and entering.) Residents should check and be sure the doors are properly locked when their move is finished.

- Just because you have observed a stranger in the building and escorted that person to the outside door does not mean security has not been breached. This person has had an opportunity to become familiar with the building layout and could very easily have taped or disabled the lock, making it possible to re-enter the building at a later time.

- If someone rings your doorbell for any reason whatever, except for business in your apartment, refer the person to the resident manager, who alone is responsible for admitting all workers, salespeople, future residents, and other nonresidents. If you notice a stranger loitering in or around the premises without any apparent reason for being there, notify the resident manager immediately.

- It is to your advantage to get to know your neighbors and others living in your building, both to know who belongs in the building and to assist each other in times of emergency.

- Do not wait until your apartment has been ransacked or a fire has destroyed your personal property. Neighbors watching out for and helping one another is the essence of community watch programs.

- Keys should never be lent to casual acquaintances. Lost or stolen keys should be reported to the resident manager, who will change the lock and issue a new key. Any stranger seen using a key will be escorted from the building (burglars do have ways of obtaining master keys). If you do give a key to a friend who does not reside in the building so he or she can take care of your mail, water your plants, or feed your pet while you are away, please inform the resident manager so that proper security can be maintained.

- When you vacate your apartment, all keys have to be returned to the office. Keys should never be left in your apartment or with anyone other than the resident manager.

Other Guidebook Contents

Although it may be desirable to create a specific security guidebook, there are other general "house rules" and safety precautions as well as information regarding emergencies that apartment residents need to know. A single source that incorporates all these types of information is the most practical approach—it helps if "everything residents need to know" is in one place.

Security in Parking Lots and Garages

People are robbed, assaulted, even murdered in parking lots and garages. Cars are stolen or damaged, or their windows may be broken and car stereos and other items of personal property stolen. Motor vehicle-related incidents of all sorts can also occur—e.g., hit-and-run accidents, driving under the influence of alcohol or drugs (DUI). The list can go on and on. That is why it is important to be aware—and make your residents, your tenants and their employees, and your own employees aware—of potential problems.

It is also important to police parking areas regularly. Accumulated snow, icy conditions, untended shrubbery, and litter (cans, paper, debris)—a general lack of custodial maintenance—send a clear message about your managed property that is received by potential criminals as well as your patrons. The message that no one cares is not only a "welcome" sign for the criminal element, but a strong negative perception for residents or tenants of the property (and their customers). The consequences include loss of residents and tenants as well as criminal incidents.

Security Issues

The security requirements of a parking facility will depend on its location and whether it is an open lot or an open or enclosed garage. The people who will be using the facility and its hours of operation are also considerations.

Employee Parking.   Before new employees start work, they should be advised exactly where they are expected to park. Commercial properties often differentiate parking areas for tenants' employees and property management staff from those reserved for visitors. However, at shopping centers, areas designated for employee parking are often in remote parts of the parking lot or garage so that availability of close-in parking is maximized for retailers' customers. Similarly, at residential properties, management staff may have to park behind the building while spaces near the front entrance may be reserved for visitors and prospective residents, and current residents may have assigned spaces or access available spaces on a first-come, first-served basis.

It is a good idea to remind management employees periodically that it is important to be aware of their surroundings at all times. They should also be encouraged to report any suspicious persons or activities in the parking area to security personnel, who can conduct proper follow-up on reported incidents, criminal or otherwise. The same cautions should be shared with residents or with commercial tenants so they can pass the information along to their employees.

Reserved Parking.   In a commercial setting, there is also the issue of reserved parking, especially for business executives. Cars parked in reserved spaces that are marked with a person's name or a position title (e.g., J. Smith or President) are more likely to be vandalized by unhappy employees than one parked in a space that is simply marked "Reserved" and carries no name or title. Vanity license plates with names are another way of identifying the owner of a car (i.e., J SMITH if John Smith is president of the company) although vanity plates that carry a slogan or personal message rather than a name can still be a signal to potential vandals if their significance is known.

Parking for Company Cars and Trucks.   Tenants' company cars and trucks can be parked in a secured environment or fenced-in area. Trucks or containers on trailers may hold raw materials or finished goods representing potential revenue—and profits—for the company and desirable material for thieves who can "fence" it for twenty cents on the dollar. Trucks and trailers need to be locked with proper padlocks and seals. Parking the vehicles close to the wall or backed up to the wall or even back to back will make rear access doors more difficult to open.

A business may have appropriate accountability procedures and invoice controls in place, but these are usually operative only when the goods are *inside* the firm's facility. Considering how many people in a company know the contents of its trucks—at a minimum, the driver, shipping clerks, dock workers, and accounting personnel, and probably the maintenance workers assigned to the area—it is important to establish security procedures and monitor loading and storage areas.

Real estate managers need to be aware of potential problems and make recommendations to commercial tenants regarding their facilities. How-

---

Personal Precautions in Parking Facilities

• Park in well-lighted areas—try to find space in areas of heavy traffic.

• Make sure the motor is turned off and the gear shift is in "park"—do not leave a vehicle unattended with the motor running.

• Stow purchases and personal items in the trunk of the car—do not leave valuables in plain sight.

• Be sure car windows are closed tight and storage areas (glove compartment as well as trunk) are closed and locked—use a steering wheel locking device (e.g., The Club) as an added deterrent.

• Lock the vehicle and take the keys with you—spare keys should not be left anywhere in the vehicle.

• Look alert and project confidence—give the impression you know where you are going and can take care of yourself.

• Be aware of your surroundings—survey the parking lot or garage and the area near your vehicle so you know where exits and emergency call boxes are located.

• Report suspicious persons or activities to property security personnel or call the police.

These cautions and other information can be compiled and shared with residents and tenants. Consultation with the local crime prevention officer may yield additional specific suggestions for a particular parking lot or garage.

---

ever, since industrial tenants, in particular, are most likely to have an extensive fleet of trucks, it should be the tenants' responsibility to secure parking and loading areas in their leased space. Cooperation with and approval of the property management company will ensure a maximized effort on the tenants' behalf.

Other Vehicles.   If bicycles or motorcycles are popular in your area, it may be desirable or necessary to designate areas for parking these vehicles. This arrangement will also necessitate establishing rules about securing the bikes and not leaving personal belongings on them. These rules and precautions can be communicated by incorporating them into the signage designating the area for two-wheeled vehicles.

Security Measures

A variety of measures, employed together, help to deter criminals from entering a parking facility and thus avert criminal incidents. The measures themselves are not infallible—some criminals will stop at nothing to commit a crime—so awareness and follow-up are critical components of a parking security program.

Patrolling Parking Lots and Garages.   Parking facilities can be patrolled in several ways. The most popular method uses Cushman three-wheel, gasoline or electric (battery) powered vehicles designed specifically for patrolling parking facilities. These vehicles work effectively and are able to move at the proper speed through narrow passageways and along walkways. Bicycle patrols are also popular, and at some large shopping centers, guards mounted on horseback monitor open parking lots. While bicycles facilitate mobilization and maneuverability in limited spaces, mounted patrols provide a broader perspective for monitoring because of the rider's elevated position. Sometimes it is practical to have dogs accompany guards on patrol, especially at night.

Walkie-talkies, cellular phones, or phones on direct lines to the company switchboard or security office add to the package by allowing rapid access to security personnel for assistance.

Signage.   For purposes of information as well as deterrence of undesirable behaviors, different kinds of signs are often installed in parking lots and garages. The suggested wordings that follow serve different purposes. The first ones are intended to announce a policy and a penalty (#1–#3)— or simply to discourage (deter) unlawful activity (#4)—while the last ones identify limited uses.

Sign No. 1	No Trespassing—Parking by Permit Only
	Violators Will Be Towed at Owner's Expense
Sign No. 2	Private Property
	No Trespassing
	Illegally Parked Cars/Violators Will Be
	Towed at Owner's Expense
Sign No. 3	No Parking
	Violators will be prosecuted
Sign No. 4	For Your Protection
	This Parking Lot
	Is Being Video Taped
Sign No. 5	Reserved Space—No. 36
Sign No. 6	Disabled/Handicapped Parking Only

Large areas also require geographic markers to help people locate their vehicles. Colors, alphanumeric codes, and other ways of naming sections of a parking lot (e.g., animals, directions, seasons) are all viable alternatives.

Note that parking for people with disabilities requires larger spaces for vehicles plus an allowance for wheelchair access. Usually the space also has to be marked with the wheelchair symbol. These spaces are required to be located nearest or immediately adjacent to a building. (The Americans with Disabilities Act has established specific requirements for placement and dimensions of parking designated handicapped. Practical information on parking lot design, zoning requirements, security, signage, and other issues can be obtained from ULI—The Urban Land Institute in Washington, D.C.)

Towing of Vehicles.   Before towing a vehicle that is parked illegally or in violation of management company policy (stated in signage), it is imperative to have a specified procedure in place. Components of a towing procedure might include the following:

- Notify local police.
- Call towing company.
- Inspect violating vehicle for scratches and dents before it is removed.
- Write a report—
  —Include a listing of all property visible inside the vehicle.
  —Indicate the reason why the vehicle is being towed.

Because this type of action has legal and liability implications, it is a good idea to have your corporate counsel and your insurance carrier review the policy and procedure and the intended signage *before* implementation. They can provide insights regarding acceptable language and permissible actions to ensure compliance with local ordinances and avert problems with insurance coverage for damage to vehicles or general liability. Also, local ordinances may specify where (how far apart, how high on the wall or pole) signs may or may not be placed and require certain sizes of signs and lettering on them, as well as sign construction (e.g., metal signs may be required, with poles). These requirements have to be met, and an inspection and/or a fee for a sign permit may also be required.

Facility Usage.   The types of signage needed and the specifics regarding towing will, to some extent, depend on usage of the parking facility. Residential properties have three categories of users—residents, site management or contract (service) personnel, and visitors; the latter include prospective residents as well as guests of current occupants.

In general, the parking facilities at residential properties have to be accessible around the clock. At commercial properties, however, while the variety of users is expanded, the hours of access usually can be limited. In addition to management staff and tenants' employees, parking must be available for visitors to the property. At an office building, this category might include tenants' clients, vendors, and contractors as well as various service providers (deliveries, janitorial cleaning, etc.). If there is a retail component, the general public becomes an added user. Note, however, that "office hours" are no longer merely 9:00 A.M. to 5:00 P.M.; flex-time strategies implemented by different commercial entities are likely to extend the peak activity period to cover 6:00 A.M. to 9:00 P.M., meaning parking will have to be accessible (and monitored) at least 16 hours a day.

At shopping centers, the users of parking include shoppers as well as tenants' employees and suppliers. Shopping hours as well as merchandise delivery schedules will determine hours of active use, which may typically span the hours between 8:00 A.M. and 10:00 P.M. (or later) and require monitoring for as much as 16 hours. Although lots entered directly from the street via multiple access points can be difficult to close off entirely, round-the-clock patrols and monitoring can help deter vandalism and abandonment of vehicles during the time a center is closed. The presence of 24-hour businesses (supermarkets, drug stores, restaurants) makes round-the-clock security imperative, although this may be arranged directly by the commercial tenant.

Lighting.   Parking areas need to be saturated with light. An even distribution of cost-effective lighting fixtures such as those using metal-halide or high-pressure sodium-vapor lamps usually will provide an optimum level of illumination. Lights can also be focused to illuminate the parking area without causing glare. Such lighting helps deter crime and enhances visibility for users and monitors (patrols). In addition to the parking areas, walkways and entrances to buildings need to be well lighted. To maximize visibility, it is important to position lights so that structural elements and landscaping components (e.g., trees and shrubbery) do not cast shadows or create "blind spots" that can become hiding places. (The Illuminating Engineering Society of America in New York City publishes lighting standards and provides information and assistance with technical problems. The National Lighting Bureau in Washington, D.C., has developed guidelines for interior and exterior lighting requirements, including lighting for safety and security. They can provide comparison information on types of lights, illumination they provide, and related costs.)

Garage Security—Special Considerations

Parking structures create additional security considerations. Elevators require specific monitoring, and the degree of enclosure will determine the amount of natural light available to supplement interior lighting. More often these days, access is controlled, either by issuing tickets that record entry time (usually for parking paid by the user) or by doors or gates activated by a card reader (mostly private parking limited to select users—e.g., residents, tenants' employees). This is also an area where closed-circuit television (CCTV) allows monitoring of remote areas on a continual basis either in addition to or instead of security patrols.

Lighting. In enclosed parking facilities, it is not the type of light that is important but the foot-candles of illumination generated. Fluorescent, mercury-vapor, or high-pressure sodium-vapor lamps are adequate to the task. (Metal-halide lamps are increasingly desirable as a means of ensuring good color discrimination. They present a more natural appearance of buildings and their surroundings and facilitate rapid identification of vehicles by patrons on foot.) However, high-pressure sodium-vapor lights are superior in terms of efficiency. Efficiency, cost, and glow are all important. The lighting standards available are basically guidelines for achieving an even distribution of light.

Both perimeter lighting and structural lighting are needed to aid in the operation of CCTV and facilitate detection of unauthorized personnel and activities. More light is needed at egress points so people on foot can see their surroundings. It is also desirable to have emergency lighting available in stairwells and elevators as well as at random locations throughout the garage.

Interior "Finishing." Underground and other completely enclosed parking garages can maximize illumination by painting the walls white. Painting the columns a different bright color will enhance the available illumination from light bouncing off (reflected by) the white walls. Graphics and signage also play an important role—larger numbers of clearly readable signs are needed, with placement at levels that catch the light from low-beam headlamps. Adequate ventilation is needed to remove carbon monoxide. A review of OSHA requirements is also advisable because of the enclosed environment.

Elevators. Because elevators in garages operate slowly, people often have to wait for them. Glass surrounding walls (enclosures) and glass-walled elevators provide excellent opportunities for natural surveillance. CCTV targeting elevator doors and, preferably, inside each cab allows close monitoring of elevator use as well as potential for (and actual) criminal activity.

Access Control. Both entrance and exit points need to be controlled. Card-activated gates are common. However, if a card system is used elsewhere for access (e.g., to enter the building or limit access to controlled areas of a building), it is preferable to have an operation in which one card operates all access points. (Most card systems are programmable to limit individuals' access if that is necessary.) An anti-passback feature is needed even for a card system in a parking operation. A limited system might be employed for night-time access if daytime activity requires generally open access.

Closed-Circuit Television (CCTV).   CCTV is especially useful in monitoring enclosed parking facilities. Minimally, cameras need to be focused on or set to include in their area of view:

- Aisles
- Ramps
- Elevators
- Ingress and egress areas

An adjunct intercom system is needed in case gate arms have to be activated manually (e.g., because a card does not release the gate or someone misplaced or lost their card). Alternatively, a keypad may be used to operate the gate or as an override option.

Additional Precautions.   Regardless of the types of vehicles being parked in an open lot or enclosed garage, it is prudent to post notices stating that the management is not responsible for the condition of vehicles or their contents. Notices need to be prominently displayed, preferably adjacent to elevators or egress stairways as well as at the entrance.

Some residential properties require proof of insurance coverage for vehicles regularly parked on the premises. This requirement may be appropriate for commercial properties or leased parking facilities where specific spaces are leased on a monthly or other long-term basis. Proof of insurance helps protect the management of the facility as well as the vehicle owner from liability and related claims.

Leased Garages

Often a garage will be leased to a subcontractor or concessionaire whose own people are brought in to operate the facility. In this situation, the users are not only residents, or tenants and their employees, but also the general public (i.e., pay-as-you-go parkers); and the facility has become a source of revenue for the property and its ownership. However, such a change can give rise to additional concerns because the garage is no longer operated as a strictly private facility. Usually residents' assigned parking area would be separate from that of commercial users, secured from floor to ceiling and isolated from the general public. As an added security measure, some garages will have "panic buttons" strategically located throughout the facility and require a roving security officer to respond to calls from those locations.

When facilities that are open to the public utilize ticket booths, the personnel charged with collection of parking fees not only need to be protected, they also have to be able to view their surroundings. Booths that are equipped with holdup or panic buttons and have glass on all sides (including the door) will meet these needs. In addition, the glass has to be kept clear of postings (no memos or signs—it is not intended to be a bulletin board). Attendants need to know the most current policy and procedures for the facility as well as emergency and other necessary phone numbers and guidelines for dealing with different types of money-handling situations. Booths are typically located in exit areas, and these need to be well lighted at all times so attendants can see oncoming vehicles and their drivers as well as be aware of the comings and goings of people on foot.

Security at Other Commercial Properties

The primary security issue for commercial properties is unauthorized access. For properties that are located away from the central business district—e.g., office and industrial parks—the two principles of security are:

1. Make it difficult for an unauthorized person to get in, and
2. Make it as difficult as possible for an intruder to get out.

Likewise, there are two areas to be addressed in providing effective security of a premises: external and internal.

In an attempt to make the premises more secure you need to consider several factors. Your goal should be total defense—not one measure, but the sum of all practical and possible measures. The degree of security should be commensurate with the perceived threat and the value of the contents of the property. You also need to consider that the amount of time, money, and effort you can justifiably spend on security is governed by the threat to which the property is exposed—i.e., the risk factor. It is essential that a survey of the property and the recommendations for security measures that come out of that survey take into account all three of these factors. This chapter will focus on the security needs of an industrial property and specifically those of industrial tenants.

Factors to be considered are the type of operation, what it values, the location of the premises and its nature, and its potential to be a crime site.

- Type of business or trade—manufacturing, assembly of manufactured components, and storage (warehousing) operations all differ in the challenges they present and the security measures they need.
- Nature and value of material(s)—Raw materials or component parts, though costly, generally are of lesser value in themselves than are the

finished goods manufactured or assembled from them. Sophisticated computer-controlled process equipment has greater value than tables that simply provide a work surface for assemblers.

- Location—The neighborhood surrounding an industrial property contributes to the degree of crime risk. Other commercial uses can be a lesser risk factor than entertainments that attract undesirables (bars, adult book stores, etc.) or rundown housing.

- Nature of the premises and security requirements—How the building is constructed, the number of entrances, the presence of loading docks, and similar factors determine the types of security measures needed.

- History of criminal incidents on the property and in the immediate area—You need to find out what types of crimes have been reported in the immediate vicinity and at the property itself and whether these were crimes against people or property or both.

When considering security, all properties have one factor in common—the need to provide "defense in depth."

Defense in Depth

Defense in depth embraces good perimeter security, adequate physical security features for the building, appropriate intruder detection systems, and appropriate work practices and procedures.

Perimeter Security.   Adequate exterior lighting is an elementary security technique. Lighting is needed at the perimeter to enable police or other patrol personnel to observe the area between the boundaries of a property and the building, as well as the building itself. Ideally, the lighting would be directed toward the building. Locations that may be susceptible to attempted breach (unauthorized entry) would also be illuminated.

The street number should be prominently displayed, preferably using reflective numbers that are at least three inches high. Numbering painted or otherwise applied on the curbing is usually required to be black on a reflective white background. However, you will need to be aware of and comply with local ordinances, which may require additional or different placement of the street numbers and specify acceptable methods and materials.

Gates and fences should be intact and functioning optimally—e.g., gates installed so they cannot be lifted from the hinges and locked using hardened-steel close-shackled padlocks with heel and toe locking. The degree of security provided by the lock should be commensurate with the perceived threat and comparable to the security provided by the fence.

It is a good policy to keep gates locked when the premises are not in use and to keep keys separate from the locks at all times to prevent duplication or lock substitution. Consider using a hardened-steel plate or pad-lock bar for additional protection.

Fencing should be securely fixed to posts and base. If there is barbed wire on the top of the fence, it should be placed to maximize its effectiveness and securely attached, particularly at corners or returns. If there is no barbed wire, consideration may be given to adding it on top of existing perimeter fences or walls. The degree of protection afforded by the fence should be equivalent to that provided by the gate and its lock—they are not separate entities.

Doors in perimeter walls need adequate locks supported by hinge bolts (hinge pins) if necessary. A security patrol can be instituted to provide some supervision of the premises after hours. Closed-circuit television (CCTV) monitoring of the perimeter is another option.

Inner Perimeter and Parking Areas.   Because they may be used as steps to gain entry over walls or to store stolen items for later retrieval, empty crates or Dumpsters (industrial waste bins) should be located away from perimeter fences or building walls. Ideally, all material of value should be located in secure areas. (Removable large-size items of merchandise and equipment are as subject to theft as small ones.)

Vehicles left in parking lots on site can be targets for theft with the additional possibility of being used to remove stolen property from the premises. They may also be used as a step to gain access to the roof of the building. Parking space assignments should preferably be marked with a code or number for internal use, *not* with the number (address) of the leased premises. If the parking space marked with the number of the leased unit is empty, it can signal that the unit is unoccupied. To prevent car theft, vehicle owners should be cautioned about locking their cars and setting the gearshift in the park position. Vehicles can be fitted with alarm systems to signal unauthorized entry; use of anti-theft devices (e.g., a steering wheel lock) is an added deterrent. Additional security is provided if vehicles, especially vans, are parked back to back. Contents will be more secure if rear doors cannot be opened easily.

The Building Exterior.   All openings present opportunities for unlawful entry. Entry by removing bricks, galvanized iron, fiber cement, glass areas, and grilles should also be anticipated if the target is attractive. Instead of asking only, "What can be opened?" you should also consider, "What can be kicked in?" and "How can the building be entered from above and below?" Noise does not deter a determined criminal, especially at an industrial site.

Doors should be solid wood and fit well in the doorjamb which, in turn, should be securely fitted to the wall. The door can be strengthened by adding steel sheeting and reinforcing the door frame. Steel doors are another possibility. Hinge pins or hinge bolts will provide additional security for doors that open outward.

Sliding doors that move sideways should have guide rails of sufficient strength that are securely mounted to the building. The fittings securing the door to the rails should be adequate to ensure that the door cannot be lifted from the rail. If two doors are locked together, they should not be movable together in one direction.

Access to loading or storage areas is usually provided by roller shutter doors. Often the area inside these doors is sufficient to allow a vehicle to be driven into the premises and loaded after the lock has been broken. (Manufacturing and warehousing operations that bring transport trucks inside the premises to load and unload are most vulnerable.) Steel roller shutter doors provide the most secure closure. Guide rails need to be mounted to the wall securely.

Ventilation shafts are yet another possible access route since they are often large enough to accommodate an adult. Unless there is some obstruction in the shaft (e.g., a fan), external protection will be needed at the outlet of the shaft (e.g., a security grille).

Locks.   The degree of security required of the lock depends on the perceived threat. Frequently, locks designed for residential applications are used at business premises, and security is easily compromised. Four-point locking devices provide a high degree of security, as do many of the locks available for industrial applications. It is important for locks to be well fitted to the doors and for the bolts to have an adequate throw (effective extension distance) protruding into the strike plate on the doorjamb. To preclude an intruder from cutting a bolt that is accessible, the bolt should be made of hardened steel or have roller inserts or similar mechanisms (e.g., a shim). Unfortunately, good quality locks are often fitted to inadequate doors. Often it is as important to replace the door as it is to replace the lock.

The better-quality mortise lock with the bolt mechanism embedded in the door and the strike plate on the doorjamb generally provides an acceptable degree of security. (This requires a solid-core door of sufficient thickness that its strength will not be compromised by hollowing out a space for the lock.) If double doors are to be locked together, concealed or lockable bolts are preferable. Often additional locks are fitted to support existing systems.

The quality of the locks should be commensurate with the degree of security necessary to deter or deny entry to unauthorized persons. It is especially important to match the lock to the material of the door. Entrances featuring aluminum frames and doors require locks designed for maximum effectiveness in that specific application.

Because there is a wide range of locks available and some locks have very specific applications, it may be wise to consult a locksmith before making changes in locking systems or devices. In a commercial setting, key control is vital.

Glass Areas. Modern commercial buildings often have glass exterior walls as well as plate glass doors. Such expanses of glass are an invitation to problems. Glass may be broken or removed to permit access to a property or entry to a building. To make a building more secure, expanses of glass can be replaced with glass blocks or regular bricks. However, if a window is essential for aesthetic reasons or to provide natural light, additional security can be provided by installing a grille behind the glass or in front of it, with the grille securely fixed to side walls or appropriate returns. Glass doors can be similarly protected.

Display windows can be protected by installing a grille behind the display area or applying a security film to the glass. Replacing plain glass with a tempered variety is another possibility. Roller grilles or roller shutters on the outside will provide added protection. Skylights and glass areas in roofs can also be protected by installing grilles or bars.

Entrance Control

One of the most secure methods of entry control is a system of anterooms. Access is granted only after the person responsible for admission is satisfied that the caller's credentials are valid. A reception area that is open to the public may be separated from the general work area by a locked door, and there may be an intermediate area or passage to be traversed as well. (At an industrial site, a guardhouse or gatehouse may provide the initial entry screening function.) Direct entry to a secure area is prevented because the inner door is opened only when the outer door to the public area is closed and locked.

The form of entry control should be commensurate with the risk factor attributed to the premises. At some commercial premises, strict control of entry before and after normal business hours is essential.

Frequently, large amounts of valuable merchandise are held at one location for distribution to the display area before a store opens for business. This presents an attractive target to potential thieves. Entrance to these premises should not be permitted during such high-risk periods. If entry is essential, the credentials of the person seeking admittance should be established before the door is opened.

A keypad or card reader or an intercom or visual monitor such as a closed-circuit television (CCTV) camera can be used to control the admission of staff members and customers. Convex mirrors also permit views of people seeking entry and, like CCTV, extend the field of vision to include vehicles or people near the entrance.

For staff entry, the system can include ways for them to indicate if they are under duress when entering the secure area, thus providing warning to a security service without alerting the offender. A code word or number or a sensor mechanism might be considered, depending on the need.

Spotlight
on
Security Measures

Approaches to Providing Security

Protection of assets is where the concepts of security meet and merge with the devices and the people who safeguard the lives and property of residents and tenants and their personnel. People should be the primary consideration because strategies for protecting them generally also safeguard their belongings and the managed property.

Dead-bolt locks, door chains, and peepholes may be considered low-tech security devices, and they are. However, when used properly, they are effective means for residents, in particular, to safeguard themselves and their personal property. They offer the specific advantage of being resident-driven: They provide ways that residents can control their own environment. Card access systems and closed-circuit television (CCTV) surveillance, on the other hand, are clearly high-tech measures. They utilize computers or their equivalents, are dependent on electricity, require additional high-tech control devices, and often rely on others for monitoring.

Regardless of the level of technology involved, any security device or system is only as effective as the people who control it. A dead-bolt lock is not a security measure if it is not used. In use, it may not stop a forced entry by a determined intruder, but it may delay the person's entry long enough to allow a call to 911 for police assistance. Similarly, a CCTV camera that is not operational or that is not consistently monitored—either directly (a person watching one or more TV screens) or indirectly (someone reviewing videotape recordings after the fact)—is not likely to deter an intruder once the operational situation is known. Nor will it effectively assist in identifying an intruder who succeeds in entering the building. High-tech systems need to be monitored and maintained, and a back-up power source is required in case of a brownout or a power outage. These extras that are not provided

---

Planning for Security

The key to providing cost-effective security is planning. First of all, you have to decide what you want to accomplish. The following are some of the questions to consider.

- How large is the area to be protected?
- What potential problems—i.e., criminal opportunities—exist there?
- What are the expectations of ownership, management, and residents or tenants as to how much and what type of security will be provided?
- How much money is available to provide security?

The best recommendation is to work with a professional security consultant. From your goals, an inspection of the premises (i.e., a security survey), and established budgetary parameters, a security professional can determine different ways the goal might be accomplished at different levels of expenditure. From the array of alternatives, you will need to evaluate and compare features and benefits of the different approaches or systems and their attendant costs.

You also need to keep in mind that any security provisions you implement will create expectations. You can add to or enhance a system as necessary or appropriate in the future. Changing needs and newer technologies are reasons to re-evaluate established security measures at any time. However, change should be approached with caution: Any change you make may be perceived as a reduction in security, so it is very important for residents and tenants to understand *what* is being changed, *why* it is being changed, and *how the change will benefit them.*

---

by the system vendor along with the hardware are important considerations that should not be overlooked when selecting security equipment and systems. Economics are also a consideration. As with any technology-based security measures, the more sophisticated the system, the higher the cost.

Among the most sophisticated measures are integrated security systems, which include access control that relies on identification of authorized individuals with cards or other devices, multiple CCTV cameras positioned strategically and sometimes housed in domes (for protection of the camera, to conceal it, or both), all tied into a computer monitoring and control center along with intrusion and fire alarms. Integrated systems are designed and tailored for the specific security requirements of a company or a property, and they are perhaps more generally applicable in commercial settings because of the complexity and the cost.

Among the physical security measures that can be implemented are systems for limiting or denying entry to a premises. "Access Control" discusses some of the high-tech keypad and card systems that are commonly used. Often these measures are part of a more comprehensive integrated security system. There is also information about the low-tech and very basic access control system: a lock and key. This chapter identifies some key control considerations.

"Intrusion Alarms" describes the different types of warning devices available and how they function in use. While they are often independent systems, intrusion alarms can also be incorporated into more complex monitoring systems or be one of many components of a comprehensive integrated security system.

In "Fire Alarms," James H. Cullity describes how different devices detect the stages of a fire. While not a security measure in itself—there are penalties for signalling a false alarm, even if the non-fire emergency is critical—the fire alarm is an important life-safety measure required under local building codes. Like intrusion alarms, fire detection devices can also be incorporated into an integrated security system that includes other devices and technologies.

In selecting devices to warn occupants of the building of a danger (i.e., signal that the premises should be evacuated), the type of signal is an important consideration. The need to accommodate individuals with disabilities may commend an alarm system that uses both audible (bell, chime, buzzer, horn, or siren) and visible (a strobe or other flashing light) signals.

"Closed-Circuit Television (CCTV)" outlines some of the components of this type of surveillance system. This technology presents the opportunity of monitoring more than points of ingress and egress and sensitive areas. As the size of cameras has been reduced, it is easier to make their presence less obvious. Those who employ CCTV also need to consider some questions regarding privacy issues: Will any hidden cameras be used? If so, where? Why? What policies are being implemented or served by such surveillance? Will the presence of hidden cameras be disclosed to those who are being monitored (and/or videotaped)? Because hidden cameras can, in some contexts, introduce potential for liability, their use needs to be considered carefully.

As CCTV technology matures, services have been established that can monitor and document activities at a host of properties across the United States simultaneously. The cameras are all integrated into a single system, and hook-ups to local police (and fire) departments allow the service to notify law enforcement, as well as the property's ownership and management, when an incident occurs. This approach can expedite capture of an intruder or resolution of other security problems in the absence of on-site security personnel. This remote visual monitoring technology is described by John I. Kostanoski in "Visual Monitoring via CCTV."

In spite of all the technology available, the human presence is often the deciding factor in handling a criminal incident or other on-site emergency. "Security Guards" outlines some of the issues that should be considered in contracting for guard services. One of the most important values of security guards is their *visibility*. It may not matter whether the guard force that patrols a property numbers two or ten or more individuals. The number may depend on the amount of territory to be covered on patrol, the frequency of patrols, and the extent of the patrol procedure (e.g., punch clock time checks, location checkpoints, testing whether doors are locked), among other things. No matter how many people are involved, guards that are not visible will not be an effective deterrent. Guards that are not available cannot serve as employee or customer escorts. Guards who only monitor a CCTV screen cannot know what is going on in areas that are not surveilled directly by the cameras. Visibility, availability, and an active duty routine are important to the *perception of security* as well as the reality.

In the final chapter, Christopher A. Hertig talks about the specifics of "Security Training." He rightly points out that security personnel cannot function optimally unless they become an integral part of the management and operations team. He also outlines the various roles a guard force plays and emphasizes the need to provide guard personnel with general training in addition to the security-specific training.

Something that is not addressed specifically in these technology-oriented chapters is the variety of measures for protecting valuable records, whether in paper form or stored in a computer. Papers can be stored in locked fireproof filing cabinets or a safe or a specially designed vault. The sheer volume of paper generated in any business is overwhelming, and the specific value of individual documents varies substantially. In real estate management, more specific documents are likely to be considered valuable and worthy of safeguarding because of the manager's contractual relationship as the property owner's agent.

Computer files pose challenges of limiting access, maintaining backup (paper and floppy disks or tapes), and safeguarding the confidentiality of financial information acquired in the manager's fiduciary role as the owner's agent. Because computer technology is moving forward at an extremely rapid pace, it is prudent here to only touch on some highlights. Passwords within an existing system can authorize and control access to specific computer systems, software programs, and individual files or documents. While encryption programs are available, only someone knowledgeable about computers in general and the hardware and software in a particular system can properly advise about digital document protection measures. Inventory controls that include records of assigned codes and equipment serial numbers coupled with devices that anchor computer equipment to desks are straightforward minimal approaches to protecting these valuable business assets.

Other safeguards that protect personnel and equipment include careful pre-employment screening of all job applicants that includes credit and criminal histories as necessary or appropriate and consistent thorough checking of references. Bonding of employees who handle clients' funds

Safes

There are many types of safes available on the market today. They range from wall units to blowtorch-proof floor units. A variety of locking mechanisms is also available (e.g., combination, time-delay, two-key operation). In choosing a safe, as in other security measures, the notion of "commensurate with the risk" applies.

In developing selection criteria, one should consider the items of greatest value likely to be held (cash, documents) and the holding period. This type of security needs to be evaluated regularly because the amount of cash held in a safe usually increases over time, and the protection provided by the safe concurrently diminishes in proportion to the value of the contents.

A floor safe often meets the requirements of those whose cash holdings are lower. A model with a slot or chute allows deposits to a portion of the safe that is otherwise inaccessible. Two keys are usually required to open the secured area, and often one key is held by an armored transfer service employed to remove the cash to a bank.

The location of the safe is important. Safes should be securely attached to floor joists or wall studs to make removal more difficult—safes weighing less than 1000 kg. (around 455 lb.) are classed as portable. Appearances can be deceiving; sometimes safes that look substantial are easily breached. The construction of the safe selected—materials and assembly—should be adequate to the need for protection. Also, the area surrounding the safe should be well-lighted. Illumination provides an added deterrent and facilitates observation of an intruder via CCTV.

Security can be increased by installing an alarm system to signal any attempts at unauthorized access. Detectors used to integrate a safe into an alarm system usually are triggered by a noise, heat, light, or vibration. It is also possible to incorporate a duress signal into a combination lock on a safe. The potentially easy access by unauthorized personnel to safes with keyed locks necessitates strict security measures to safeguard all keys to the safe.

and financial records provides a management company with some protection against theft or dishonesty. Having employees sign nondisclosure and/ or noncompete agreements helps to safeguard company confidential information and provides remedies if the agreement is violated.

Pre-employment screening of security personnel—whether your own employees or those of a contracted service—is especially important because they are being entrusted with responsibility for protecting people's lives as well as company property and employees' personal belongings. Once on board, they need to be fully integrated into your work force, which means that security guards should receive the same general training as is given to all your employees, including and especially training in the communications and interpersonal skills they need to properly perform their security role.

Access Control

Access control systems using cards or keypads or other devices continue to gain in popularity. Businesses use such systems internally to limit access to their facilities. In some situations, certain employees may not be authorized to access some areas of the business, and programmable keypads and card systems facilitate this type of exclusion. Office buildings may control access by requiring tenants' employees to show an identification card to a security guard or other monitor at the building entrance, and a keypad or card system may be operational only during non-business hours and weekends. New residential properties are being built with access control systems in place, and some older properties have been replacing keyed locks with keypads or card systems at their front (and rear) entrances, if not on the apartments themselves.

Access control technology is very sophisticated. In the mid-1990s, the types of devices available range from the simplest designs with keypads or cards to computer-controlled systems integrated with closed-circuit television monitoring. The areas in between the single device and the integrated system include bar code technologies and biometric identification systems based on such parameters as hand prints (thermal scan), retinal images (eye scans), and voice prints. *Star Trek* is alive and well in the 1990s.

When choosing any type of access control device or system, it is important to decide what features and capabilities are needed and how much you are able or willing to spend before beginning to look. In general, the greater the security provided by a technology, the more it will cost. For most managed properties, the simpler, lower-cost devices and systems will be adequate.

Keypads

Keypads are usually installed adjacent to the doors they control. They may have actual buttons to push, and the buttons may be in a horizontal or vertical series. Each pushbutton may be numbered; some are double-numbered—for example, a five-button system might have 10 numbers, and the top button might respond to both number 1 and number 2. Other models have a smooth surface that has to be touched by those wishing to gain access. Like pushbuttons, they respond to finger pressure. These, too, may be single- or double-numbered.

The keypads are operated by completing an electrical circuit when the proper sequence of numbers is "punched," releasing the electrically controlled lock in the door. A five-button keypad may operate on any number of digits up to five. (More complicated code sequences can be difficult for authorized personnel to remember.) The number sequence can be changed, for example when an employee is terminated from an individual business; but such a change may not be necessary at each employee turnover if access to the building is separately controlled at the entrances. A manual override allows personnel who are not authorized to enter—e.g., a technician who services business equipment and needs access on a one-time basis—to be "buzzed" through the locked door. The override, in turn, precludes giving the access code to temporary or part-time workers. In most situations, the override will be operated by a receptionist or a security guard on duty.

Multiple entrances to a building or a business can each be fitted with the same type of device and the same code. Alternatively, the technology can facilitate enforcement of a policy requiring all doors, except perhaps the front street-level entrance of an office building, for example, to be kept locked at all times.

The capacity of a keypad is generally unlimited; access is controlled by limiting the number of people to whom the code is distributed. However, there is also a substantial likelihood of keypad controls being breached, not only because an unscrupulous employee or resident may give the number code to an unauthorized person, but because someone could figure out the code if given enough time. The key to minimizing the likelihood of a breach is to make sure that employees or residents understand that the purpose of the device is *to protect their lives and their property* and will govern their actions accordingly.

Card Systems

Card systems also come in a variety of sizes, shapes, and complexities. In some of the card technologies, information is programmed onto a chip embedded in the card. These cards may have to be inserted into a slit in the scanning control device, or they may have to be pressed onto the controller or held near it (proximity devices). Other card technologies code the authorization information onto a magnetic strip, much like the ones on the backs of credit cards. The latter are passed through a slit in the control device attached to the wall next to the door, and the information is scanned to complete an electrical circuit and release the door lock.

Like keypads, it is possible to control multiple entrances with duplicate devices. However, the more sophisticated programming involved permits exclusion from access to certain areas or use of certain entrances if such limitations are desired. In a commercial setting, such control facilitates protection of company trade secrets and ongoing research and development as well as safeguarding the lives and property of individual employees.

The capacity of a card access system is limited by the memory capacity of the card reader. Card systems are more difficult to breach than keypads, but it is not impossible. Again, an unscrupulous individual might pass an authorized card to an unauthorized person, and some types of cards can be counterfeited.

Choosing a Card System.   In selecting an access control method or system, there are numerous factors to be weighed and evaluated, among them cost, system expandability, programming and reprogrammability, and the availability of different types of controls within the system.

- Cost—Major enterprise access control systems with national coverage can cost hundreds of thousands of dollars—know your budget limitations.
- Cards—Cards should be tamperproof, and replacement cards should be readily available.
- System Capacity—Consider your current and future needs, including sufficient capacity to allow for temporary authorization of part-time employees, official visitors, and contract workers. Expandability is also important—the system should be able to grow with the needs of the company.
- Programming—Look for easy on-site programming by authorized personnel. Although there are access control bureau services available, it is preferable to rely on on-site programming and use such services as a supplement.
- Other Desirable Features and Safeguards—
  —Time zone capabilities that allow management of individual access on the basis of time and date.
  —Card reprogrammability, preferably on site.
  —Anti-passback capability that denies users the chance to enter and then slip the card back under the door to an unauthorized person outside.

—A back-up supporting battery and an alarm on the main line to ensure retention of data files in the event of a power failure.

—A lock-out function that denies access for a programmable period after a number of attempts to gain unauthorized access have been unsuccessful.

—An alarm that will sound if the door is held open too long—this feature should also permit a legitimate bypass of the system for an emergency evacuation.

—An alarm that will sound and deny entry if the card reader is tampered with.

—A duress signal incorporated into the reader that can be activated if an authorized user is being forced to open the door for an unauthorized person.

These are just a handful of the possible features card systems offer. Card access control systems are frequently used by those using an automated teller machine (ATM) at a bank or other location. Private corporations use the technology to restrict access within their facilities. Security guards can use a version of the technology for their walking tours, to "clock in" at established checkpoints. Some cards incorporate photographs and are worn in holders or clipped onto clothing, serving both as access control and as photo identification of personnel. Still others include identification capabilities via encoded biometric data—so-called smart cards.

Card Access Technologies.   The major technologies are Wiegand, proximity, and magnetic stripe, which account for 90 percent of the applications. The major points in evaluating a technology are:

1. Encoding security
2. Reader life
3. User convenience
4. Initial cost
5. Maintenance cost

Wiegand is a magnetic pulse-generating technology (magnetic wires are embedded in the card). It offers maximum encoding security, maintenance-free readers, moderate cost initially, and low cost over the long term.

Proximity systems use radio frequency to make contact between the reader and the card. They provide good encoding security and offer convenience for users (cards may be presented to the reader from a short distance away—typically 18 inches to 2 feet), but they are subject to interference and have moderate costs both initially and over the long term. Some proximity systems use tokens rather than cards, and these are typically round (a "button") and can be read from someone's hand or a pocket on their clothing.

Magnetic (mag) stripe systems encode information into a black strip on

Card Reader Technologies Compared

Features/Technology	Wiegand	Proximity	Mag Stripe
Encoding Security	High	Moderate	Low
Reader Features	Long Life	Subject to Interference	High Maintenance
Card Features	Convenient	Easy to Use	Short life
Initial Cost	Moderate	Moderate	Low
Maintenance Cost	Low	Moderate	High

the back of the card. It is read by being passed (swiped) through a slit or opening in the reader. This technology's encoding security is low; reader maintenance is high and card life is short. While initial cost is low, long-term cost is high.

Although the cost is greater than that of a key cylinder, there are strong advantages to a card system. For example, when a company downsizes, sometimes no one collects the outstanding keys, and it can be difficult to collect them after the fact. With card access control, the individual cards are simply deleted from the system.

Key Control

Conventional locks and keys are still the most common means of controlling access to properties and buildings. The critical factor in keeping this lesser technology viable is *key control*. The following are examples of policy strategies that can help real estate managers control keys at their properties.

- Having a key control policy in effect and understood by personnel who implement it.
- Inventories and inspections conducted periodically by the designated key controller to ensure compliance with the policy (the policy and procedure stating how often this is to be done).
- Keys stored in a lockable fireproof cabinet that is kept locked at all times except when keys are being removed or returned.
- Master keys devoid of markings identifying them as such.
- Locks and keys to all buildings and entrances controlled by one designated person who is given overall responsibility for issuance and replacement of locks and keys.

- Keys issued only to authorized personnel.
- Key control documentation that includes—
  —Buildings or entrances for which keys are issued.
  —Location and number of master keys.
  —Location and number of duplicate keys.
  —Location of keys and locks held in reserve.
  —The name of the person to whom each key is issued.
  —Identification of the key issued (number or other code).
  —Time of issuance and return of the key.
- All requests for reproduction or duplication of keys to be approved by the designated key controller (better still, any duplication of keys would be arranged by that person and the copies tracked in the system).
- Employees prohibited from removing property keys from the premises.
- Locks changed immediately upon loss or theft of keys.
- Loss or theft of keys investigated promptly by the designated key controller.
- Locks changed (moved from one location to another) at least semi-annually as an added safeguard.
- Manufacturers' serial numbers obliterated on combination locks.
- Locks on inactive gates in storage facilities required to be sealed, and locks and seals checked periodically by guard personnel.
- Measures implemented to prevent unauthorized removal of locks on open cabinets, gates, or buildings.

A good place to start in setting up a key control program is to have a professional locksmith examine your building or property. The locksmith can review your current key-handling practices and set up a key control program. There will be a cost for this service as well as the attendant administrative costs of controlling keys on a day-to-day basis. (Locksmiths are listed in the Yellow Pages of the telephone directory.)

As with other types of professional services, it is wise to interview locksmiths whom you wish to consider. You should ask about their years in business, hours of operation, location, and whether or not they are bonded. References are also a must. Because keys and locks are part of security, it is important for the selected vendor to be trustworthy. You may wish to establish a working relationship so the locksmith can be called upon in the future to install locks, make copies of keys, and replace lock cylinders, as well as provide advice on managing locks and keys.

An Ounce of Prevention

One of the surest deterrents to crime and criminals is to reduce the opportunity for a crime to be committed. One of the most effective ways to accomplish this is to control access to a property or a building. Keeping unauthorized (and unwanted) people out protects the lives and property of those residents, employees, and others who are authorized to come in. Although high-tech systems and equipment are available, sometimes just controlling the low-tech systems (e.g., keys and locks) will accomplish the goal more cost-effectively. The type of property, its location and configuration, and its tenancy are key factors in determining the degree of access control needed.

Intrusion Alarms

Alarm systems should be considered an accessory to good physical security, not a substitute for it. An alarm system will only advise of unlawful entry; it will not prevent a smash-and-grab incident. It does not provide an immediate response, nor does it buy time for victims. To do all that—and more— requires a balance between electronic and physical security.

Selecting an Alarm System

The deterrent value of an alarm system should also be considered in conjunction with the cost of providing the same level of deterrence by other means. Among the issues to be considered are:

Building location and construction,
Methods of detection, and
Quality of equipment to be used.

Building *construction* will be one of the governing factors in the selection of activation devices. Another factor will be the type of protection required. The alarm system may be necessary for general perimeter protection or to secure an area or an object (e.g., a safe).

Basically there are two methods of detection: Alarms may be located at the perimeter of the building or property to advise of intrusion and within units on the premises to advise of entry after the perimeter has been breached. A combination of the two basic methods may also be used.

Control panels may comprise a mechanism for simple alarm initiation or enable control of separate sectors or zones that include a number of detectors. The range of equipment available will necessitate selection and installation of detectors by a professional with the necessary knowledge to ensure that:

1. False activation is minimized.
2. The signal transmission is appropriate for your requirements.
3. The end users (management personnel, tenants' employees, residents) are advised of how the system operates.

In selecting alarm equipment, dual-tech sensors, audible horns, and UL-listed equipment should be considered for all uses.

Consideration should be given to how much security is needed, what requires specific protection, and what exactly is to be detected. If it is expensive and not essential to protect the entire perimeter of a property, then the concept of "detection upon entry" should be considered in choosing an alarm system.

Intrusion alarms are very common today. More and more people have alarm systems in their homes and businesses. The fact that they are common means there are many choices of systems, equipment, and service. The real estate manager charged with selecting an alarm system or service or evaluating equipment to recommend to the property owner needs some basic information about alarms and alarm companies.

Selecting an Alarm Company

There are two approaches to selecting an alarm company. One is to contact an associate who manages the same kind of property and ask two questions:

1. Who provides your alarm service?
2. Are you satisfied with the company's performance?

The other approach is to look in the Yellow Pages of the phone book for alarm company listings (under burglar alarms, fire alarms, etc.), checking in particular for UL-listed vendors. As with any equipment investment or service contract, it is wise to request information and bids from several vendors. Although you may be able to develop some specifications related to your requirements, it is likely the vendors will want to visit the property and evaluate the areas to be alarmed. Regardless of how you identify potential vendors, they should all be asked to provide customer references, and these should be checked out thoroughly before proceeding. What you should be looking for is the customers' experiences with the alarm company regarding the following:

- Its service charges.
- How the company responds to service requests.
- The quality of its service.
- The quality of work performed by its technicians.

Checklists for Selecting an Alarm Company

Important considerations in selecting an alarm company and defining the service to be provided can be addressed with the following checklists.

Six points regarding the security system company:
1. At least ten customer references in your area.
2. At least five years of operation under present management.
3. Membership in the National Burglar and Fire Alarm Association.
4. Disclosure of the company's Dun and Bradstreet Credit Report.
5. Agreement to pay any equipment-related false alarm fines.
6. UL 611 accreditation by Underwriters Laboratories, Inc.

Five points regarding installation and service:
1. Installation by company-trained technicians (not subcontractors or moonlighters).
2. Managers on call for you—at all times.
3. Proof of workers' compensation insurance (to protect you from personal liability).
4. Service by National Burglar and Fire Alarm Association-certified technicians—24 hours each day.
5. An annual inspection and preventive maintenance service program.

Seven points regarding the system and monitoring:
1. A "hands-on" trial, in advance, of how to operate it.
2. Full disclosure, in advance, of all equipment makes and models.
3. Protection against service disruption from severed telephone lines.
4. Wire splices soldered—this is vital!
5. Monitoring center owned and controlled by the installation company.
6. Monitoring center locally situated, subject to your inspection, and UL-listed.
7. Automatic test signals to monitoring center—at least weekly.

More information about alarm company selection can be obtained by contacting Underwriters Laboratories or the National Burglar and Fire Alarm Association.

Remember one rule of thumb: The biggest may not be the best. Your goal should be to select a reputable company that installs alarm systems and services them cost-effectively. (A series of checklists that can help guide your selection of an alarm company can be found in the accompanying box.) Characteristics of alarm companies that can be checked out for comparison include the types of equipment they use and the monitoring services they offer.

Central Station.   The alarm company should have a central station operating twenty-four hours a day and staffed by at least two people at all times. It should have a back-up generator (automatic) in the event of a power failure. Be sure to ask how alarm signals are transmitted to the central station because this factor determines what will be installed at the property and affects your service costs. Signals may be transmitted over data lines (multiplex), by direct wire (hard wiring), using a McCulloh Loop, or digitally via telephone lines.

Central Station Control Panels.   How alarm signals are transmitted to the central station depends on the receiving (and sending) equipment.

- *Multiplexing* allows transmission of multiple signals over a single pair of wires with the signals "separated" (reproduced and identified) at the receiving end. This offers the advantage of fewer wires being required to connect a number of alarms into the system; it also provides greater line security while reducing leased-line charges.

- *Direct wire* requires hard-wiring from the user account premises to the central station. Telephone line installation and monthly charges are usually higher. It has only one signal. The system may have line security; it does have a line trouble signal and may be used for a police department connection.

- *McCulloh loop* requires a leased line into the telephone exchange from the central station. The system is similar to multiplex in that line trouble can be isolated by interrogation from the central station receiver. It may have line security (not subject to circumventing with battery or alligator clips). The user is required to pay a telephone company installation charge and a monthly leased-line charge. Multiplex signals are possible. This is the least-expensive leased line.

- *Digital communication* uses existing telephone lines. The alarm system dials into receivers with the account number and alarm condition. There is no line supervision and no monthly leased-line charges.

Upon receipt of an alarm signal, the central station notifies the appropriate authority and then anyone else designated by the subscriber.

Types of Monitoring Services.   Various types of monitoring services are available. Depending on your needs, the alarm response may be specified or limited. Residential properties which are "open" twenty-four hours a day will have different response needs than commercial properties, which may be open only designated hours and days of the week.

In *straight monitoring* service, the alarm company takes action on alarm only. In *opening and closing monitoring,* however, the subscriber will designate opening and closing times (including weekends and holidays). The alarm company will then monitor to ensure the alarm is set and disarmed at the designated times, and if not, appropriate action will be taken as specified by the subscriber. Also, if the alarm system is disarmed during off-hours, the alarm company will take the appropriate (prespecified) action. Normally everyone who is to have access will be provided with a card bearing their personal identification (ID) number. In order to disarm the alarm at an off-hour, they will have to call the alarm company first and give their system code and personal ID number. A report of openings and closings is typically sent to the subscriber each month; if additional reports are needed (e.g., weekly or bi-weekly), these would be made available at an extra charge.

Testing is advised at least monthly. The subscriber is urged strongly to test the system frequently to be certain everything is in working order. To do this, the subscriber is required to call the central station first and give the system code number, then run the test. Each time the system is tested, a different device should be tripped or violated, and the alarm company has to be called back to verify that the signal was received.

In addition to providing a warning and alerting authorities in the event of an intrusion, alarm companies can monitor other systems and equipment that have built-in control devices—e.g., sprinkler systems, temperature, moisture, water level, generators, pumps, industrial processing (furnaces, etc.), HVAC, electric power. Since vital operating systems can be vulnerable to sabotage, it may be appropriate and cost-effective to include monitoring of them as well.

On-Site Control Panels. Control panels for installation on site come in different shapes and sizes, designed to monitor a single zone or multiple zones. They may be used for fire alarms as well as intrusion alarms. The control panel for an alarm system should be placed in a protected area that is not accessible to passersby. It is also advisable to locate the control away from heavy machinery or anything that vibrates sufficiently to trip the alarm mechanism.

Arming Stations. The devices that permit the subscriber to arm (turn on) and disarm (turn off) the alarm system are called *arming stations*. They may be on the control panel or remotely located and may include a "panic button."

An arming station on the control panel may be a key pad or a digital pad. This type requires a time-delay circuit for the entrance door to allow the subscriber to disarm and re-arm the system at opening and closing, respectively. (Contacts inserted in the door and door frame make a closed circuit when the door is closed; opening the door breaks the circuit and trips the alarm.) Usually the control panel is not located immediately adjacent to the door.

An inside arming station may likewise be a key pad or digital pad. Any motion detectors between the entrance door and the arming station need to be on a similar delay or follower circuit. In addition, a Sonalert or other small buzzer mechanism may be installed at the arming station. This buzzer is triggered when the door is opened and reminds the subscriber to disarm the system upon entry. (It may also sound when the system is re-armed, giving the subscriber a set time period in which to exit and lock the door or else the alarm will be tripped.) As for the door lock, a Medeco cylinder is virtually pick-proof, and its keys cannot be duplicated by ordinary key machines.

If the key pad is an outside remote installation, it is usually key operated only. Nothing need be on a delay circuit. If an outside arming station is tampered with, an alarm condition will be signaled. Unfortunately, this type of installation can be vandalized.

As a general rule, all arming stations used by the alarm company should have two light-emitting diodes (LEDs), one that glows red when the system is armed and one that glows green if the protective circuit is closed and the system is ready to be armed. There are some exceptions to this, however.

False alarms may be caused by subscriber error, faulty alarm equipment, or a telephone line malfunction, all of which need to be investigated and corrected promptly. Once an alarm system has been installed, it needs to be maintained and tested regularly. Regardless of the type you have, alarms need to be checked periodically to ensure that all components are operating properly. They also need to be serviced by a reliable company at least once a year. In addition, it is important to teach your staff how to use the system and how to respond when an alarm is triggered.

Types of Detection Devices

A variety of devices can be installed to trigger the alarm. Some may use a magnetic contact that maintains an electric circuit: When the contact is broken, an alarm is signaled. Motion sensors detect physical changes in the area being monitored. Panic devices allow an individual to intentionally trigger an alarm in a dangerous situation. Each type of detector has advantages and disadvantages in regard to a specific application. Often it is best to consult with experts who can evaluate your property, your operations, and your alarm needs. They can advise you on what would be your best and most cost-effective choices and recommend ways to maximize detection potential while also controlling costs. Usually there is an installation fee (based on time, materials, and complexity of the job) and a periodic (monthly is typical) fee for the monitoring service. (Some companies will give a discount if the monitoring fee is paid annually.) So that you can be prepared to work with an alarm company and speak their language, brief descriptions of several types of detection devices are provided.

The *passive infrared (PIR) motion detector* is probably the most common type in use. It is designed to detect rapid temperature changes, as from body heat. PIR motion detectors have to be positioned carefully. They work best at detecting movement (e.g., walking) across the field of view. False alarms can be caused by:

- Air-conditioning or heating units (avoid placement too close to them or aiming directly at them).
- Sunlight (avoid aiming at windows).
- Drafts (avoid locating near overhead doors).

Depending on the model, a PIR detector will "cover" an area within 40 to 150 feet from the device.

An *ultrasonic motion detector* emits high-frequency sound waves from a transmitter into the detection area and back to a receiver. When both transmitter and receiver are in one unit, it is called a *transceiver.* The transceiver is the most common type of ultrasonic motion detector in use. Motion in the detection area causes a shift that increases or decreases the frequency of the transmitted sound waves. If the receiver detects a change, the unit signals an alarm. Ultrasonic motion detectors are best used in office areas and should not be used in machine shops; the monitored area also needs to be heated. False alarms are caused by sound and motion:

- Air movement (turbulence created by fans, heaters, air conditioners).
- High-pitched sounds (noises emitted by motors, fans, steam radiators; may not be audible to the human ear).
- Objects in motion (loose hanging objects such as mobiles; drapes; blueprints tacked to a wall—items easily disturbed by drafts or other air movement).

Ultrasonic motion detectors work best in an area approximately 20 by 20 feet—the best catch-path is into or away from the device.

"Panic" devices (hold-up indicators) come in many forms and are most often used in banks, retail establishments, and other businesses that handle cash transactions in person. A simple *push-button* device is least expensive but prone to false alarms from being bumped accidentally. A *squeeze-type* device has to be pressed on both sides to activate it. It has to be key re-set, making it easy to identify which button was used in the event of multiple stations. The *money clip* device is inserted in a cash register drawer; when the last bill is pulled out, contact is made. This is more difficult to wire but easier for a cashier to use. A *foot rail* is unobtrusive and easy to use but more expensive than buttons, and it is subject to false alarms from kicking. When a panic device is used with a *digital communicator,* a separate signal can be transmitted to signal a hold-up. However, if only one *direct wire* is used, only one signal can be transmitted.

Switch mats are usually installed under carpets, rugs, or runners. They are "normally open" devices; when stepped on, they close a circuit. Since some burglar alarm systems use "closed circuits," a converter may be nec-

Intrusion Alarm and Space Protection Terminology

Alarm Circuit An electrical circuit of an alarm system that produces or transmits an alarm signal.

Alarm Condition A threatening condition (e.g., an intrusion or fire) sensed by a detector or signaled by the potential victim (e.g., a hold-up).

Alarm Signal A signal produced by a control unit indicating the existence of an *alarm condition* (e.g., bell, siren, strobe light, digital communicator, tape dialer, etc.)

Area Protection (Space Protection) Protection of the inner space or volume of a secured area by means of a *volumetric sensor.*

Capacitance The property of two or more nonconducting objects which enables them to store electrical energy in an electric field between them. Capacitance varies inversely with the distance between objects; the change of capacitance with relative motion is greater the nearer one object is to the other. The basic unit of measure is the *farad.*

Capacitance Alarm System An alarm system in which the protected object is electrically connected as a *capacitance sensor.* The approach of an intruder causes sufficient change in capacitance to upset the balance of the system and initiate an alarm signal. Also called *proximity alarm system.*

Capacitance Sensor A sensor that responds to a change in capacitance in a field containing a protected object or in a field within a protected area.

Closed-Circuit System A system in which the sensors of each zone are connected in *series* so that the same current exists in each sensor. When an activated sensor breaks the circuit or the connected wire is cut, an alarm is transmitted for that zone.

Contact The two (paired) metallic parts of a switch or relay which, by touching or separating, make or break the electrical current path.

Doppler Effect (Shift) The apparent change in frequency of sound or radio waves when reflected from or originating from a moving object.

Double Loop System An alarm circuit in which two wires enter and two wires leave each sensor.

Dual-Sensing Detector A detector that incorporates two detection technologies to sense an intruder, both of which must be activated before an alarm signal can be transmitted. Typical devices combine microwave and passive infrared (PIR) *or* ultrasound and PIR.

End-of-Line Resistor Circuit An alarm circuit that uses a resistor to terminate an electrically supervised circuit. Resistance changes may be caused by a sensor, tampering, or circuit trouble.

Floor Mat (Mat Switch) A flat area mechanical switch used under carpeting; pressure when it is stepped on triggers an alarm.

Intrusion Alarm System An alarm system for signaling the entry or attempted entry of a person or an object into the area or volume monitored by the system. *Signaling* may be by audible (bell, siren) or visual (flashing lights) annunciation or both. *Monitoring* is via a device that can detect entry (door or window contact, motion detectors). The two are passive and must be activated by an alarm control in order to establish a *system.*

Alarm Terminology *(concluded)*

Microwave Frequency Radio frequencies in the range of approximately 1.0 to 300 gigahertz (GHz; 1 GHz = 1,000,000,000 hertz = 10^9 cycles per second).

Microwave Motion Detector A sensor that detects the motion of an intruder through the use of a radiated radio frequency (RF) electromagnetic field. The device operates by sensing a disturbance in the generated RF field caused by intruder motion, typically a modulation of the field referred to as *Doppler Shift* or *Doppler Effect,* which is used to initiate an alarm signal.

Multiplexing A technique of transmitting two or more signals over the same wire in either or both directions concurrently.

Normally Closed (NC) Switch A switch in which the contacts are closed when no external forces act upon the switch (e.g., magnet or voltage to coil).

Normally Open (NO) Switch A switch in which the contacts are open (separated) when no external forces act upon the switch.

Open-Circuit System A system in which the sensors are connected in *parallel.* When a sensor is activated, the circuit is closed, generating a current which activates an alarm signal.

Passive Infrared (PIR) Sensor A sensor that detects natural radiation or radiation disturbances but does not itself emit the radiation on which its operation depends.

Perimeter Protection Protection of access to the outer limits of a *protected area* by means of physical barriers, sensors on physical barriers, or exterior sensors not associated with a physical barrier.

Photoelectric Sensor A device that detects a visible or invisible beam of light and responds to its complete or nearly complete interruption.

Radio Frequency (RF) Interference Electromagnetic interference in the radio frequency range.

Sound Sensing Detection Device An alarm device that detects the audible sound caused by an attempted forcible entry into a protected structure (such as breaking glass). The device consists of a microphone, an amplifier, and contacts. Sensitivity of the unit is adjustable so that ambient noises or normal sounds will not initiate an alarm signal.

Strain Gauge Alarm System An alarm system that detects the stress caused by the weight of an intruder as he moves about a building. Typical uses include placement of the strain gauge sensor under a floor joist or under a stairway tread.

Ultrasonic Motion Detector A sensor that detects the motion of an intruder through the use of *ultrasound* generating and receiving equipment. The device operates by filling a space with a pattern of high-frequency sound waves; an increase or decrease in frequency initiates an alarm signal. This principle is referred to as the *Doppler Effect.*

Volumetric Sensor A sensor with a detection zone that extends over a volume such as an entire room, part of a room, or a passageway (e.g., ultrasonic or sonic motion detectors).

essary to create an open circuit. If there are guard dogs or large rodents within the detection area, switch mats should not be used even though so-called pet strips are available for this application.

A *proximity detector* is a capacitance device used to protect safes and cabinets. A single wire from the safe or cabinet to the alarm is all that is required. Highly sensitive circuitry will detect an intruder upon *approaching* the safe. The safe or cabinet should be mounted on insulators (provided with the proximity alarm) and positioned at least six inches from walls. A proximity detector is the best device for alarming safes.

Magnetic contacts are the oldest and still most widely used form of detection device. A magnet is attached to the moving part of a window or door, and the switch is hard-wired onto the stationary window frame or doorjamb. When aligned, they form a closed circuit. If the magnet is moved, the circuit opens and an alarm is activated. Steel doors require larger (wide-gap) contacts because their mass will affect the magnetic circuit; overhead doors require special large contacts with leads armored in cable. False alarms result from incomplete circuits caused by:

- Loose-fitting doors (easily moved by the wind).
- Warped doors (not aligned with the frame).
- Contacts on steel doors too small.

In a hostile environment (dampness, corrosive chemicals), concealed contacts should be used; otherwise, exposed contacts may be "jumped out" (i.e., a circuit may be opened signaling an alarm). Also, exposed contacts are more easily tampered with and defeated.

Glass Protection.   In addition to contacts (which protect against intruders opening a window), there are other types of devices that signal an alarm condition in the event an intruder merely breaks the glass and does not open the window.

A ⅜-inch-wide *metallic foil tape* can be fastened to the glass around the perimeter of the window, approximately 3 inches in from the frame. This tape becomes part of the alarm circuitry via take-off blocks with terminals. It is covered with a clear protective shellac-like substance. When the foil tape is broken, a circuit is opened and an alarm is signaled. Foil is the oldest, most-reliable form of glass protection, but it has some drawbacks: It can be scratched or otherwise damaged. Over time, it can become brittle and crack or pull away from the glass. It may be affected by exposure to sunlight, condensation, extreme dryness (lack of humidity), and other environmental conditions. In addition, it usually requires frequent service.

Shock sensors may be mounted on walls or roofs as well as on glass. This type of sensor detects energy shocks caused by severe hammering, chopping, breaking, etc. Though aesthetically more pleasing than foil, shock sensors are more expensive, and some models require a processing module in addition to the shock sensor. Shock sensors are mounted on the mullion (frame) of the window and generally on every other frame intersection on multiple windows. Sensitivity is adjustable, and the area covered varies from 50 to 150 square feet. False alarms can be triggered by loose windows or frames.

The presence of an alarm system may deter a potential intruder, but the primary function of an alarm is to signal the presence of an intruder. Although alarms and the types of detection devices discussed here can be used independently, intrusion alarms and their triggering mechanisms can also be components of more comprehensive integrated systems designed to control access to a property, a building, or a defined area or to monitor whole buildings.

Fire Alarms

James H. Cullity

The fire alarm system is probably the least thought about detection system you have, yet it is there and it is always ON. One important rule of thumb is to have your system completely checked on an annual basis. (Most municipal codes include a requirement for such periodic testing.) Fire alarm systems are accredited by Underwriters Laboratories, Inc. (UL), Factory Mutual System (FM), and the National Fire Protection Association (NFPA), whose guidelines cover installation and transmission of alarm signals.

Fires and Fire Detection

There are three basic causes of fires: accidental, natural, and arson. A cigarette that is not extinguished may be dropped in a wastebasket containing paper that can start a fire accidentally. Lightning striking a building and igniting combustible construction materials would be a natural cause. Any fire set intentionally is considered arson, which is a criminal act.

Fires develop in four stages. In the *incipient stage,* invisible combustion products are given off as the fire is beginning. No visible smoke, flame, or appreciable heat is present yet, but fire is starting. A short circuit in the wiring inside a wall or ceiling, an oily rag, an overheated element in an appliance, any one of thousands of potential causes can exist without anyone knowing it is there. (This stage may be detected by a *gas detector.*)

In the *smoldering stage,* combustion products are apparent as smoke, but flame or appreciable heat is still not present. *Photoelectric smoke detectors* signal a fire at this stage.

In the *flame stage,* actual fire now exists. While appreciable heat is still

---

Causes and Detection of Fires

Three Basic Causes of Fires

- Accidental
- Natural
- Arson

Four Stages of Fire/Methods of Detection

1. Incipient Stage—Detected by gas detectors.
2. Smoldering Stage—Detected by photoelectric smoke detectors.
3. Flame Stage—Detected by flame detectors.
4. High Heat Stage—Detected by heat detectors.

NOTE: Gas-sensing fire detectors (a specialized application) are not commonly used.

---

not present, it will follow almost immediately. This stage is signaled by *flame detectors.*

In the *heat stage,* uncontrolled high heat and air that is rapidly expanding unite to make a dangerous combination that destroys property and claims lives. This stage is signaled by *heat detectors.*

Fire Detection Devices.   There are several types of devices for detecting fires and sounding alarms, all working on different principles. Some of the more common ones are described here.

Gas Detectors.   Gas detectors may be hard-wired or battery operated. They are placed at a specific location to detect a specific gas.

Smoke Detectors.   Smoke detectors may be hard-wired or battery operated, and they can be set up to serve a number of different functions, such as:

- Shut down air handling equipment.
- Start exhaust fans.
- Close fire doors.
- Provide elevator capture (preventing access except by fire fighters).
- Trigger extinguishing devices.
- Notify local fire department.
- Provide early warning to inhabitants.

Ionization-type smoke detectors respond to invisible particles of combustion. A small amount of radioactive material ionizes the air in the sensing chamber, thus rendering it conductive and permitting a current to flow through the air between two charged electrodes. This effectively gives the sensing chamber an electrical conductance. When smoke particles enter the ionization area, they decrease the conductance of air by attaching themselves to the ions, reducing the ions' mobility. When the conductance is below a predetermined level, the detector circuit responds by sounding an alarm. Ionization detectors are better for detecting fast-flaming fires. However, they can be affected by dust, humidity, and air currents.

Photoelectric smoke detectors respond to visible products of combustion. They commonly employ light scattering for detection. *Beam-type* detectors project a beam of light to a photo cell. Smoke between the light and the photo cell reduces the amount of light reaching the cell and triggers an alarm. In a *spot-type* detector, light is projected to a photo cell from a source positioned at a 90-degree angle to the photo cell. Smoke entering the chamber reflects the light into the photosensitive cell causing an alarm condition. Photoelectric smoke detectors are better for detecting slow-smoldering fires.

Other types of smoke detectors include *two-wire detectors* in which power to the detectors and alarm transmission are carried on the same pair of wires and *four-wire detectors* in which power to the detectors and for alarm transmission is supplied by separate pairs of wires. This type of smoke detector requires supervision of the power.

Duct detectors generally employ sampling tubes to monitor the air in supply and/or return ducts for the presence of smoke. (Typically, air output from the HVAC system is pulled through a sampling tube.) Detectors should be positioned six duct widths, minimum, from a 90-degree bend in the duct. They can be used to shut down the air-handling system in case of fire.

Flame Detectors.   There are two basic types of flame detection devices. The *ultraviolet (UV) type* detects flame which can be seen by the human eye; the *infrared (IR) type* detects flames not visible to the human eye.

Heat Detectors.   These devices are activated by rising temperatures, either directly (thermostats) or indirectly (rate-of-rise detectors). *Thermostat-type heat detectors* activate at a given temperature (e.g., 135°F, 190°F) or a given rate of change in temperature (15°F in one minute or faster); UL-listed thermostat contacts close when an alarm condition exists. Thermostat-type detectors are fixed devices that cover an area 15 by 15 feet (225 square feet) to 30 by 30 feet (900 square feet). They are available with three different types of elements.

1. Restorable bimetallic—This is similar to a home heating thermostat. The element flexes at a given temperature.

2. Replaceable eutectic element—The heat collector element melts at a given temperature and is replaceable.

3. Nonreplaceable eutectic element.

Fire Alarm Terminology

Air Sampling-Type Detector This type of device consists of piping or tubing distributed from a detector unit to the area to be protected. An air pump draws air from the protected area back to the detector through the air-sampling ports and piping or tubes. At the detector, the air is analyzed for fire products.

Heat Detector A device that detects abnormally high temperature or rate of temperature rise.

Line-Type Detector A device in which detection is contained along a path. Typical examples are rate-of-rise (ROR) pneumatic tubing detectors, projected-beam smoke detectors, and heat-sensitive cable.

Nonrestorable Detector A device whose sensing element is designed to be destroyed in the process of detecting a fire.

Rate-of-Rise (ROR) Detector A device that responds when the temperature rises at a rate exceeding a predetermined number of degrees.

Restorable Detector A device whose sensing element is not ordinarily destroyed by the process of detecting a fire; restoration may be manual or automatic.

Smoke Detector A device that detects the visible or invisible particles of combustion.

Spot-Type Detector A device whose detecting element is concentrated at a particular location. Typical examples are bimetallic detectors, fusible alloy detectors, and smoke detectors.

Thermal Lag When a fixed-temperature device operates, the temperature of the surrounding air will always be higher than the operating temperature of the device itself. The difference between the operating temperature of the device and the actual temperature of the air is commonly spoken of as *thermal lag* and is proportional to the rate at which the temperature is rising.

A *rate-of-rise (ROR) heat detector* is a pneumatic-type device which detects a sudden rise in temperature (approximately 15 degrees in 60 seconds). These units will also trip at a fixed temperature. The device contains an air chamber with a calibrated vent hole. If air expands faster than it can be vented, pressure moves a diaphragm which closes the contact. These detectors cover an area 15 by 15 feet (225 square feet) to 30 by 30 feet (900 square feet), and units self-restore after rate-of-rise action. Some ROR heat detectors also incorporate a fixed temperature eutectic element which destroys the entire detector when activated.

Other Alarm Devices. While not detection devices themselves, *pull stations* are commonly employed alarm devices. In buildings, they may be mounted behind glass that must be broken to access the pull mechanism, which is used to manually activate an alarm. The device is mechanically latched to prevent the activator from restoring it to the "normal" position.

False Alarms.   False alarms can be caused by a variety of factors, among them:

- People problems (human errors).
- Smoke detector location.
- Improper installation of alarms.
- Humidity.
- Insects.
- Noncompatibility.
- Radio frequency (RF) interference.
- Induced smoke.
- Smoke detector sensitivity.

False alarms can have undesirable consequences, including residents and tenants not bothering to investigate alarms, volunteer fire departments not responding to a real alarm, and fire chiefs reducing their engine assignments.

Fire Extinguishing Equipment

There are two types of *sprinkler systems.* In a "wet" system, water in pipes maintains a certain pressure holding a clapper closed. When the sprinkler head releases, water flows and extinguishes the flames. In a "dry" system, air pressure in the pipes holds the clapper closed, and air pressure is maintained by a compressor. When the sprinkler head releases, the air pressure drops rapidly, the clapper opens, and water flows to extinguish the flames. Switches in the sprinkler systems respond to water flow or low pressure which triggers the release of the sprinkler head.

Fire extinguishers are available in four different types. Each type is designed for different applications based on the type of material involved in the fire. Fire extinguishers should be inventoried and recharged as needed; usually local fire ordinances require extinguishers to be checked on an annual basis and certified to be in operating order. Your local fire department may be able to do a survey of your property for the purposes of identifying problems and making various recommendations for corrections that will reduce your risk of fire.

Fire Prevention and Protection

A variety of resources are available to assist real estate managers in developing fire prevention and fire protection programs as part of a property's

---

Fire Extinguishers

Class A—water-based—use to extinguish fires in paper, wood, etc.
Class B—chemical-based—use to extinguish fires involving grease or other flammable liquids.
Class C—dry-chemical—use to extinguish fires in electrical equipment.
Class ABC—multipurpose—can be used against all types of fires.

---

operations. Those listed in the following sections are generally national in scope. Some sources closer to home include your insurance agent and the local fire department.

Inspection Manual.   One readily useful aid for inspection is the *NFPA Inspection Manual*. This pocket book is designed to be carried by individuals on actual inspections. It includes references to items that are most frequently needed, and it covers inspection procedures for all types of properties, common and special hazards, building features and accessories, fire brigades, inspection of fire protection equipment, and many other items.

Building Codes.   Building codes are designed to control construction, alteration, repair, moving, and demolition of buildings. Building codes may also establish fire limits and define the type of construction that may be erected within them. There are five recognized model building codes in current use in the United States and Canada in addition to certain state building codes. The following codes differ considerably in form and arrangement, but they are all revised periodically to keep them up to date.

National Building Code, available from American Insurance Association, 1130 Connecticut Avenue, NW, Suite 1000, Washington, D.C. 20036 (phone: 202-828-7100).

Uniform Building Code, available from International Conference of Building Officials, 5360 Workman Mill Road, Whittier, California 90601 (phone: 800-336-1963).

National Building Code of Canada, available from National Research Council, Government of Canada, Ottawa, Ontario, Canada (phone: 613-954-8211).

Southern Standard Building Code, available from Southern Building Code Congress International, 900 Montclair Road, Birmingham, Alabama 35213 (phone: 205-591-1853).

Basic Building Code, available from Building Officials and Code Administrators International (BOCA), 4051 West Flossmoor Road, Country Club Hills, Illinois 60478 (phone: 708-799-2300).

Fire Prevention Code.   The Fire Prevention Code is a set of regulations recommended by the American Insurance Association of the United States. A similar set of regulations, National Fire Code of Canada (cited as the Fire Prevention Bylaw), is recommended by the National Research Council for Canada. These regulations govern conditions that are hazardous to life and property from the standpoint of fire and explosion. They also govern the storage and handling of hazardous materials and devices. The codes further regulate conditions that result from the use or occupancy of buildings or premises. The Fire Prevention Codes provide safeguards which are necessary for the protection of life and property from the use of flammable liquids, gases, hazardous chemicals, and explosives.

The Fire Prevention Code is revised every few years to keep it current. The various editions have been adopted by hundreds of communities and no community can afford to be without a fire prevention code. Where state laws permit, many cities adopt the code by reference. This practice requires a brief "adoption ordinance."

Other Sources.   There are also many organizations and agencies that actively promote the various phases of fire prevention and fire protection and whose services may be used by those engaged in fire protection work. A partial list includes:

> American Insurance Association (AIA)
> Bureau of Explosives
> Canadian Underwriters Association
> Factory Insurance Association
> Factory Mutual System (FM)
> Federal Fire Council
> International Association of Fire Chiefs
> International Association of Fire Fighters
> International Fire Service Training Association (IFSTA)
> National Bureau of Standards (NBS)
> National Fire Protection Association (NFPA)
> National Safety Council (NSC)
> Southeastern Underwriters Association
> Underwriters Laboratories, Inc. (UL)
> United States Department of Agriculture (USDA)
> United States Department of Interior (DOI)

Closed-Circuit Television

For years people have been intimidated by closed-circuit television (CCTV)—they tend to think of it as "Big Brother is watching." There are also those who think dummy cameras are a good idea, but they are not because dummy cameras imply surveillance when none is actually taking place.

CCTV is not complicated—its purpose is surveillance and deterrence. The basic system comprises a camera, a monitor, and a time-lapse recorder. The quality of the equipment will determine the capabilities of the system and the quality of its imaging. It is best to see demonstrations of several different systems before committing to a particular one. Your surveillance requirements and goals should guide your choice of equipment. Warranties, service, and the ability to be upgraded or expanded in the future can be important considerations. Other questions that should be explored before selecting a CCTV system include the following:

- What is the application?
- If an indoor application, is the lighting adequate?
- If an outside application, what kind of weather and climatic conditions have to be anticipated?
- What kind of resolution is needed?
- What range of distance is to be surveilled?
- Is there any blockage of view in the area to be surveilled?
- In selecting a camera, is consideration being given to the possibility of a pan and tilt type?
- In selecting a lens, is consideration being given to the distance to be covered? How the images will be used? Lighting requirements? Weather?
- Who will be monitoring the cameras and for what purpose?

- Will everything be monitored? Or, will monitoring be triggered when movement within range occurs?
- What type of backup is provided if a camera fails?
- Will video placement disturb intrusion sensors?
- What is the possibility of an intruder bypassing the proposed system?
- What is the available budget?
- What will it cost to upgrade the system? Can it be upgraded?
- What other functions will the CCTV fulfill?

Adequate lighting is imperative for indoor applications, while for cameras set up outdoors, weather conditions may necessitate a housing to protect the camera from moisture and/or temperature extremes.

Choice of camera lens is also important—be sure to buy the correct lens for the intended application. Do you need a wide-angle or telephoto lens, or will a standard lens suffice? Each type of lens provides a different picture ranging from a large area with extraneous details (wide-angle) to a highly focused close-up (telephoto) or somewhere in between. Cameras with zoom lenses include a range of view. The choice of lens should be based on the area to be surveilled and the goals of that surveillance.

Monitoring is another important aspect of a CCTV installation. Surveillance without analysis of the activity under observation is operationally inadequate and not cost justifiable. However, it may not be practical to monitor everything all the time. Limiting monitoring to movement within camera range may be a preferable approach. This is referred to as viewer-initiated video.

In choosing a company to install a closed-circuit television system, the best approach is one of care and caution. CCTV equipment should be installed by company-trained technicians (not subcontractors or moonlighters), and the firm should have managers on call at all times to troubleshoot problems. As with any contractor, the installer should be required to provide proof of workers' compensation insurance. Ideally, the contract will provide for periodic inspections and preventive maintenance service and protection against service disruption from severed telephone lines if the system requires remote transmissions. The contract should also include a full disclosure, in advance, of all the equipment makes and models that will be used in creating a system for you. (Anticipated costs of the equipment, installation, and ongoing service should also be disclosed.) Finally, it is desirable to have a "hands-on" trial, also in advance, to help you and your personnel understand how the equipment operates and its surveillance capabilities. In sophisticated systems, there may be banks of TV screens and one or more control panels, or the entire operation may be controlled through a computer. You should ask yourself how sophisticated a system you need to accomplish your surveillance goals efficiently and cost-effectively. You will also need to assess the potential for the proposed system to be bypassed and consider enhancements to the system to minimize that potential.

Visual Monitoring via CCTV

John I. Kostanoski

The purpose of a visual monitoring system is to provide visual information of a loss event in real-time—as opposed to time-past, as is the case with photography. Security can react to a crime, and camera observations recorded with time-date-location framing can be used as evidence in court because they show *what* took place and *when* it took place. In effect, a crime can be detected and a criminal recognized and identified *before* the perpetrator can escape from the crime scene.

Visual monitoring offers a novel approach to avoiding the false alarm problems of commercial, institutional, industrial, and governmental organizations. Both police and security—and, consequently, businesses, through fines—pay a heavy price for false alarms. For example, the Toronto Metropolitan Police Department has estimated a cost factor of $130 per call, and false alarms occur frequently—9 to 9.5 of every 10 signals issued. It is not uncommon for police and security to be devoting a sizable proportion of their service calls to alarm signals, with limited resources being expended on responses to false alarms. Toronto is not alone: Cities in the United States—Chicago and Los Angeles, for example—estimate they spend $10 million and $25 million, respectively. Visual monitoring of crimes against businesses can end much of this waste by allowing a remote operator to inspect a building via CCTV before calling security or the police. If an intruder is present, the person can be "captured" on tape, and the monitor operator can direct security to the intruder's location or provide police with a "hard copy" description. Visual monitoring is an approach with a twenty-first century solution; by comparison, other false alarm reduction programs are obsolete.

On-Site and Off-Site Visual Monitoring

The Security-Imaging Systems Laboratory, a technology transfer center of the State University of New York at Farmingdale, currently houses technology with which to demonstrate the design features and protection functions of both local and remote visual monitoring systems (*top* image in accompanying box).

Local Visual Monitoring.   The task in on-site monitoring is to connect the cameras to a recording device such as a video recorder. The new and improved way is to use a digital multiplexer. A multiplexer sends multiple camera images to a single monitor and also prepares multiple camera outputs for recording onto a single two-hour videotape. The old and cumbersome way was to use a video switcher which would run through the camera images sequentially. The problem was that the switcher would dwell on each camera view for 4–5 seconds before moving to the next camera. In a sixteen-camera system, one "cycle" would take up to 80 seconds (nearly 1½ minutes) to be completed; the multiplexer performs the same task in .26 second (more than 300 times faster). Obviously, with the use of a video switcher, much surveillance intelligence would be lost because the image from any one camera would not be picked up again for 80 seconds.

The multiplexer sends as much information as possible in the shortest amount of time. Essentially, it is a recording control system. It differs from the video switcher in that it gathers complete pictures from multiple cameras through a process known as time division multiplexing—a process that first digitally slices and then combines video fields to produce full frames for human viewing. It is extremely fast. If a video switcher were to run through camera images sequentially at anywhere near the speed of a multiplexer, the monitor operator would not be able to understand what he or she was looking at because the human mind is unable to absorb so much information in such a short period of time.

Another advantage of a multiplexer-based visual system to a property manager is cost reduction. A multiplexer limits the number of monitors needed in a multiple-camera system. Then, too, it limits the amount of property space, the number of personnel, and maintenance needed to operate a security control center. A control center could conceivably be one security desk, as it is theoretically possible to have as many as 128 cameras flashing across a single monitor screen.

Multiplexer Keyboard Control.   The multiplexer keyboard (*bottom* image in box) enables an operator to manage the following visual functions:

Full Screen: Any one camera in the system can be selected, and its field of view will occupy the whole screen.

CCTV Visual Monitoring Controls

Top: The technology engine that drives the visual monitoring system of the Security Imaging System Laboratory is a Dedicated Micros Uniplex Series 2 Duplex Multiplexer *(top unit)* for local or on-site visual monitoring, and a Dedicated Micros Digital Video Storage and Transmission (DVST) transceiver *(bottom unit)* for remote or off-site visual monitoring.

Bottom: The keyboard at the top of the photograph operates the Uniplex multiplexer; the dark keyboard below it operates the DVST transceiver.

Photographs by Gary Moo Young. Courtesy of John I. Kostanoski and Security-Imaging Systems Laboratory, State University of New York at Farmingdale.

Four-Way Split: The screen can be split into quadrants, and four separate cameras can be selected to occupy the individual quadrants.

Multiscreen: The screen can be split into five different multiscreen modes:

8 plus 2 cameras—8 cameo and 2 quadrant sized pictures;
12 plus 1 camera—12 cameo and 1 quadrant sized pictures;
16 cameras—16 cameo sized pictures;
4 plus 3 cameras—4 cameo and 3 quadrant sized pictures; and
9 cameras—the screen is divided into 9 equal-sized cameo pictures.

Picture-in-Picture (P-in-P): A quadrant-sized picture is superimposed on a full-screen camera display. The superimposed picture can be an image from a single camera or a quadrant-sized picture with 4 separate compressed images from 4 different cameras. Also, the P-in-P "screen" can be located in any one of the four corners of the monitor screen.

Live, Encode, and Decode Modes: A multiplexer compresses up to 16 (or more) camera pictures onto a single monitor screen nearly simultaneously. This is the *live* mode and includes all the various screen displays (full, four-way, multiscreen, picture-in-picture) as well as the time, date, and camera location at the base line of the picture(s). Also, the multiplexer records selected images or all of the camera pictures to a single videotape—this is the *encode* mode. Video recordings can be viewed on the monitor screen, and all of the screen displays are available to the viewer—this is the *decode* mode of the multiplexer. The multiplexer featured in the photograph (*bottom* image) is a duplex type, which means it can encode camera pictures to a video recorder while simultaneously producing camera images in the various screen displays on the monitor.

Sequence: Any or all of the cameras can be included in a sequence mode, and the speed at which sequencing occurs is user-programmable.

VCR: The VCR key displays camera pictures being sent for processing and recording to the VCR.

Telemetry: The telemetry function operates up to 16 pan-tilt-zoom lens cameras. Numeric arrow keys control a camera's pan movement (horizontal) as well as its tilt movement (vertical) and offers up to ten preset and focused camera positions. Zoom and focus keys allow for manual operation of both near and far camera views. Any camera can be programmed to randomly move throughout all preset positions in preset time modes to conduct proactive on-site security patrols.

Remote Visual Monitoring. Digital video storage and transmission (DVST) technology serves two very important functions for the property manager:

1. It provides visual verification of an intrusion event at a property site and thus reduces false alarms as well as fines; and

2. It conducts proactive visual patrols of remote property sites and thus reduces the recurring costs of security guards.

In effect, DVST can remotely monitor—and therefore help control—violence, theft, and other crimes against businesses across a street, a state, the nation, and around the world in a price-conscious manner (i.e., the cost of a phone call).

In terms of the first function (verification), DVST can monitor and react to alarms and emergencies as a camera locks into the location of a disturbance and transmits a full-screen picture to the monitoring desk. That is, the transceiver (a unit that both transmits and receives) *automatically* calls the monitoring desk and freeze-frames its picture (with time, data, camera number, and location) onto a monitor screen until acknowledged by an operator. The operator clears the screen and allows other pictures to come in and, in the event of a verifiable intrusion, records the violation to provide security or the police with a "hard copy" description of the violator.

With reference to the second function, a monitor operator can conduct proactive security patrols and move cameras sited at distant properties both horizontally and vertically, thus offering broad sweeping views of the interiors of facilities (which may be located nationally or internationally). Its motorized zoom lens moves across different focal length ranges, offering both near and far views, from telephoto (close-up) to wide-angle fields of view. In this way it can capture the facial features of an intruder—i.e., make an acceptable recording—to meet the legal test of identification in a court of law. It is one thing to recognize a person and quite another to identify him or her—a distinction marked by the number of pixels an intruder's facial features fills on a television monitor screen. The difficulty here is that intruders do not like to be seen because they do illegal things. For them, intrigue is existence. For the DVST transceiver, the unveiling of an act cloaked in subterfuge is the rationale of its existence. Remote operation of a camera's pan-tilt-zoom lens allows a monitoring operator thousands of miles away to move the camera in concert with the movements of the intruder and record characteristics unique to that individual and, with what has to be regarded as an ingenious telemetry capability, achieve the all-important goal of identifying him or her.

DVST Keyboard Control.   The DVST keyboard depicted in the photograph (*bottom* image) enables an operator to manage the following remote visual functions:

Full Screen: Same as multiplexer keyboard control.

Four-Way Split: Same as multiplexer keyboard control.

Multiscreen: Up to 16 cameo-sized pictures are displayed.

Telemetry: Same as multiplexer keyboard control but with remote capabilities.

Color: Transmission of remote picture can be in color.

HiLo: Transmission of remote pictures can be either in high or low resolution as well as full screen, multiscreen, or quadrant size. The rate of picture transmission is determined by the size, resolution, and color of the images. For example, a low resolution black-and-white quadrant size picture can be sent at the rate of about 5 frames per second, full-screen black-and-white at .88 second, and full-screen color at 1.2 seconds.

Line: The DVST transceiver sends, receives, and records full-frame images through the integrated service digital network (ISDN) basic rate interface service. ISDN provides 128 kilobits per second of transmission as the two "B" channels of the service which are rated at 64K each are utilized simultaneously. The charge per minute by NYNEX, the phone company serving the New York–Long Island region in which the SUNY Laboratory is located, is 10 cents per minute. The cost of a long-distance call incurred by the Laboratory as a result of the remote monitoring of cameras in a facility in Reston, Virginia, was 26 cents per minute; and the cost of installing ISDN service is the same as installing ordinary phone service. In fact, DVST can be used over ordinary voice-grade phone lines, but video images are transmitted at a slower rate, a full frame every 6 to 13 seconds.

Freeze Framing and Digital Zooming: Camera pictures can be frozen in the full-screen display for closer examination and study. An area of interest of the picture can be enlarged (doubled in size) with a digital 2× zoom. Each segment of a single picture can be enlarged in this manner. The picture is not being digitally altered; rather, the pixels in the picture are being magnified.

Sequence: Same as multiplexer keyboard control. DVST utilizes the Joint Photographic Experts Group (JPEG) standard of digital video compression and does not "conditionally refresh" or "digitally alter" video images, an important police and security feature that has legal implications.

The Technology of the Future

In the past, intrusion-detection systems reported alarm signals digitally as tones over voice-grade phone lines to a central station alarm company. The data were translated into a numeric code to indicate the source of the alarm as well as the zone that had been violated, presumably by an intruder. Enter

DVST. It, too, sends signals over the phone lines—analog video signals that are converted into a compressed digital form and transmitted from a property site to a transceiver at a remote monitoring station. The signal is translated back into analog form and transferred onto the pixels of a monitor screen to "paint" pictures, each worth more than a thousand words to a jury.

It is as if one has been time-warped into a new dimension in which buildings are no longer buildings but starships in cyberspace. The functionality of the technology seems no different than those sophisticated sensor probes launched into deep space by the U.S.S. Enterprise in *Star Trek*. Good science may or may not flow from good science fiction, but security clearly is traveling on the information superhighway with a real-time visual presence and profound interactive capabilities. Security as a function no longer needs to be limited to only one time and one place; a new digital technology is instantaneously transferring the function to multiple property sites in the here and now of cyberspace.

Security Guards

Security guards are hired for the purpose of protecting assets—both people and property. The following is a checklist of points to consider in the utilization of security guards.

- The extent of the service needed—Ask the prospective guard company to conduct a security survey of your property to identify vulnerabilities. The survey should include a review of your key control policies and practices as well as evaluation of doors, locks, windows, lighting, and signage. This information is needed to determine how many security officers are needed.

- The type and amount of training needed—What specific training will security officers be given before coming on your property? What additional training will they have to be given?

- The intended duties of the guards—Guards' duties may include patrolling the premises, monitoring interior and exterior locations via CCTV, escorting employees and others to their vehicles after hours (or when it is dark), controlling access to the property or the building (or monitoring the equipment for access control), or all of these and more. The specific duties often depend on the number of officers per shift assignment and the unique features of the property as well as its location and use or occupancy.

- The extent of patrol—By what routes and how often will guards patrol the property? What procedures and/or equipment are needed to validate the patrol activities? Consider that it is important to vary the patrol routes and schedules so a "routine" will not be obvious to an observer intent on unauthorized entry.

Qualifying a Security Guard Company

- Determine whether the security guards are salaried employees of the guard company or independent contractors.

- Verify proper licensing in compliance with local and state law. Note that simply being told by a guard company that it is licensed is not sufficient. The landlord or manager should check this out personally.

- Verify that the guard company has an adequate screening process, possibly including a standardized psychological test such as the Minnesota Multi-Phasic Personality Inventory. Likewise, verify that the guards have passed an annual physical examination, which ensures that their guards meet all state and local requirements.

- Consider requiring a clear criminal record. (Special attention should be paid to the security guards' criminal records, if any.)

- Other requirements might include the ability to communicate well in English, literacy, having a driver's license, etc.

- Verify that the guard company will not overwork its guards, providing fatigued, less-than-fully-capable individuals.

- Make it clear that the guard company is an independent contractor.

- Specify guard company duties and include penalties for failure to meet contract obligations.

- Provide an "out" for the landlord to terminate the security guard contract for any reason.

- Authority of the guards—What provisions will be made for supervising the guard force? What chain of command will be in effect? What will be the priority of people to be contacted by guards in the event of a breach of security, a criminal incident, or other emergency?

- Company policies—Will guards interact with other employees or building occupants, or will they keep a low profile and work in the background?

- The type and extent of documentation of incidents—How will guards' activities be recorded and reported? How widely will such documentation be circulated?

In addition to training by the guard company and by the hiring company (guards need an orientation to the property and the people and facilities on it), a security guard force will need policies and procedures to follow. They will also need lists of emergency contacts—supervisors, executives, property management staff members, lock companies, locksmiths, companies that service other security devices and systems, and local community resources (police, fire, ambulance)—and the types of emergency situations in which to call upon these people.

Guards' logs and incident reports should be reviewed daily, and security officers' procedures and protocols should be evaluated periodically. These may need revision because of installation of newer equipment, a change in the number of security personnel, or an incident that has revealed a weakness in the property's security.

Usually guard service is provided under a *contract.* The agreement should spell out all the duties to be performed, the numbers of individuals to be assigned to your property, and the requisite qualifications of those personnel. Provision for replacing individuals or groups of guards whose performance is unsatisfactory should be included, as should a provision allowing you to terminate the contract if the terms are breached and corrective measures are not implemented. Requirements for guards to wear uniforms (or not) and the issues of firearms and use of force are other important contents of the contract. Responsibility for payroll and employee benefits for the guards, assignment of replacement personnel when guards are absent (for illness, vacation, etc.), and appropriate insurance coverages (liability, worker's compensation) should also be addressed.

The importance of high levels of liability insurance (in the range of $5 to $10 million) should not be overlooked. The guard company should have adequate liability insurance and provide proof of such coverage in the form of a *certificate of insurance* before starting the assignment. (The contract should require the property owner and the management company to be identified as additional named insured parties on the policy.) It is prudent for the property owner or the manager to verify the coverage with the insurance carrier (certificates of insurance have been falsified). As an added safeguard, you can check the insurance company's rating (A. M. Best Company in Oldwick, New Jersey, is an independent source for such data), and it is a good idea to establish a minimum acceptable ranking (e.g., no lower than B+). It should also be noted that many insurers will not provide coverage on liability claims for armed guards that are not certified peace officers (e.g., off-duty police), so the issue of firearms needs to be looked at very carefully.

Hiring a contract guard service is an area where the property manager can benefit from advice of legal counsel and one's insurance carrier. Compliance with applicable laws as well as changes in the insurance status of the property (also its owner and the management company) are important considerations to be explored *before* a guard service is employed. Local law enforcement agencies may be able to make general recommendations about property security needs and legal implications as an added preparatory step.

Once guard service is in place, its role can be increased but rarely decreased. Perceptions of increased versus decreased security among building occupants—residents, commercial tenants and their employees—are

Characteristics of Different Levels or Qualities of Security Guard Service

High-End Service

1. Uniformed, high-profile guards who are former police officers and who are particularly well trained.

2. Such guards might walk through an entire building or project, punching in with a system that verifies that the entire premises is being patrolled properly and in a timely manner.

3. If they are in a motor vehicle, it would be an "official" vehicle, bearing the emblem of the guard company.

4. They may or may not be armed, but they would certainly have a means of readily communicating with the on-site or off-site "central station."

5. At this level, the landlord might also expect the security officer to make a log entry of any vehicle coming onto the premises and any people who might seek to gain access.

6. For after-hours assistance, such a guard might carry a beeper so that tenants working late could secure an escort for the walk to their automobile.

7. Supervisory personnel might check on the on-site personnel at irregular intervals.

Low-End Service

1. Non-uniformed, low-wage personnel who have no substantial security training.

2. No patrols of the premises or no mechanism for verifying that the guard has patrolled.

3. The guard's personal vehicle, with no special markings.

4. No means for the guard to communicate with the "central station" except, perhaps, a public pay phone in the lobby or an elevator phone.

5. No logging of people coming onto the property.

6. No easy method for tenants to contact the guard.

7. No spot-checking by supervisory personnel.

another important consideration in choosing to use a guard service and selecting the company to provide the guard force.

As with any contracted service, issuing specifications or a request for proposal (RFP) to several qualified vendors is recommended. More precise specifications and requirements should allow vendors to develop proposals that can be compared. Then, in your evaluation of proposals or bids, it is important to look at more than the "bottom line." Some questions to be asked are:

- How do the hourly (or other) rates compare among bidders?
- What is included in the regular service fee?
- Does the guard company provide ongoing training and refresher courses for its personnel?
- Are you contracting for union or non-union labor? (Union contracts typically define working conditions as well as wages and benefits.)
- How does the vendor qualify the personnel it hires? (Educational requirements and background checks are key considerations. Use of psychological profile tests is also helpful.)
- How do business references characterize the vendor? (Satisfied clients who can attest to the quality of personnel and service are preferred references to contact as well as the vendor's financial institution. A guard service contract is often a major financial commitment for the purchaser of services.)

In the qualifying of individual guards, it is desirable for them to have a "clear" criminal record. This may be difficult to address satisfactorily, but it should be possible, at a minimum, to distinguish what is a clearly unacceptable record (e.g., conviction for burglary or assault) from minor infractions that are not relevant to the assigned duties (e.g., a long-ago arrest for a single incident of driving under the influence). The ability to communicate is another important requirement. In addition to English, it may be necessary or desirable for guards to be able to communicate in whatever other language is spoken where they are assigned.

What you will receive for the dollars charged, the reputation of the guard company, and the caliber of the personnel who would be assigned to your property are all important considerations. In security as in other services, biggest is not necessarily best, nor is the lowest fee a guarantee of cost-effective service.

Security Training

Christopher A. Hertig

For the overwhelming majority of organizations in the protection industry, training is conspicuous by its absence. It is talked about and written about but rarely happens. The following is a frank and informal discussion of the realities of security training today—why it does not happen as well as how to make it happen. The idea is to *manage training to minimize losses and maximize profits.*

Training Non-Security Personnel

Non-security personnel should receive instruction that is appropriate for their roles and functions. This varies for every employee, and a job task analysis will reveal the necessary customization of training for each position. Before undertaking a comprehensive job task analysis, there are a few simple questions that can be asked to help determine the subjects for instruction of non-security personnel.

- What are their normal job duties?
- What are their duties during emergencies?
- What duties do they share—in whole or in part—with security personnel?
- Which employees have contact with the public?

Addressing these questions will provide guidance for managers in determining the WHAT of training non-security personnel. The question regarding public contact can be used to group personnel based on such issues as:

Training

Training can be defined as an intense learning process whereby job knowledge, skills, and abilities are positively enhanced. The training process incorporates various teaching/learning methods. It involves significant amounts of practice. It should be tested or validated in some manner.

Training is an intensive process. It involves significant amounts of practice in developing the skill necessary to perform the job task in question. It does not consist of a briefing by a manufacturer's representative on how to operate the new access control system. It is not a single lecture from an attorney on the lawful use of force. Nor is it a sole class on public relations. In order to be effective and not a waste of time and money, training must consist of continuous learning—there must be enough practice for the trainee to develop to an appreciable degree the skills being taught.

Who comes into contact with visitors? Who is likely to answer the phone when a bomb threat is received?

A review of your existing crisis or emergency plan can uncover some training gaps. If there are functions that need to be performed and employees have not had the necessary training to perform them, this gap needs to be filled via some type of instruction, or the emergency plan should be revised, or both. Simply assessing what has transpired during prior incidents is another strategy to find gaps in training. A group discussion, individual interviews, or a survey form will aid in this discovery.

In general, both security and non-security personnel should have some training in the following areas:

Communications

Interpersonal relations

Reporting loss-causing (or merely suspicious) events

Fire protection, prevention, and response

Emergency situations (natural or man-made disasters, bomb threats, hazardous materials incidents)

Safety

While this is a very rudimentary analysis, the astute manager can see the obvious importance of certain topics because they carry over into the realm of security and safety but are important in their own right: Communication skills are critical for good business practice as well as emergencies. Interpersonal relations facilitates dealing with customers, clients, tenants, and employees in regular business settings as well as being a real asset when one is confronted by a violent person.

Advantages of Security Training

- More productive employees who are more efficient, doing the job the right way in less time.
- Enhanced relations between employees and management as employees understand management's objectives and priorities.
- Increased professional identity of employees who feel more committed to their jobs.
- More job satisfaction by employees who also feel pride in their work— managers will feel this way, too.
- Increased loyalty to the employer who has demonstrated an interest in and commitment to employees by training them.
- Decreased turnover due to greater satisfaction among employees who are better prepared to solve problems on the job.
- Fewer accidents and mistakes.
- More ethically correct decisions—employees doing the right thing in the right way.
- A degree of protection from allegations that management is negligent in preparing personnel to do their jobs—in civil liability parlance: failure to train, instruct, and/or supervise.

The Role of Security Personnel

Although most people do not realize it, security officers are actually adjunct members of the management team. As management representatives, they make a variety of decisions on behalf of management. Security personnel are the ambassadors of the organization; they are an extension of its public relations efforts. They also serve as intelligence agents, compliance enforcers, and resources regarding a number of legal issues.

Management Representatives. Security personnel are often the ones through whom management speaks to employees, customers, visitors, vendors, clients, tenants, etc. In many situations, a security officer is the first person visitors see when entering a building or property and the last person they see when leaving it. In addition, security sometimes provides customer service. For example:

> Years ago there was a shopping mall that advertised its security services through the varied customer services the security force provided. Officers carried pocket directories of store tenants with each one's phone number and a description of its merchandise. This worked very well when answering shoppers' questions and giving directions. Officers also read menus from the various restaurants in

the mall as part of their training so they could respond to customers' wishes for a particular type of food or service. They jump-started automobiles and provided a variety of other individualized customer services as well.

One area in which security personnel play a key role is in victim assistance when an incident occurs. How a victim is attended and what he or she is told is very important. Victims who are treated poorly are not likely to take the side of management in legal affairs! A professional victim-assistance program staffed by customer-oriented security personnel is simply good business. Having all security force members assigned to public sites trained in first aid and CPR is a first step. In the mall environment mentioned previously, staff wearing Red Cross First Aid patches on the left shoulder of their uniforms seemed to generate positive reactions from patrons. Paramedics were included in the security force whenever possible. Additionally, the supervisor carried adhesive bandages and other first aid supplies in a pouch on his belt. A security officer putting a bandage on a small child was greatly appreciated by many a mother.

Intelligence Agents.   Security officers obtain all types of useful information for management. I remember doing a survey for the manager of a shopping mall on what effect moving the bus stops would have on tenants' business. My subordinates regularly reported on which stores closed early (a potential lease violation). We also kept this manager informed about the general state of business at the mall, the success of promotional efforts, and other aspects of mall operations. The manager was smart—he made the security staff work for their money and he got his money's worth. He also made the job stimulating and enjoyable.

There are organizations that have security officers delivering mail. While it may be arguable whether or not this is a true security function and whether or not it detracts from the vigilance required of security personnel, delivering mail allows the officers to interact with people throughout the facility. In this way, they are in a position to learn what is going on.

Compliance Enforcers.   Security officers are the ones who have to see that people who come onto the property comply with the rules and regulations developed by management. This needs to be done in an effective, professional manner.

Legal Resources.   Perhaps not as obvious as the other roles security officers play, their function as resources regarding various laws is important nonetheless. People generally do not think about how the security officer relates to the law. In some cases, they have a very myopic perspective, believing that only criminal law is relevant or that civil liability is the security officer's prime concern. However, much of what a security officer does affects people's jobs, so the officer is dealing with labor law. Also to be considered is regulatory law administered by federal, state, or local agencies: Security operations are intimately tied in with OSHA, EPA, and a host of other administrative agencies.

The Rationale for Training Security Personnel

There are numerous benefits to be derived from properly training security. One important one is that untrained officers can create problems. In particular, trained security officers can help *minimize losses* by:

- Uncovering loss exposures before they blossom into loss events.
- Responding properly to emergency situations.
- Assisting and developing a positive relationship with victims.
- Meeting and exceeding legislated training standards so that management is not negligent in the criminal or civil arena.
- Reporting loss events completely so that management has the best chance of defending itself against negligence claims.

Trained security officers can also help *maximize profits* by:

- Enhancing relations with the public. Because contact with visitors, tenants, and employees is usually through the security department, security personnel can be very productive as a public relations resource.
- Enhancing relations with police. This is critical. In emergencies and during investigations, considerably less management time is spent "cleaning up messes" if relations with police are positive and productive. The same is true in working with other emergency services (fire department, emergency medical services).
- Helping the operation run more smoothly. There are innumerable ways in which a well-run security department can help management of a facility or organization simply by being "the grease in the machine." One security department I know of is responsible for safety, fire protection, worker's compensation, employee communications, and the employee store in addition to security.

On the other hand, untrained security personnel can be the cause of such difficulties as:

- Inadequate, overly expensive asset protection. Because untrained officers will not identify the various loss-causing situations that management needs to know about, small problems can become big ones. Accidents, maintenance problems, and encounters with violent individuals can mushroom into major loss events.

- Civil liability for "failure to train." Companies with an untrained contract security force—or a well-paid but untrained proprietary force—are easy targets of lawsuits. Such suits are not hard for a plaintiff to win—or to gain a handsome settlement—because all that is needed are answers to a handful of key questions:

  Was the incident in question reasonably foreseeable?
  What training did the security personnel have regarding the incident in question?
  What documentation exists to support the assertion that the officers were trained?
  How much and what type of instruction was given?
  What were the credentials of the instructor who gave the training?
  Was the training material current and well researched?

Reasons Why Officers Are Not Trained

Companies that employ security personnel, whether under contract or as a proprietary force, often choose not to provide adequate or appropriate security training. There are a variety of reasons for this, including prejudice against security personnel, a tradition of not training them, and over-reliance on supervisory discretion and police response. Often there is no budget allocation for security, and there may be confusion as to what "training" really is. Scheduling conflicts, managers' lack of knowledge about training, and a shortage of appropriate training materials are other reasons often given. Management egos sometimes get in the way, adding to the complexity of the training issue. Misrepresentation by security contractors as to the training given to their officers is another, though external, aspect of the problem. All of these "reasons" will be addressed in what follows.

Prejudice.   Security officers are discriminated against to a great degree. The media reflect prejudice in the ways security personnel are portrayed in movies, and this fosters negative perceptions among the general public. Managers manifest prejudice by cutting budgets, looking for the cheapest—rather than the most cost-effective—means of staffing the security function.

Tradition.   Simply put, there has been no tradition of training security personnel in the United States. Outside of the nuclear arena where the U.S. Nuclear Regulatory Commission has mandated extensive training, there is still very little training required by government entities in this country. Even the Department of Defense doesn't require training for security personnel at its contractors' facilities.

Over-Reliance on Supervisory Discretion. The *theory* here is that "smart" supervisors will make "the right decisions" and that line officers do not need training. There is a certain amount of validity to this assertion. When there is strong leadership, people will perform better than when leadership is absent. It is the first-line supervisor who forms the backbone of an organization. Unfortunately there are several problems with this:

1. Supervisors cannot be everywhere at once making all decisions. Since the security officer is the person in charge after hours, it is simply logical that he or she should be competent to make discriminating judgments. In addition, some decisions have to be made under emergency conditions—there is no time to ask for direction from a supervisor. Other decisions are trivial—asking a supervisor for input on each and every small decision is simply not practical or desirable.

2. Some organizations promote security supervisors from the ranks of the untrained guard force. Wearing a white shirt does not make someone a *trained* supervisor.

3. Supervisor training is not technical in nature. Generally speaking, supervisors' training is related solely to supervision. Such training does not teach them about the use of force, traffic management, crowd control, incident scene investigation, bomb threats, fire protection, or other security-specific issues. A supervisor needs a basic mastery of these technical areas in order to direct others effectively.

Often supervision is used to sell security contracts. The standard sales pitch goes something like this: "Let's face it. We're all competing for people from the same labor pool. We pay our people the same wages as our competition. What makes our company different is the level of supervision." The amazing point is that some of these same firms *recruit their supervisors from the ranks of their untrained guard forces.* I reiterate: A new title or a white shirt does not make a trained supervisor.

Over-Reliance on Police Response. The traditional thinking here is that the police will respond and take care of any serious problems that occur; the security officer's role is simply to "observe and report" incidents. This may have been an appropriate perspective in the past, but certainly not in the 1990s. Here are a few reasons why exclusive reliance on the police can be detrimental.

1. *First aid*—the immediate and necessary care given to the victim of a medical emergency. In an emergency medical situation, the first few minutes count the most. Police or ambulance services arriving on the scene several minutes later do not solve the immediate prob-

lem. Additionally, police, fire, and ambulance response may become slower in the future. With the full utilization of 911, there are often too many calls to handle. Municipal budgets are also severely strained. Police deal with more calls for service per officer than they did in the past; they will probably have a heavier workload in the future.

2. *The media!* An incident can be videotaped by members of the public immediately. In one instance, a former student of mine who became a police officer killed a dangerous suspect, and three different videos of the incident were aired on local television. These videos were all taken by ordinary citizens who happened to be at the public event where the shooting took place. Cellular phones and satellite uplinks make local news stories of a few years ago into international events within a few short minutes. The only story that gets shown in such a situation will be how security officers handled the incident.

3. *A general avoidance mentality* settles in and sets up management for civil liability. One of the problems common to shopping centers is the handling of incidents by several different entities. While an individual tenant (bar, store, game room) will handle the problem individuals initially, mall security will become involved eventually, and still later the police may be called in. Liaison problems can and do occur. If the incident leads to a lawsuit, the plaintiff may name a variety of defendants who will then try to blame each other for the problem (a strategy of "divide and conquer"). In such situations, the organization with the least-trained, least-professional security staff has the greatest liability exposure.

An avoidance mentality also tends to demoralize and confuse the security staff. My own experiences in a shopping mall security operation were filled with thoughts of waiting for police response as I had been instructed. Realistic, assertive actions were not always taken, and incidents quickly degenerated into "mini-riots" on several occasions. If management sends a message to "not do anything, just call the police and wait for them," the effectiveness of security personnel will be decreased significantly. Additionally, if the officers are not trained in and oriented toward effective problem-solving, the situation usually gets worse. Once the police arrive, the security staff may be blamed for the problem.

Because the avoidance mentality is not motivating to security officers, they may vote with their feet—i.e., terminate their employment—and management then has to deal with all the problems of personnel turnover (among them, increased overtime, demoralization, decreased levels of customer and client service, the expense of hiring and training new officers).

Interestingly, the same phenomenon can occur when other protective forces are part of the mix:

- *Site security* at an entertainment complex is told that an entertainer's own personnel will handle disorderly persons coming on stage. The on-site security force is not trained in crowd management or eviction procedures for such situations, even though they will most likely interact with the entertainer's security force as well as have to control disorderly persons who are not on the stage.

- *Mall security* is not trained in retail theft laws because this is considered the individual retailer's responsibility, even though the mall security force will respond to calls for assistance from a store's security personnel.

Absence of Budgetary Allocation.   Many would say this is the biggest impediment to security training. Most organizations allocate very little money for training; some allocate nothing at all. Sometimes when money is designated for training, the security manager uses it to attend conferences rather than for the improvement of subordinate staff members.

When there is no budget, it is difficult to train people. It is also difficult to defend against allegations of negligence. Obviously there should be a training budget. Another strategy that may be employed on an interim basis is to apply funding from other sources to training.

Confusion about Training.   Very few people truly understand what "training" is. They confuse training with education, thinking that a learning experience (a lecture, a class, reading something out of a manual) is training. While such learning experiences are useful, they cannot be depended on to substantially impact job performance. Education may change the way one thinks; training should change the way one behaves. Training is more intensive than education and includes extensive practice.

A former chief training officer of mine put it this way: "When you are done with the handcuffing class, I want everyone to have red wrists." If everyone has red wrists, this is a basic measurement of adequate practice in applying the handcuffs. Compare this with the all too frequent approach to training of simply demonstrating a task and having the class members practice it a few times. I even remember attending a baton class where the instructor read out of a book and then demonstrated techniques with which he was not familiar.

Scheduling Difficulties.   A person can only be in one place at a time. Security personnel are often on duty 24 hours a day, 365 days a year. If everyone is to be trained during a classroom session, the class will have to be scheduled *at least twice.* If no one gets sick or takes vacation that day, or no new people are hired after the class, the entire security force may be trained in two class sessions. In addition,

> Managers have to pay overtime for people to be in class;
>
> Only a single topic will be addressed within a class, and
>
> People are only attentive 20–25 percent of the time while in class.

It is fairly easy to figure out that classroom training does not work too well for security forces.

Obviously, the main emphasis should be on having security personnel learn outside of a classroom environment as much as possible. Distance education via home study or work study programs, reading material and answering questions on it, viewing videotapes at home or listening to audio cassettes on the way to work are all strategies that can be used. Procedural manuals can be read and questions about them answered. The only face-to-face "training" time is when a supervisor briefly reviews the material with individual workers to ensure the employee's comprehension.

Managers' Lack of Training Know-How.   Lack of knowledge—and imagination—among managers regarding how to train is an ongoing issue. Most people think training is something that occurs in a classroom with an instructor. That is the familiar model. However, training need not follow that model. It can and should take various forms. This ties in with scheduling difficulties as well as the lack of budgetary allocation. Training must be given, but it cannot be only via classroom experience.

Training Materials.   There are not a lot of materials available for security training. Fortunately, this is changing for the better every day. (At the conclusion of this discussion is a list of some resources that may be consulted.) On the other hand, it is often decided not to purchase existing instructional material because it is not a perfect "fit." Managers will review a packaged training program or video and decide not to buy it because it does not address their particular needs. The problem with this is in the alternative, which is *not* training. The choice not to purchase a particular training package is fine; but regardless of the particular purchase choice, the need for training still exists. In most cases, however, there is simply no training. Typically, a more pressing matter comes along, and training is forgotten until the next security-related problem arises.

Ego.   The security manager's ego may be the biggest obstacle to security training. Very few of them will admit to their painfully obvious shortcomings in the training arena. Most will say something like the following:

> "I think we do a pretty good job emphasizing that area with our supervisors," or

"We have excellent cooperation with the local police," or even

"We have a series of professionally produced videotapes that all of our employees view."

While all of the preceding statements sound good, they are dodging the issue of what training the security force is actually being given. Some managers will brag about the wonderful guest lecturer they had or the great class that a few of their people attended. Again, this avoids the issue of providing adequate training to *all* members of the security force.

Misrepresentation in Contractors' Marketing.   This occurs when contract security services promote their firms via the training they provide. Usually it goes like this: "All our officers receive eight hours of training prior to being assigned to a client's job site. Once assigned to a client location they receive site-specific training."

What this means is that the officers are "trained" on their first day of work—in between filling out W-2 forms, getting fitted for uniforms, being interviewed, etc. Actual time spent in a learning mode is considerably less than eight hours. Most of the actual training time is spent watching a video and answering a few simple questions based on it. There is no active learning and no interaction with an instructor.

Subsequent on-site training consists of being told where to park and being shown around the job site—in other words, a superficial orientation to the property. While not unimportant in and of itself, this "training" is simply not enough to develop a productive security officer.

Companies sometimes market this way when they have a sophisticated training program or state-of-the-art instructional equipment—at their headquarters. Customers are told of the wonderful training program or gadgets that exist, but they are at headquarters, not the "field" offices. Few of the security officers actually benefit from the program because they never get to headquarters.

Another approach they may take is to tell clients that "people from the company" have undergone certain instruction—e.g., the FBI National Academy, the local police academy, or the National Crime Prevention Institute. Unfortunately, those particular people will not be the ones protecting your property.

Training Strategies and Tactics

There are several steps in strategizing the training of personnel responsible for security at managed properties, among them:

- Hire personnel capable of being trained.
- Train new hires before they start to work.

- Use off-the-shelf materials whenever possible. (It is more economical than starting from scratch, and the material can be supplemented with situation-specific examples.)

- Use videotapes and other "distance learning" options to maximize productivity and minimize costs.

- Use classroom training when necessary and appropriate and reinforce the learning experience with individual study and distance learning.

- Make learning a continuous process and measure people's progress.

- Train security and non-security personnel together for the benefit of both groups.

- Develop information resources that help trainers—and trainees—keep current.

Hiring and Training.   Hire experienced, educated personnel who can be trained. This does not mean you should hire people who have training already and neglect to train them yourself. It does mean you should hire the person with the most potential for benefitting from the training.

Once people are on board, they should be given as much pre-service instruction as possible. Reducing the number of unpleasant surprises on a new job is key to keeping employees happy and preventing problems. Security officers are no different. In fact, it is more important for them to be prepared to deal effectively with emergency situations and critical incidents. Security personnel can be effective ambassadors for the company only if they are well-integrated into the organization. They have to understand management's perspective and believe they are members of the management team if they are to represent management in a positive manner.

Training Materials.   For most training, programmed instruction is effective. Off-the-shelf materials save tremendous amounts of time and development costs. While they may not be a perfect match for your needs, they are considerably more beneficial than no training at all. Creative resource management is key here: Some vendors will work out payment plan options, and you may be able to share resources with other departments or divisions or organizations. Local security organizations can be a great asset in this regard.

You can also save time and money by utilizing distance education. In this way, you avoid paying overtime wages to people who are in a nonproductive classroom mode. A little distance education interwoven with other learning strategies (e.g., classes, job aids) goes a long way.

Some subjects can only be taught in a classroom or training center environment—first aid, CPR, defensive tactics, and similar "skills" that re-

---

Training Assessment Grid

Topic	Pre-Service	On-the-Job	CPO Program	In-Service Classes
Report Writing				
Legal Aspects				
Crime Scene				
Interviewing				
Safety				

---

quire demonstration and evaluated practice. However, these topics can and should be introduced beforehand—and reinforced afterward—via individual study and distance-learning media.

Continuous Learning.   Learning and growing should be a continuous process. Learning comes in episodes. People learn from attending and participating in a class, reading an article, critiquing how an incident was handled, or watching a video. The learning is reinforced by answering questions about the information presented to them via the different media. Relying on only a single episode or instructional strategy to train will not develop your personnel.

You also need to keep track of what security officers are learning and when. Whether or not training is adequately dispersed throughout the individual's employment can be assessed in a structured way by constructing a grid (see the abbreviated example in the accompanying box). In the left column, you can list the key topical areas, and in the other columns identify whether or not they are taught at each juncture of the individual's work experience. If there are supervisory reviews of an officer's reports during the officer's initial probationary period, then yes can be written in under on-the-job next to report writing. Report writing is covered in the Certified Protection Officer (CPO) program, and the employee who undergoes that training would rate a yes in the CPO column. If there are periodic in-service classes on report writing, then yes can be written in that column. Obviously, honesty is essential here. If no is entered for some subjects in one or more columns, the training process may have to be restructured. Ideally, a completed form for each employee would have a yes in each column for each subject or skill.

One way to approach continuous learning of classroom topics is to have the class members do *pre-work* prior to the class, *class work* in the class, and *post-work* after the class is finished. This approach gets learners warmed up for the class by having to think about what they are going to be learning—pre-work prepares the learner for the classroom experience. Post-work continues the learning process after the class. It also makes both the learner and the instructor accountable—post-work provides a means of evaluating the learning that took place.

Organizations that use the Certified Protection Officer (CPO) program can easily give pre-work assignments. All they need do is have the officers read a chapter in the course text, *The Protection Officer Training Manual*, and answer the questions at the end of the chapter. (There are 30 chapters in the text.) For a class on report writing, for example, the learner would simply read and answer the questions in the chapter on report writing. (A pre-work exercise for a class on emergency procedures could take the form shown in the accompanying box. This approach can be used for either security or non-security personnel.)

Once the class session is under way, the leader might simply review the emergency plan with a chart or a projected slide or overhead transparency (approximately 90% of learning is visual) and then go over the pre-work. This review could start with question #4, which could be an introduction or "icebreaker," or key points for dealing with various types of emergencies could be presented on an overhead. There are numerous approaches that can be taken to tailor the session so it addresses the specific learning needs of the organization. At the same time, this introductory activity can serve as a think tank or brainstorming session for upgrading and revising the emergency procedures already in use.

The class work itself could consist of a 10–20-minute problem-solving exercise using a specific example such as a power outage. This could start with a scenario developed along the following lines:

It is 9:00 P.M. on a Friday evening. All power has been lost. Address the following considerations:

Notification of appropriate personnel.
Investigation of the power loss.
Establishing alternate communications links.
Ensuring that vital records, equipment, and/or processes are not adversely affected.
Maintenance of safety in the building.
Controlling access to the area.

You have 10 minutes to complete this exercise.

This outline of a structured scenario illustrates how the class can be made an active-learning, problem-solving experience. It forces the class members

---

Sample Emergency Procedures Pre-Work Exercise

On *[insert scheduled date]* we will be having a training session on Emergency Procedures. Prior to class attendance it is imperative that the following questions be completed so that the answers may be shared with other class participants.

1. List your duties in a general emergency.

2. Which of these duties do you find to be most difficult?

3. List any emergencies that you have had to deal with while employed here.

4. What do *you* wish to learn from the class session on *[insert scheduled date]*?

---

to focus on real-world problems and ensures that learning is transferred from the classroom environment to the work environment.

As a subsequent post-work exercise employees could be assigned to re-write the emergency procedures for this type of situation; or the instructor could conduct a drill, or the class could be given a written evaluation to assess their learning. The latter might take the form of a take-home test. There are many approaches to post-work, and each instructor has to tailor these exercises to the needs of the organization.

Security as Part of the Team. Finally, security and non-security personnel should be trained together. There are numerous courses from which employees with different work assignments can benefit. Customer service, interpersonal communications, and business writing are some examples of non-security subjects about which security officers can learn something relevant to their job functions. Having officers attend the types of training given to other staff members can provide numerous benefits.

- Integration of the officers with the rest of the organization can occur more quickly and completely because of the shared learning experience.

- Training costs can be reduced or eliminated because specific training sessions are already set up—all that is required is to allow a few extra seats for the security officers.

- One outcome will be a better image of the security force and enhanced communications between the security department and the rest of the organization. As an integral part of the staff, security officers will be more likely to receive input from other employees about security problems that are developing.

- Previous learning will be reinforced, and that learning will be expanded as it is applied in different areas.

Information Sources.   To ensure continued successful training, you should get into the information pipeline. Many organizations simply appoint someone to coordinate training without giving that person access to the necessary information. Being on the mailing lists of publishers and video vendors is essential to finding out what instructional materials are available. Membership in local security and safety groups is key to lining up speakers and finding ideas for growing the training program and keeping its content current. Attendance at local and national seminars facilitates networking and helps you see the "big picture." Membership and participation in professional security organizations such as the American Society for Industrial Security (ASIS) provide educational and networking opportunities for all security personnel, regardless of their staff or supervisory position.

Training Resources

Organizations

The American Society of Law Enforcement Trainers (ASLET), 102 Dock Road, P.O. Box 361, Lewes, Delaware 19958-0361 (phone: 302-645-4080; fax: 302-645-4084).

ASLET is a group of more than 5,000 persons who teach, manage, and consult. Members have a vast array of specialties and they actively network with each other. Benefits include a subscription to the *ASLET Journal*, which is filled with reports on current research, opinion pieces, and book and video reviews, as well as tips and resources for teaching. Members also receive a *Directory and Resource Guide* along with discounts on books, training supplies, classes, and other items.

International Foundation for Protection Officers (IFPO), Bellingham Business Park, 4200 Meridian, Suite 200, Bellingham, Washington 98226 (phone: 360-733-1571; fax: 360-671-4329).

In Canada: 7500 MacLeod Trail S., Calgary, Alberta, T2H 0L9 (phone: 403-251-5227; fax: 403-251-5237).

The IFPO is a nonprofit educational organization dedicated to upgrading the professional status of security officers and supervisors. The organization has certified thousands of security officers throughout the world. Individuals who desire the Certified Protection Officer (CPO) certification must have a minimum of 6 months full-time experience as a protection officer (or the part-time equivalent), complete a distance-education course based on *The Protection Officer Training Manual,* and list several security or law enforcement supervisors as references. The CPO program was designed to make professional growth opportunities available, comprehensive, and recognized.

Managers who wish to send their personnel through the CPO Program can obtain *A Guide to Using the Certified Protection Officer Program as a Means of Organizational Development* from the IFPO at no cost. The *Guide* provides tips and strategies for incorporating the CPO Program with existing training as well as information on setting up training programs. The IFPO also has a certification program for supervisors. Candidates for certification in the Certified Security Supervisor (CSS) program must first complete a distance-education course titled "The Security Supervisor Program." They must then be nominated by several persons in supervision and/or management and meet the experience requirement (18 months full-time security experience with at least 6 months in a supervisory position).

Other Foundation programs include publications on crime prevention, careers in security, private investigation, security resources, civil liability, and other topics. There is a newsletter, and Associate Membership status is available for officers and supervisors. Associate Members receive their choice of a complimentary publication, a newsletter, discounts on Foundation publications and programs. There are also discounted life and health insurance plans available. Corporate memberships are available for employers wishing to enroll their entire staff as Associate Members.

Training Resources *(continued)*

American Society for Industrial Security (ASIS), 1655 North Fort Myer Drive, Suite 1200, Arlington, Virginia 22209-3198 (phone: 703-522-5800; fax: 703-243-4954).

ASIS is a multinational organization with 25,000 members who are security managers and directors responsible for loss prevention and security for private and public organizations. The ASIS Certified Protection Professional (CPP) program includes specific training in assets protection and examinations based on the training materials. Candidates must provide proof of professional experience (nine years of full-time security experience with at least two years in a supervisory role) plus professional references. To maintain standards of conduct, CPP applicants must adhere to a prescribed Code of Ethics.

ASIS also publishes a monthly journal *(Security Management)* and provides a variety of services to members, including publications of their own and from other publishers.

Professional Security Training Network (PSTN), 1303 Marsh Lane, Carrollton, Texas 75006 (phone: 800-942-7786; fax: 214-716-5352).

PSTN produces a wide variety of video programs on topics such as crowd control at special events, use of force continuum, and high rise security and safety. They also have a twelve-part Basic Security Officer Training Series which comes with instructor guides and test materials. PSTN offers a means of documentation for their programs as well as a subscription service.

Training Materials

Professional Training Resources (PTR), P.O. Box 439, Shaftsbury, Vermont 05262 (phone: 802-447-7832; fax: 800-998-9400).

PTR markets more than 200 different books and videos. Titles are available from various publishers and producers. Topical areas are crime prevention, security management, supervision, defensive tactics, etc. PTR also provides consultation in the area of supervisory development for security operations.

York College of Pennsylvania, Special Programs Office, Country Club Road, York, Pennsylvania 17405-7199 (phone: 717-846-7788; fax: 717-849-1607).

The Special Programs Office offers a wide variety of classes on the York College campus as well as at client locations. Classes on report writing, crowd management, defensive tactics, violence prevention, crime scene awareness, public relations, and other subjects are available. Additionally, the Special Programs Office sells the participant materials for these programs separately to people who are unable to attend classes or those who wish to develop their own classes. Each packet consists of a detailed subject matter outline, learning exercises, and sources of additional information.

Training Resources *(concluded)*

Publishers

Butterworth-Heinemann, 225 Wildwood Avenue, Woburn, Massachusetts 01801 (phone: 800-366-2665; fax: 800-446-6520).

Butterworth-Heinemann is the premier publisher of security books. Titles include *The Ultimate Security Survey; The Protection Officer Training Manual; CCTV Surveillance; The Security Officer's Handbook: Standard Operating Procedures; Office and Office Building Security, Second Edition,* and many others. Videos on certain topics such as defense against stalking and kidnapping are also available.

Communicorp, Inc., 220 Westmore/Meyers Road, Lombard, Illinois 60148-3041 (phone: 800-367-9274; fax: 630-629-7106)

Communicorp, Inc., produces an assortment of videos on such topics as patrol, courtroom procedures, courtesy in the function of security, and liability issues, among others. Selected tapes and testing materials are also available in Spanish.

Recommended Reading and Resources

For those interested in particular aspects or tools of security, we commend the books and publications listed here as additional reading and resources. They address in greater detail many of the concepts introduced in this text, and while some are technical in nature, they often include illustrations that aid understanding.

Books and Publications

Barnard, Robert L.: *Intrusion Detection Systems* (2d ed.; Boston: Butterworth-Heinemann, 1988).

Baron, S. Anthony: *Violence in the Workplace: A Prevention and Management Guide for Businesses* (Ventura, Calif.: Pathfinder Publishing of California, 1993).

Before Disaster Strikes: Developing an Emergency Procedures Manual (Chicago: Institute of Real Estate Management, 1996).

Broder, James F.: *Risk Analysis and the Security Survey* (Boston: Butterworth-Heinemann, 1984).

Capel, Vivian: *Security Systems and Intruder Alarms* (Boston: Butterworth-Heinemann, 1989).

Coverston, David Y., and Coverston, Sam S.: *Security Training and Education: A Handbook with Questions and Answers* (Ocala, Fla.: Security Seminars Press, 1990).

Craighead, Geoff: *High-Rise Security and Fire Life Safety* (Boston: Butterworth-Heinemann, 1996).

Crowe, Timothy D.: *Crime Prevention Through Environmental Design* (Boston: Butterworth-Heinemann, 1991).

Cumming, Neil: *Security: A Guide to Security System Design and Equipment Selection and Installation* (2d ed.; Boston: Butterworth-Heinemann, 1992).

The Dimensions of Parking (3d ed.; Washington, D.C.: NPA—the National Parking Association and ULI—the Urban Land Institute, 1993).

Fay, John: *Butterworths Security Dictionary: Terms and Concepts* (Boston: Butterworth-Heinemann, 1988).

Fennelly, Lawrence J.: *Effective Physical Security: Design, Equipment and Operation* (2d ed.; Boston: Butterworth-Heinemann, 1996).

Fennelly, Lawrence J. (Ed.): *Handbook of Loss Prevention and Crime Prevention* (3d ed.; Boston: Butterworth-Heinemann, 1996).

Fennelly, Lawrence J.: *Security Applications in Industry and Institutions* (Boston: Butterworth-Heinemann, 1992).

Fites, Philip, and Kratz, Martin P. J.: *Information Systems Security: A Practitioners Reference* (New York: Van Nostrand Reinhold, 1993).

Gigliotti, Richard, and Jackson, Ronald: *Security Design for Maximum Protection* (Boston: Butterworth-Heinemann, 1984).

Guy, Edward T., and Merrigan, John J.: *Forms for Safety and Security Management* (Boston: Butterworth-Heinemann, 1981).

Grover, K. R.: *Retail Security Policy Manual* (Boston: Butterworth-Heinemann, 1992).

Healy, Richard J.: *Design for Security* (2d ed.; New York: John Wiley & Sons, Inc., 1983).

Healy, Richard J., and Walsh, Timothy J.: *Principles of Security Management* (New Rochelle, N.Y.: Professional Publications Division of Harris & Walsh Management Consultants, Inc., 1983).

Hughes, Denis, and Bowler, Peter: *The Security Survey* (Brookfield, Vt.: Ashgate Publishing Company, 1982).

IREM SMART Partners® Program: Better Properties through Stronger Communities (Chicago: Institute of Real Estate Management, 1994).

Isaacs, Richard B., and Powers, Tim: *The Seven Steps to Personal Safety* (New York: The Center for Personal Defense Studies, 1993).

Jacobs, Roger B., and Koch, Cora S.: *Legal Compliance Guide to Personnel Management* (Englewood Cliffs, N.J.: Prentice-Hall, Inc., 1993).

Keckeisen, George L.: *Retail Security Versus the Shoplifter: Confronting the Shoplifter While Protecting the Merchant* (Springfield, Ill.: Charles C Thomas Inc., 1993).

Kidd, Stewart: *Dictionary of Industrial Security* (New York: Routledge, Division of Routledge Chapman and Hall, Inc., 1987).

Kruegle, Herman: *CCTV Surveillance: Video Practices and Technology* (Boston: Butterworth-Heinemann, 1995).

Kyle, Thomas C., and Aldridge, James: *Security Closed Circuit Television Handbook: Applications and Technical* (Springfield, Ill.: Charles C Thomas Inc., 1992).

Lighting for Safety and Security (Washington, D.C.: National Lighting Bureau, 1994).

Lyons, Stanley: *Security of Premises: A Manual for Managers* (Boston: Butterworth-Heinemann, 1988).

National Crime Prevention Institute: *Understanding Crime Prevention* (Boston: Butterworth-Heinemann, 1986).

O'Block, Robert L., et al.: *Security and Crime Prevention* (2d ed.; Boston: Butterworth-Heinemann, 1991).

Petruzellis, Thomas: *The Alarm, Sensor, and Security Circuit Cookbook* (New York: The McGraw-Hill Companies, Inc., 1994).

Pike, Earl A.: *Protection Against Bombs and Incendiaries: For Business, Industrial, and Educational Institutions* (Springfield, Ill.: Charles C Thomas Inc., 1973).

Purpura, Philip P.: *Retail Security and Shrinkage Protection* (Boston: Butterworth-Heinemann, 1993).

Purpura, Philip P.: *Security and Loss Prevention: An Introduction* (2d ed.; Boston: Butterworth-Heinemann, 1990).

Rosenblatt, Richard J.: *A Customer Oriented Approach to Safe Shopping* (Baltimore, Md.: The Center for Social and Community Research at Loyola College, 1995).

Ruthberg, Zella G., and Tipton, Harold F. (Eds.): *Handbook of Information Security Management* (Boston: Auerbach Publications, 1995).

San Luis, Ed; Tyska, Louis A., and Fennelly, Lawrence J.: *Office and Office Building Security* (2d ed.; Boston: Butterworth-Heinemann, 1994).

Schaub, James L., and Biery, Ken D., Jr.: *The Ultimate Computer Security Survey* (Boston: Butterworth-Heinemann, 1995).

Schaub, James L., and Biery, Ken D., Jr.: *The Ultimate Security Survey* (Boston: Butterworth-Heinemann, 1994).

Schnabolk, Charles: *Physical Security: Practices and Technology* (Boston: Butterworth-Heinemann, 1983).

Security: A Guide to Specifying and Obtaining Services by Contract (Silver Spring, Md.: Property Management Association, 1994).

Security and Safety: Issues and Ideas for Shopping Center Professionals (New York: International Council of Shopping Centers, 1989).

Sennewald, Charles: *Effective Security Management* (2d ed.; Boston: Butterworth-Heinemann, 1985).

Siljander, Raymond P.: *Introduction to Business and Industrial Security and Loss Control: A Primer for Public Law Enforcement and Private Security Personnel* (Springfield, Ill.: Charles C Thomas Inc., 1991).

Stallings, William: *Network and Internetwork Security: Principles and Practice* (New York: Macmillan, Inc., 1995).

Standard for Safety for Surveillance Camera Units, UL983 (5th ed.; Northbrook, Ill.: Underwriters Laboratories, 1993).

Sustaining SMART Partners®: A Community Approach to a Community Watch (Chicago: Institute of Real Estate Management, 1995).

350 Tested Strategies to Prevent Crime: A Resource for Municipal Agencies and Community Groups (Washington, D.C.: National Crime Prevention Council, 1996).

Traister, John E.: *Design and Application of Security-Fire-Alarm Systems* (rev. ed.; New York: The McGraw-Hill Companies, Inc., 1990).

Tweedy, Donald B.: *Security Program Design and Management: A Guide for Security-Conscious Managers* (Westport, Conn.: Quorum Books, Greenwood Publishing Group, Inc., 1989).

Tyska, Louis A., and Fennelly, Lawrence J.: *Security in the Year 2000 and Beyond* (Palm Springs, Calif.: ETC Publications, 1987).

Uniform Building Security Code (Whittier, Calif.: International Conference of Building Officials, 1994).

Walker, P. N.: *Electronic Security Systems: Better Ways to Crime Prevention* (2d ed.; Boston: Butterworth-Heinemann, 1988).

Walsh, Timothy J., and Healy, Richard J.: *Protection of Assets Manual* (4 vol. set; Santa Monica, Calif.: The Merritt Company, 1995).

Working Out SMART Partners®: Practical Concerns for Every Property (Chicago: Institute of Real Estate Management, 1995).

Periodicals

The *Journal of Property Management (JPM)*, published by the Institute of Real Estate Management, and *Security Management,* published by the American Society for Industrial Security, are recommended resources on the subjects addressed in this book. Both publications also offer compilations of article reprints on selected topics, making it easier to access information. Security issues are frequently addressed in real estate and business sections of major metropolitan area newspapers as well as business publications such as *The Wall Street Journal.* Other periodical resources include the following:

Buildings published by Stamats Communications, Inc., in Cedar Rapids, Iowa.

Building Operating Management published by Trade Press Publishing Corporation in Milwaukee, Wisconsin.

Crime Prevention News published by CD Publications in Silver Spring, Maryland.

Empower published by GreaterData, Inc., in Minnetonka, Minnesota.

Multifamily Executive published by MGI Publications, Inc., in Yardley, Pennsylvania.

Security published by Cahners Publishing Company, New York, New York.

Security Technology & Design published by Locksmith Publishing Corp. in Park Ridge, Illinois.

Shopping Centers Today published by the International Council of Shopping Centers in New York, New York.

Shopping Center World published by Argus, Inc., in Chicago, Illinois.

ToolKit published by GreaterData, Inc., in Minnetonka, Minnesota.

Urban Land published by ULI—The Urban Land Institute in Washington, D.C.

Legal Issues. A number of newsletters directed to real estate managers include information on court cases and their outcomes, including liability lawsuits claiming negligence on the part of a property's ownership or management in providing security. Others occasionally discuss security issues, including negligence and liability, in a larger management or marketing context. Following are some of these publications.

Commercial Lease Law Insider published by Brownstone Publications, Inc., in New York, New York.

Commercial Leasing Law and Strategy published by Leader Publications, a division of The New York Law Publishing Company, in New York, New York.

Landlord Law Report published by CD Publications in Silver Spring, Maryland.

Landlord Tenant Law Bulletin published by Quinlan Publishing Company in Boston, Massachusetts.

Managing Housing Letter for Managers of Private, Assisted & Public Housing published by CD Publications in Silver Spring, Maryland.

Professional Apartment Management published by Brownstone Publications, Inc., in New York, New York.

Sales & Marketing Magic for Apartment Managers published by The Sales & Marketing Magic Companies in Palm Harbor, Florida.

Security Measures. The manufacturers and distributors of the various security devices and systems are the best information source for particular details. *Security* (published by Cahners Publishing Company) generally reviews current security issues and the devices and strategies that can be implemented to address them. Each issue also contains numerous advertisements for security products and services. (Product information can be accessed on-line at: http://www.secmag.com.) *Security Technology & Design* (from Locksmith Publishing Corp.) is another publication devoted to security issues but with a different focus, as indicated by its title. It offers articles and substantial numbers of advertisements.

Also, any issue of *Security Management* (published by the American Society for Industrial Security) will have advertisements from several providers of locks, personnel identification systems, access control devices and systems, CCTV equipment, and integrated security systems. There are also advertisements from security guard contractors and services that test and verify the credentials of both security and non-security employees. Articles describing various security technologies and techniques and their applications are included in a variety of other professional publications, including *Buildings* magazine, *Journal of Property Management, Multifamily Executive,* and *Shopping Center World.*

Professional Organizations

Professional associations serving the real estate management and security industries are also possible resources on specific security issues. Many have their own publishing programs or distribute publications that focus on the information needs of their members.

Security Organizations

American Society for Industrial Security (ASIS), 1655 North Fort Myer Drive, Suite 1200, Arlington, Virginia 22209 (phone: 703-522-5800; fax: 703-275-3043). Maintains Certified Protection Professional (CPP) certification program for security managers and directors and distributes publications on security subjects. ASIS can be accessed on the Internet at: http://www.asisonline.org. ASIS also publishes *Security Management,* which can be accessed on the Internet at: http://www.securitymanagement.com.

Computer Security Institute (CSI), 600 Harrison Street, San Francisco, California 94107 (phone: 415-905-2626; fax: 415-905-2218). Publisher of *Computer Security Handbook* and an annual *Computer Security Buyers Guide.*

International Association for Shopping Center Security (IASCS), P.O. Box 55199, Atlanta, Georgia 30308 (phone: 770-934-2749). Publisher of *Security Standards for Shopping Centers.*

International Foundation for Protection Officers (IFPO), 4200 Meridian, Suite 200, Bellingham, Washington 98226 (phone: 360-733-1571; fax: 360-671-4329). Maintains Certified Protection Officer (CPO) and Certified Security Supervisor (CSS) designation programs for personnel who provide physical security and publishes booklets relevant to officer training.

National Burglar and Fire Alarm Association (NBFAA), 7101 Wisconsin Avenue, Bethesda, Maryland 20814 (phone: 301-907-3202; fax: 301-907-7897). Members are dealers and installers of burglar and fire alarm equipment.

Real Estate Organizations

Building Owners and Managers Association International (BOMA), 1201 New York Avenue, NW, Suite 300, Washington, D.C. 20005 (phone: 202-408-2662; fax: 202-371-0181). Offers Real Property Administrator (RPA) certification. Publishes and distributes materials related to office building management and maintenance.

Institute of Real Estate Management (IREM), 430 North Michigan Avenue, Chicago, Illinois 60611 (phone: 312-329-6000; fax: 312-661-0217). Maintains Certified Property Manager® (CPM®) designation program and has extensive educational and publications programs, including the bimonthly *Journal of Property Management.* Access IREM on the Internet at http://www.irem.org.

International Council of Shopping Centers (ICSC), 665 Fifth Avenue, New York, New York 10022 (phone: 212-421-8181; fax: 212-486-0849). Offers Certified Shopping Center Manager (CSM) designation and publishes materials related to all aspects of shopping center management.

National Apartment Association (NAA), 201 North Union Street, Suite 200, Alexandria, Virginia 22314 (phone: 703-513-6141; fax: 703-513-6191). Awards Certified Apartment Manager (CAM) certification and publishes and distributes books on apartment management.

National Society of Environmental Consultants (NSEC), P.O. Box 12528, San Antonio, Texas 78212-0528 (phone: 210-271-0781; fax: 210-225-8450). Encourages awareness of environmental risks and regulations and their impact on real estate value.

Property Management Association (PMA), 8811 Colesville Road, Suite G106, Silver Spring, Maryland 20910 (phone: 301-587-6543; fax: 301-589-2017). Publishes materials relevant to property management.

ULI—the Urban Land Institute (ULI), 625 Indiana Avenue, NW, Suite 400, Washington, D.C. 20004 (phone: 202-624-7000; fax: 202-624-7140). Association of real estate developers, architects, and others responsible for urban planning, community development and land use. Publishes books and other materials relevant to development. ULI can be accessed on the Internet at: http://www.uli.org.

Other Organizations of Interest

American Institute of Architects (AIA), 1735 New York Avenue, NW, Washington, D.C. 20006 (phone: 202-626-7300; fax: 202-626-7421). Association of professional architects. Publishes books and materials on related subjects.

American Insurance Association (AIA), 1130 Connecticut Avenue, NW, Suite 1000, Washington, D.C. 20036 (phone: 202-828-7100; fax: 202-293-1219). Publishes books on insurance and liability laws and their implications.

Illuminating Engineering Society of North America (IESNA), 120 Wall Street, New York, New York 10005-4001 (phone: 212-248-5000; fax: 212-248-5017). Technical society of lighting engineers, architects, contractors, and others who deal with illumination; publishes lighting standards.

Insurance Information Institute (III), 110 William Street, New York, New York 10038 (phone: 212-669-9200; fax: 212-732-1916). An association of property and casualty insurance companies that provides insurance information and educational services to the general public.

International Association of Fire Chiefs, 4025 Fair Ridge Drive, Fairfax, Virginia 22033 (phone: 703-273-0911).

International Association of Fire Fighters, 1750 New York Avenue, NW, Washington, D.C. 20006 (phone: 202-737-8484).

International Fire Service Training Association (IFSTA), Oklahoma State University, 930 North Willis, Stillwater, Oklahoma 74078-0118 (phone: 405-744-5723).

Lighting Research Center, Rensselaer Polytechnic Institute, Troy, New York 12180 (phone: 518-276-8716). Offers numerous publications on lighting topics (manufacturer-specific comparisons, performance issues, standards), including equipment and applications (e.g., parking lots).

National Association of Fire Investigators (NAFI), P.O. Box 957257, Hoffman Estates, Illinois 60195 (phone: 847-885-8304).

National Association of Mutual Insurance Companies (NAMIC), 3601 Vincennes Road, P.O. Box 68700, Indianapolis, Indiana 46268-0700 (phone: 317-875-5250; fax: 317-879-8408). Compiles and analyzes information on insurance and loss prevention and loss reduction.

National Fire Protection Association (NFPA), 1 Batterymarch Park, Quincy, Massachusetts 02269 (phone: 617-770-3000).

National Lighting Bureau (NLB), 2101 L Street, Suite 300, Washington, D.C. 20037 (phone: 202-457-8437; fax: 202-457-8411). Trade association of companies involved in lighting; promotes the concept of lighting energy management via various publications.

National Safety Council (NSC). 1121 Spring Lake Drive, Itasca, Illinois 60143 (phone: 630-285-1121).

Risk and Insurance Management Society (RIMS), 655 Third Avenue, New York, New York 10017 (phone: 212-286-9292; fax: 212-986-9716). Supplies information to assist in the purchase of insurance.

Underwriters Laboratories (UL), 333 Pfingsten Road, Northbrook, Illinois 60062 (phone: 847-272-8800; fax: 847-272-8129). Operates product safety certification laboratories and programs; publishes safety standards. Other locations in Melville, New York; Santa Clara, California; and Research Triangle Park, North Carolina.

Index